THE TRIALS OF MARGARET C

The Trials of Margaret Clitherow

Persecution, Martyrdom and the Politics of Sanctity in Elizabethan England

PETER LAKE AND
MICHAEL QUESTIER

continuum

Published by the Continuum International Publishing Group

The Tower Building	80 Maiden Lane
11 York Road	Suite 704
London	New York
SE1 7NX	NY 10038

www.continuumbooks.com

First published 2011

British Library Cataloguing-in-Publication Data
A catalogue record for this book is available from the British Library.

ISBN: HB: 978-1441-15134-6
        PB: 978-1-441-10436-6

Typeset by Pindar NZ, Auckland, New Zealand
Printed and bound in Great Britain

Contents

PART II

Acknowledgements

About ten years ago, the authors of this volume, for rather different reasons, became interested in the famous martyr, Margaret Clitherow of York, who was pressed to death on 25 March 1586 for refusing to plead when she was charged with the crime of harbouring Catholic seminarist clergy. We are grateful to the editors of *Past and Present* for allowing us to draw on some of the material in an article which appeared in that journal in 2004 under the title 'Margaret Clitherow, Catholic Nonconformity, Martyrology and the Politics of Religious Change in Elizabethan England'. We would also like to thank those who have read and commented on part or all of the text, notably Caroline Bowden, Gerard Boylan, Pauline Croft, Ginevra Crosignani, Claire Cross, Simon Healy, Julie Hirst, James Kelly, Christina Kenworthy-Browne, CJ, Gerard Kilroy, Miri Rubin, Nicholas Schofield, William Sheils, Caroline Watkinson and Rivkah Zim. We are indebted to Sir Thomas Ingilby of Ripley Castle, North Yorkshire for permission to reproduce the portrait of his sixteenth-century relative, the priest Francis Ingleby. Michael Questier is grateful to the warden and fellows of All Souls College, Oxford, for a visiting fellowship in Michaelmas 2007, during which term some of the research for this volume was completed.

List of Plates

Preface

What happens when the authority of the State is confronted and challenged by the presence of a refractory religious minority within its midst? As often as not, the minority proclaims its political loyalty to the regime of the day. And, almost certainly, the majority of the minority actually means what it says. Others – admittedly a small minority of the minority – are not willing to pledge their loyalty quite so unequivocally. Under certain circumstances, they are prepared to resort to courses designed to undermine and even to overthrow what they regard as an illegitimate and intolerable expression of temporal political power. The State responds to this challenge to its authority by rehearsing what it takes to be orthodox and acceptable attitudes, indeed platitudes, about the nature of society and the proper role of government in sustaining the commonwealth. It says also that the particular beliefs of the dissenting minority are not its concern. All it wants is a guarantee of political obedience. Increasingly, however, it comes to regard at least some members of that minority as either potentially or actually subversive. Inevitably, claims are made that the minority, in league from time to time with friends and supporters in other countries, is prepared to foment conspiracies of various kinds. Some of these conspiracies have a basis in reality. Others, even if they are not pure invention, are ferreted out and brought to the public's attention primarily because of loose talk and speculation.

Faced with what it comes to see as not merely a domestic but, in the end, an international threat, the State seeks to introduce legislation that redefines subversion and disloyalty. In its dealings with at least some members of the minority, in other words those it identifies as guilty of disobedience, disloyalty and ultimately of subversion, the State and its agents become increasingly, albeit intermittently, draconian and arbitrary, often pressing up against the limits placed upon them by even their own recently enacted laws. The State's more hawkish agents are prepared to resort to (formally) unlawful acts of torture carried out in secret but authorized at the highest levels of government. In response, some members of the minority are likely to accuse the regime of cruelty, injustice, persecution and tyranny. All sorts of rumours start to fly. Some people claim that the official rhetoric about the need to guarantee State security actually brings into being the (alleged) threats which, in turn, the State can use to subvert fundamental social and political freedoms. The State now starts to stage a series of show trials designed to demonstrate both the reality of the threat and the righteousness and necessity of its own preventive measures.

In the process, a number of theoretical questions suddenly acquire sharply practical implications. How can one define what falls under the rubric of belief or opinion and what comes under the rubric of political obedience? Where is the dividing line between the internal realm of conscience and the external realm of the State and its demand for political allegiance? Where does temporal authority end and spiritual authority begin? These questions and issues can be answered and addressed in very different, indeed often in mutually exclusive, ways by the parties to these disputes. As a result, categories and values assumed to be known and constant, whose transparency and constancy are taken to underpin all social, moral and political 'order', suddenly become not merely objects of debate and anxiety but also of radical contest.

Central here are notions of religious and of political identity, of patriotism and its relationship to various sorts of religious profession and belief. While the minority vigorously protest their patriotic fervour, despite the strength and singularity of their own controversial views and allegiances, the majority, or at least certain highly placed, well-connected, vociferous, sometimes officially sponsored and sometimes self-appointed, spokesmen for the majority, claim that precisely because of the transnational attachments and allegiances inherent in the minority's beliefs, they cannot really be regarded as patriots at all. They certainly cannot be trusted. Accordingly, in the name of the security of the realm and the interests of the community, they can quite legitimately be subjected to the surveillance and suspicion, the control and indeed sometimes even to the active repression, of the State.

In response, some members of the minority, reacting in anger and desperation to what they take to be the tyranny and oppression being visited upon them and theirs by the State, turn to currently available modes of radical political thought and action. Thus they adopt ideologies that justify resistance to, indeed the violent overthrow of, what they now confidently feel able to identify as a tyranny, and they posit utopian versions of what life would be like after such acts of political revolt have successfully been accomplished. Inevitably this style of political radicalism further alarms and enrages much of the majority. In turn, this emboldens the State in its repressive measures, and appears to confirm the truth and to encourage the ever more enthusiastic and lurid deployment of the stereotypes and caricatures employed by the advocates of further repression against the minority. Other members of that minority, horrified by the violent turn that events have started to take, decide to market themselves as moderates. They seek to voice what they take to be the real and abiding loyalty and obedience of the majority of the minority, but find themselves increasingly caught between the repressive apparatus of the State, the allegations of disloyalty and subversion employed by certain highly vocal agents and supporters of the State and the activities of the radicalized members of their own community, who do not hesitate to vilify them as odious quislings and time-servers.

To some this might appear to be a description of twenty-first century Britain. Just as much, in our minds, it is one possible account of Elizabethan England. Here the minority is made up of English Catholics, and the majority we can take to be English Protestants of various kinds. What follows is an analysis of many of the ideological, social, political and cultural dynamics of the confrontation between the Elizabethan State and the Catholic minority in its midst. It is an analysis conducted by reference to one particular set of events and issues: the godly life and horrifying death of one woman, Margaret Clitherow, and contemporary concerns about religious conformity and deviance, political allegiance and religious dissent, concerns which framed both her life and her death. To some readers, particularly Catholic ones, Mrs Clitherow, the pearl of York, will be instantly recognizable and thoroughly familiar as one of the brightest stars of the English Catholic firmament, a fixed point of the period's sometimes extraordinary Counter-Reformation zeal and piety, and a glorious martyr for the faith. Furthermore, Clitherow is one of a handful of sixteenth-century Catholics who are likely to be known to those who are not members of the modern Catholic community in England; and she is also one of a very few sixteenth-century women who are likely to have been heard of by anyone at all.

We want, however, to set Clitherow and her fate within a series of contexts, familial and local, national and international, ideological and cultural, political and religious, from which she has habitually been extracted by those who have written about her. The aim of this volume is first and foremost to reconstruct a credible narrative but also, through telling this particular story, to analyse the impact of post-Reformation religious conflict on certain central aspects of contemporary English religion, politics and society. As such it represents the continuation of an ongoing project, in which both authors have been engaged for over a decade, namely to use the experience of English Catholics in the period after the Reformation to throw light on some of the central issues of that time and place.

As these opening paragraphs were intended to imply, this is not a story altogether devoid of contemporary resonance. But both authors like to think of themselves as historians, and this is a history book, so hereafter our focus will be on Mrs Clitherow and her times. The claims and concerns of the present will have to look after themselves.

Note on the Text

In the text, dates are given Old Style but the year is taken to begin on 1 January. The spelling and punctuation of quotations from early modern manuscripts and books have been modernized. Unless otherwise stated, the place of publication of all works cited in this volume is London.

Abbreviations

AAW	Archives of the Archdiocese of Westminster
ABSJ	Archivum Britannicum Societatis Jesu
'An Answere'	'An Answere to a Comfortable Advertisment with it[s] Addition Written of late to Afflicted Catholykes concerninge Goinge to Churche with Protestantes wher in all the Advertisers Reasons are Confuted and it Declared to be Unlawfull to Goe to Churche with them as the Advertiser did Allowe. By a Catholyke Preest in the Southe' (attributed to John Mush), Oscott College, Birmingham, MS 99 (unfoliated; foliation supplied). A published version of this text appeared, after the present volume went to press, in G. Crosignani, T. McCoog and M. Questier (eds), *Recusancy and Conformity in Early Modern England* (Toronto, 2010), pp. 157–243
Anstruther	G. Anstruther, *The Seminary Priests* (4 vols, Ware and Great Wakering, 1968–1977)
APC	*Acts of the Privy Council of England*, ed. J. R. Dasent *et al.* (46 vols, 1890–1964)
ARCR	A. F. Allison and D. M. Rogers, *The Contemporary Printed Literature of the English Counter-Reformation between 1558 and 1640* (2 vols, Aldershot, 1989–1994)
Aveling, *CR*	J. C. H. Aveling, *Catholic Recusancy in York 1558–1791* (1970)
BCA	Bar Convent Archives
BCA, LD	'The Life and Death of Mistris Margaret Clitherow', Bar Convent Archives, York (MS V, 69)
BL	British Library
Cross, 'An Elizabethan Martyrologist'	Claire Cross, 'An Elizabethan Martyrologist and his Martyr: John Mush and Margaret Clitherow',

	in D. Wood (ed.), *Martyrs and Martyrologies* (Studies in Church History 30, Oxford, 1993), pp. 271–81
Cross, *PE*	C. Cross, *The Puritan Earl: The Life of Henry Hastings Third Earl of Huntingdon 1536–1595* (1966)
CRS	Catholic Record Society
CSPD	R. Lemon and M. A. E. Green (eds), *Calendar of State Papers, Domestic Series* (12 vols [for 1547–1625], 1856–1872)
CSP Scotland	J. Bain *et al.* (eds), *Calendar of State Papers Relating to Scotland and Mary Queen of Scots 1547–1603* (13 vols, Edinburgh, 1898–1969)
CSP Spanish	M. A. S. Hume (ed.), *Calendar of Letters and State Papers Relating to English Affairs, preserved principally in the Archives of Simancas* (4 vols, 1892–1899)
Garnet, *An Apology*	Henry Garnet, *An Apology against the Defence of Schisme* (n.p. [printed secretly in England], 1593)
Garnet Correspondence	ABSJ 46/12/1–2 (transcripts of letters written by Henry Garnet)
Garnet, *A Treatise*	Henry Garnet, *A Treatise of Christian Renunciation* (n.p. [printed secretly in England], 1593)
Longley, *SMC*	K. M. Longley, *Saint Margaret Clitherow* (Wheathampsted, 1986)
Longley, 'The "Trial"'	K. M. Longley, 'The "Trial" of Margaret Clitherow', *Ampleforth Journal* 75 (1970): 334–64
Miscellanea IV	J. H. Pollen *et al.* (eds), *Miscellanea IV* (CRS 4, 1907)
Morris, *Troubles*	J. Morris (ed.), *The Troubles of our Catholic Forefathers* (3 vols, 1872–1877)
Persons, *Brief Discours*	Robert Persons, *A Brief Discours contayning Certayne Reasons why Catholiques Refuse to Goe to Church* (Douai [false imprint; printed secretly at Greenstreet House, East Ham], 1580)
Persons Correspondence	ABSJ 46/12/3–6 (transcripts of letters written by Robert Persons)
PRO	Public Record Office, recently given the new title of 'The National Archives'
TR	John Mush, 'A True Report of the Life and Martyrdom of Mrs. Margaret Clitherow', in

	John Morris (ed.), *The Troubles of our Catholic Forefathers* (3rd series, 1877), pp. 333–440
Trimble, *Catholic Laity*	W. R. Trimble, *The Catholic Laity in Elizabethan England 1558–1603* (Cambridge, MA, 1964)
Wadham, 'Trial'	'Saint Margaret Clitherow: Her Trial on Trial: The Case against Her by Juliana Wadham', *Ampleforth Journal* 76 (1971): 9–22
WHN	'Notes by a Prisoner [William Hutton] in Ousebridge Kidcote. From the Original Manuscript at Stonyhurst College', in J. Morris (ed.), *The Troubles of our Catholic Forefathers* (3rd series, 1877), pp. 231–330
YRR	'A Yorkshire Recusant's Relation' (attributed to John Mush), in J. Morris (ed.), *The Troubles of our Catholic Forefathers* (3rd series, 1877), pp. 61–102

PART I

1

The Controversial Mrs Clitherow

One of the best-known stories of the post-Reformation English Catholic community is the life and martyr's death of the much-put-upon butcher's wife, Margaret Clitherow. Her tale is known to us principally through the account of her compiled, shortly after her execution on 25 March 1586, by her chaplain John Mush.[1] Mush's narrative derives its compulsive and affective force from its report of the conflict between the stubborn but homely sanctity of a saint-already-in-the-making and the almost incomprehensible brutality of the authorities in her home city of York.

The reader of Mush's hagiography cannot but draw a contrast between, on the one hand, its narrative of the abuse of State power directed against this ornament of womanly virtue, and, on the other, the order and quiet discipline exerted by Mrs Clitherow, wife and mother, in her own household. Here, respectful of the authority of her husband but fiercely defending her conscience-based prerogative to practise religion as she saw fit, she decided to allow herself to be directed in a life of quiet but intense Catholic piety by a series of confessor-priests whom she welcomed into her home. From the mid 1570s, for a period of about ten years, she was subjected to constant official harassment. From time to time she found herself dragged from the security of her dwelling in the Shambles in York and imprisoned merely for her conscience-driven separation from the Church of England. Subsequently, because of the malice of her enemies, she was indicted for an offence introduced into law by parliament in early 1585. During what was, on some accounts, an episode of State terrorism, she was barracked and humiliated in farcical court proceedings, the nature of which caused concern even to one of the judges on the bench. In two separate appearances in court in March 1586, Clitherow refused to plead to an indictment under the statute of 1585, which made the harbouring of a Catholic seminary priest a felony. (Under the same statute, any such clergyman who should 'come into, be or remain in any part' of the realm would be 'adjudged a traitor'.)[2] The common law had long provided a sanction for those who refused to comply with this aspect of ordinary trial procedure: the refuser was to be crushed alive (the sickeningly barbaric medieval penalty of *peine forte et dure*). This is what happened to Mrs Clitherow on 25 March 1586 in the Tollbooth on the Ouse Bridge in York. In the gloom of that dreadful place, she was stripped naked, in an obscene, virtually pornographic, shaming ritual, and was then put to the slow and agonizing death prescribed by the law.[3]

In the catalogue of martyrs compiled in the eighteenth century by Richard Challoner, the episode is reduced to a few short lines. It is taken virtually verbatim from Richard Verstegan's illustrated account of the suffering of European Catholics, his *Theatrum Crudelitatum Haereticorum Nostri Temporis*, which first appeared in 1587, the year after Clitherow's death. She perished, wrote Challoner, during the 'violent persecution raised in those times' by the lord president of the council in the North, the third earl of Huntingdon. When charged with the crime of harbouring, 'she refused to plead' in order that 'she might not bring others into danger by her conviction or be accessory to the jurymen's sins in condemning the innocent'. She bore her 'cruel torment with invincible patience, often repeating on the way to execution "that this way to heaven was as short as any other"'. After she died, her 'husband was forced into banishment' and 'her little children, who wept and lamented for their mother, were taken up, and being questioned concerning the articles of their religion, and answering as they had been taught by her, were severely whipped; and the eldest who was but twelve years old, was cast into prison'.[4]

Challoner's easily phrased summary of these events is neither entirely accurate nor does it tell anything like the whole story. This is not to say that what Challoner's account says about her is not, at some level, true. But its combination of artless simplicity and gut-wrenching pathos tends to conceal as much as it reveals. Mrs Clitherow's appalling death, which was regarded even by some contemporary Protestants as a perversion of the judicial process, raises some crucial questions about the period to which, traditionally, there have been few answers. What was the precise nature of the relationship between the Elizabethan State and the queen's Catholic subjects? Why should the supposedly moderate Protestant settlement of 1559, designed, we are often told, to incorporate as many of those subjects as possible into the national Church, have claimed, even if indirectly, a victim such as Clitherow? Also, if recognizably Roman Catholic opinions and tastes in religion were gradually, as historians nowadays frequently insist, during the later sixteenth century becoming the preserve of a social elite, namely the gentry,[5] how was it that this expression of Catholic zeal came from a relatively humble butcher's wife? Furthermore, if her zealous Catholicism was the product of mere conscience and an intense but interior affection for Tridentine piety, why should this have so provoked the authorities in the city of York?

Much of the modern Catholic account of the confrontation between the Elizabethan State and Roman Catholicism is itself derived from contemporary narratives of that conflict. These were constructed in such a way as to gloss over many of the causes that had led the State's servants and agents to deal so harshly with the queen's Catholic subjects. In time, these same narratives were adopted and reproduced by Catholic historians. Probably still the standard Catholic account is that of the secular priest Philip Hughes.[6] Hughes largely replicated William Allen's answer to Lord Burghley's well-known *Execution of Justice* of 1583. In reply to Burghley's claim that if the law was invoked against Catholics in England it was not because of their religion but because of their political offences, Allen unleashed an uncompromising polemic that accused the regime of hypocrisy and double dealing, inflating the danger from Catholics for its own nefarious ends. Hughes, like several other Catholic scholars, reproduced the lines of Allen's argument and declared that the Elizabethan State had instituted a quasi-totalitarian terror. This was a claim which, at the date when Hughes published his work, was undoubtedly influenced by recent memories of 1930s and 1940s European fascism. Allen's *True, Sincere, and Modest Defence* argued that Catholics were scrupulously loyal to the queen. There is a sense, though, in the narratives generated by Hughes and other Catholic writers, that conscience-driven resistance to a tyrant could not be described as 'disloyalty' or as culpable at all. In Hughes's work, a deeply disdainful series of glances at Elizabeth is accompanied by a searing condemnation of the persecuting minions who, he claimed, subverted and undermined the queen's rule even as they maltreated her subjects.[7]

Most of the Catholic historians of the nineteenth and twentieth centuries did, indeed, regard the Elizabethan regime as a tyranny. They were, therefore, prepared to endorse, if only implicitly, the traces of resistance doctrine in contemporary Catholic literature. Equally, they were distrustful of those Catholics who appeared to have temporized. The thrust of the Jesuit Leo Hicks's 1960s account of the political conspiracies woven around Mary, queen of Scots, in the early 1580s is that a number of Catholics had in the end decided to betray her. They could be regarded as the worst kind of collaborators, those who had sold their souls for political advantage. For Catholic scholars such as Hughes and Hicks, the Tudor monarchy of the later sixteenth century certainly shared all the worst tendencies and excesses of the totalitarian regimes, which had turned their own century into a nightmare of intolerance, blood and destruction. Hughes opined that, for Elizabeth's government, 'it sufficed that a man was a practising Catholic, as it sufficed with Hitler to be a Jew'.[8]

We might, nowadays, smile at such an unabashed equation of the cult figure of Elizabeth Tudor with a twentieth-century totalitarian dictator. Such accounts have long since gone out of fashion. Even John Aveling, a quite confessionally committed Catholic scholar, sensed the unreality of some traditional Catholic narratives of the period:

> the persecutors . . . appear only as a shadowy backcloth to the great spiritual drama of martyrdom, a backcloth painted in a few sweeping strokes of sombre colour, grotesque figures of bloody persecutors, cruel tyrants . . . fanatically cruel "Calvinist" clergy, pathetic "schismatics", bewildered and sheep-like citizens. It is all dark and unprepossessing to the point of absurdity – very like Foxe's *Acts and Monuments*.[9]

Even if such accounts might seem *passé* to us, most scholars have still, by and large, been reasonably content to take Catholics' own accounts of their victimization by the Elizabethan State largely on their own terms, in other words as a violation of the rights of their consciences. This does not mean that the political implications of martyrdom have necessarily escaped the notice of modern historians.[10] But some of those who have looked at Mrs Clitherow have wondered how far we could ever know what it was that she really thought about the link between religion and politics or indeed about anything at all. Claire Cross, for instance, has argued that the Margaret Clitherow that has come down to us is largely a creation of Clitherow's priest John Mush and his martyrological skills and polemical agenda.[11] Placing Mush's martyrological efforts in the context of English Protestant/Catholic martyrological debate and dispute, Anne Dillon has concluded that, 'paradoxically, the more careful the reading and closer the examination' of Mush's text, the further 'the woman recedes and a series of archetypes begin to move into her place'.[12] This in many ways represents a local application – through the analysis of discourse and genre – of the wider case made by Brad Gregory in his analysis of European martyrology in the post-Reformation period. There Gregory argues, against what he takes to be the rampant reductionism of much recent historical writing on early modern religion, that only religious categories are sufficient to encompass and explain religious phenomena, of which he takes martyrdom to be the unchallengeably pure, limiting case.[13]

There is a sense, of course, that the only reason we know very much about Clitherow is indeed because Mush decided to memorialize her. Also, his account of her is deeply polemical and most of its facts cannot be verified by reference to other sources. At the same time, the fact that Mush resorted to the circulation of a polemically inflected defence of his patron so soon after her death itself allows us to ask and, in some cases, to answer questions about what was going on in York in the 1580s and how Clitherow came to be caught up in the series of events that led to her execution. So closely was Mush's narrative of Clitherow's life related to those events that it would have been pointless for him to resort to pure invention in what was not just a celebration of her but also a barbed attack on her critics and enemies. Thus, while we do not contest that, for example, Mush resorts, here and there, to literary archetypes in his account of her, we argue that he did not simply invent her.[14] Nor do we think she was merely a dupe of Mush and of other clerical handlers who, when it all went wrong, covered up their exploitation and manipulation of her by turning her into a martyr.

In fact, the materials for a new reading of this particular episode and for a reintegration of it into a series of sixteenth-century narratives, local and national, political and religious, have been lying around, in more or less plain view, and sometimes even in print, for many years. It is quite possible, by one or two exercises in archival detection and lateral historical thinking to use these materials in order to say what, in some empirical sense, actually happened to Mrs Clitherow, and what political significance her gruesome fate held for her contemporaries. There are a number of both local and national, political and polemical contexts in which both Mush's account and, behind it, Clitherow's life and death can be set which, while leaving the purity and autonomy of her religious motives and commitments untouched, expose a good deal of the wider social, political and cultural dynamics of religious change in Elizabethan England. Martyrology and indeed polemic being what they are, the relationship of Mush's text to these contexts is necessarily often tangential, their influence rendered visible almost as much by what he does not say or only half says as by what he does say. However, once these contexts have been established, his narrative can then be read against the grain to reveal much about both his own circumstances and agenda and indeed those of Margaret Clitherow herself.

Not the least of the reasons for doing this is that Margaret Clitherow was an intensely controversial figure in her time even among Catholics. The most cursory reading of Mush's famous hagiographical text reveals that all was not well within the Catholic community in York. Mrs Clitherow was not the unifying force there that so many subsequent commentators have taken her to be.[15]

We can get a sense of how controversial she was from a modern polemical exchange, printed in a Catholic journal shortly after the canonization in 1970 of the 40 martyrs of England and Wales. This demonstrated how potentially contentious the inclusion of this woman had been in the list recently endorsed by Rome for promotion to sainthood. Juliana Wadham, writing in reply to an extensive analysis by Katharine Longley of the legal proceedings against Clitherow, insisted that she should not have been canonized at all. Longley had herself been instrumental in recovering and retelling the narrative of the martyrdom of Clitherow. Well aware of the local circumstances which had informed the onslaught against Clitherow and her coterie of Catholics in York, Longley, who had published the first edition of her biography of Clitherow in 1966, declared, uncompromisingly, that 'she died untried, unheard, unconvicted, the victim of national religious politics and local York conspiracy' but, 'much more, she died a *martyr caritatis* to protect others for the love of Christ and out of care for them'.[16]

Wadham's assault on Longley replicated much of the hostile contemporary reaction to Clitherow. On Wadham's account, Clitherow's famous refusal to plead was motivated by her prideful fear for her reputation. In particular she anticipated that, if her case went to trial, the proceedings would confirm a number of salacious rumours which were being circulated about her and which detracted from her local status as a heroic Christian. Wadham argued that Clitherow was on bad terms with her husband. The whole episode of her arrest was informed by the disastrous and dysfunctional state of her marriage. So far apart had she and her husband drifted that, shortly before she was arrested, 'he deliberately left the house and, it would appear, sided with the council in York' when charges were laid against her. Wadham concedes that this may have been because he was irritated by her 'Catholicism and priest-harbouring' rather than because he credited the accusations of adultery which some were making against her. Her death, however, was virtual suicide, the product of the worst kind of extremism, though, of course, combined with self-serving fear about the damage to her sexual reputation should the rumours generated by her association with Catholic seminary priests in York be subjected to further public scrutiny. The common-law judge John Clench told her in effect that, if she were to plead to the charge against her, he 'would direct the jury to acquit her'. She brought her fate on herself by stubbornly refusing to plead. It was not, therefore, the alleged tyrannical cruelty of the Elizabethan authorities that led her to her unfortunate end. It was her own stupid stubbornness that ultimately left the judges no alternative. Wadham concluded that she was no more than 'a religious fanatic whose enthusiasm to win a martyr's crown ran away with her and took her well beyond the realms of reasonable action'. How could a 'rational woman . . . abandon life, and husband and children', in order that, as Clitherow herself claimed, a jury 'should not have the burden of her death upon their conscience'? She may not have been insane but she was implacably obstinate to the point of unreasonable zealotry.[17]

John Clitherow and Henry May, respectively Margaret Clitherow's husband and stepfather, both solid citizens of York, could hardly be blamed for their concern that she was behaving in a reckless and unbecoming fashion. Her unconcealed affection for the new Catholic clergy who came from the Continent was a threat to both of them. So they decided between them to 'give her a severe fright'. She would be arrested and prosecuted, but too little evidence would be produced, and she would be acquitted, in effect let off with a warning.[18]

In fact, there is a good deal of common ground between Wadham and Longley over the question of how far family and local political circumstances conspired to bring about Clitherow's death. Longley accepted that, in the first instance, those who led the search were not trying to arrest any of her clergy friends; they meant solely to deal with her.[19] When it became clear that she would not yield, even her stepfather, Henry May, who evidently did not like her at all, tried to persuade her to save herself.[20] He probably wanted to see her buckle. She should recant and then just shut up. He was highly ambitious, a social and political climber, and he had only recently taken up the mayoralty of York. But he did not want to see her strung up on the gallows at the Knavesmire, even though that was indeed the penalty for the offence which she had committed by harbouring Roman Catholic seminary clergy.

For Wadham, the whole episode was distasteful and unedifying, not something which should have been presented for the relevant congregation in Rome to consider as a heroic witness to the faith: 'such, then, is the evidence for a newly canonized saint, who, in my view, should never have been canonized'. Sainthood had been conferred on the basis of 'too little evidence and on the recommendation of one man', the thoroughly *parti pris* John Mush. Even if Rome's devil's advocate did not have enough evidence to 'show that she was mad, or an adulteress', all the signs were that 'her case was one of a family feud which, by being taken to court, got out of hand; so that the spite which dragged her there provoked in turn the obstinacy that led to her fearful end'. Saints do not behave thus. The whole business was really rather depressing. The Church of Rome should have had nothing to do with her.

In other words, the salacious and vicious contemporary rumours which swirled around the doomed Mrs Clitherow emerged again as modern commentators sought either to memorialize or to discredit and dismiss her. But these nasty and unpleasant stories were not purely personal. In fact, the rumours and gossip about her which passed among her neighbours were linked to some of the crucial political and religious issues of the time. The doubts that even some of Clitherow's Catholic acquaintances had about her unyielding refusal to conform have found their modern equivalents in the suspicions that the supposedly heroic Catholic account of this period masks a radical political agenda. Wadham concluded that Pope Pius V's excommunication of Elizabeth in 1570, 'declaring the queen to be excommunicate, deposed, heretical and a bastard, and absolving her Catholic subjects from their allegiance to her, virtually forced them to choose between becoming traitors to their country or disobedient to their Church'. Here we have echoes of some contemporary Catholics' doubts about the wisdom of some of their co-religionists' attacks on the Elizabethan regime. These doubts received their most vigorous expression towards the end of the century during the so-called Archpriest Controversy, which split the Catholic community down the middle and which led some Catholics to express anxiety about the motives of those Catholics who had been executed for treason. While some Catholics argued that these brave souls had given their lives in the course of a glorious struggle to preserve the true faith in England, others concluded that many of the martyrs were no better than political agitators, of whom the queen's government had had every right to be suspicious. For the nay-sayers, the so-called martyrs were in fact to be pitied rather than celebrated. They were the victims of evil Jesuitical politicking. They were no more than useful idiots who had gone to their deaths for a bad cause and had unwittingly advanced the ambitions of others who had sought to bring violent alteration to the Elizabethan polity and had, in the process, subverted and perverted true religion for their own ends.[21]

Such an account has, of course, been entirely unpalatable and unacceptable to Clitherow's modern-day champions. Katharine Longley, whose exceptional archival work in York turned up crucial biographical information about Margaret Clitherow, retaliated against Ms Wadham and her aspersions on Clitherow's character and motives. On Longley's account, Clitherow was the victim not just of a State-sponsored conspiracy but also of the venality and greed of members of her own family who ought to have protected her. The scandalous and disgusting rumours about her were the product of the filthy minds of these people who joined together in an unholy league in order to destroy this precious and pious flower of the Counter-Reformation. Longley explained Clitherow's refusal to plead by showing that some of the York officials who ganged up against her were very well known to her, and she to them. The brutal sheriff Roland Fawcett was part of her mother's social milieu and circle. The animosity towards her was entirely personal and made the heroism that she displayed in the face of so much bitterness and hatred all the more remarkable. Longley speculates that the determination of Fawcett to make sure that Clitherow did not escape was informed by longstanding personal enmity towards her. One of Fawcett's duties as sheriff was to select the juries for the city assizes. Mrs Clitherow had every reason to suspect that, if she were to plead to the indictment, she would face a 'grand jury of twenty-four and then a petty jury of twelve substantial citizens, every one of whom, probably, would have been well known to her, hand-picked by Roland Fawcett'. This, according to Longley, meant that Clitherow would have seen these jury members as 'so many souls on the brink of damnation; as well might she expect justice from a jury picked by Judas Iscariot'.[22] Clitherow was, by refusing to plead, trying to protect, exactly as she said, not just her children and servants but also her neighbour who was complicit in her activities and in whose house her liturgical paraphernalia had been found.[23] In other words, Clitherow was not motivated by any material considerations and certainly not by a desire to safeguard family property from the law's penalties, penalties which stipulated that those condemned for felony offences were liable to property sequestration (though presumably her married status would have protected her in this respect).[24] If anyone needed proof that Mrs Clitherow's virtue and valour were unstained and unspotted, it was necessary only to compare her with her appalling stepfather, Henry May, the ambitious misogynist hypocrite and *arriviste*, a toady of the equally cruel lord president, Henry Hastings, earl of Huntingdon. May had so little shame that, when his own stepdaughter had been martyred for the faith, he 'spread the story that she had chosen this death as a form of suicide, being unable to face the shame of exposure as an adulteress', and, for good measure, he also accused her of a variety of 'sexual perversions' which she allegedly practised with her priests.[25]

In Longley's version of the story, the Clitherow household was a model of piety and order, just as John Mush said it was. In reply to those who surmised that all was not well between Mrs Clitherow and her husband, Longley points to the passage in Mush's 'True Report' which describes John Clitherow's hysterical grief as he realized what was about to happen to his wife: the news of her condemnation left him 'like a man out of his wits'. He 'wept so vehemently that the blood gushed out of his nose in great quantity', as he exclaimed 'Alas! Will they kill my wife? Let them take all I have and save her, for she is the best wife in all England, and the best Catholic also'.[26]

In the end, however, the fact remains that Longley's detailed archival investigation of the circumstances of Mrs Clitherow's execution serves, as it was intended, to reinforce, relatively unquestioningly, the highly polemical narrative that was compiled by Mush immediately after these frightful events took place. Longley sees absolutely no reason to doubt that 'Margaret Clitherow died . . . to God's glory and the advancement of his Catholic Church'.[27] That, and that alone, is the lesson which we are supposed to draw from this affair.

Yet, as is clear from both a cursory glance at Mush's famous text and also from the squabbling between Mrs Clitherow's modern-day supporters and detractors, there was much more to this episode (which culminated in one of the period's great show trials, albeit one that never proceeded to a verdict because of her refusal to plead) than historians have either allowed or realized.

We propose, therefore, not just to retell the narrative of this iconic figure in English Reformation history. Instead we want to revisit that narrative and, in the process, to explore some of the most controversial and confusing issues at the heart of the contemporary English Catholic community and to open up and describe the fraught relationship between Catholics and the Elizabethan State. We want to demonstrate that Clitherow's story was integral to mid- and late Elizabethan politics, one crucial component of which was the radicalization of post-Reformation Catholicism. We aim to show how such a radicalization was possible within what so many historians have described as an essentially conservative and backward-looking post-Reformation Catholic culture. As we started to locate the relevant material it also became clear that the implications and consequences of Clitherow's martyrdom rumbled on for years after she went to her death. The issues that informed her trial and execution did not dissipate once she was dead. So we decided to adopt an extended chronological perspective and, in Part II of this volume, to spell out how her trial and killing might have been understood by contemporaries in the context of events up to the accession of James VI in 1603. In particular we decided to show how the political and religious problems that concerned her were argued about by and among Catholics in the years after the authorities in York thought they had finally put an end to her.

2

The Radicalization of the Mid-Elizabethan Catholics

At some point in the mid- and later 1570s, English Catholics started to move inexorably into a different relationship with the Elizabethan State. Up until this time, or so many scholars have tended to argue, the residual Catholic element in the national Church may have been quite widespread, but it was little more than an expression of popular conservative sentiment, essentially backward looking and largely politically inert.[1] Still, most modern narratives of the period are agreed that, for whatever reason, Catholicism subsequently turned into perhaps the principal ideological expression of resistance to the authority of the Elizabethan regime.

Margaret Clitherow was one of those who, in the later 1570s, were swept up into an, at times, vigorous campaign of civil disobedience, a campaign which focused on the stipulations of the 1559 act of uniformity and the issue of church attendance. There had always been some people who had refused to accept the Elizabethan settlement of religion. But, during the 1570s, Catholics started to separate from the national Church in a way which they had not done previously. This was taken by many contemporaries to have political implications that were both novel and dangerous.

Nowhere was this more evident than in the city of York. The most engaging yet thorough account of the emergence of recusant separation in York was written by the former Catholic monk John Aveling.[2] It was penned at a time when the historiographical fashion in Reformation studies was to discover, describe and celebrate the via media of contemporary 'Anglicanism'. Of course there were real disagreements among scholars about exactly where this via media lay, who was responsible for establishing and defining it, and whom it incorporated. But there was a considerable scholarly investment in proving that the Elizabethan restoration of a recognizably Protestant liturgy and theology within the national Church led to the construction of a broad consensus within that Church about what the national religion was. There was also a scholarly stake in using this perception to underpin an essentially Whiggish narrative of the reign of the last of the Tudors as

a triumph of moderation over extremism and also of civility and rational-
ity over superstition. Aveling, who was no particular fan of the Church of
England, himself talks about something that he calls 'nascent Anglicanism'.[3]
But, while deferring to some extent to the earlier work of the doyen of
Reformation scholars, A. G. Dickens, Aveling nevertheless had his doubts
about Dickens's efforts to discover the green shoots of Anglicanism's genius
in the North of England. Aveling discovered how much resentment there
was even in the mid-Elizabethan corporation in York towards the high commission and the council in the North when those bodies tried to impose a
Protestant conformist culture on the city's population. Important civic dig-
nitaries such as John Dinely and Robert Cripling, both of whom served in
the 1570s as lord mayor of York, found themselves called to account for
their scruples in religion. Cripling was imprisoned by the council even while
he held the mayoralty.[4] Aveling called into question Dickens's conclusion
that there was relatively little religious conflict in York itself. Dickens had
argued that the economic activity of the middling sort in places such as York
tended to erase medieval religious mindsets and behavioural patterns, and
was more compatible with a so-called 'Anglican' expression of religious faith
which was opposed to the extremes that would themselves get in the way
of economic advancement.[5]

However, Aveling found and described a mid-Elizabethan Catholic awak-
ening in the North of England, one which was directly connected with the
politics of the Elizabethan succession question and which, incidentally, is
crucial for our account of Margaret Clitherow. The first serious expression
of this kind of Catholic dissent was the northern rebellion which broke out
in November 1569. In the end this was a disastrous failure, largely because
of the lack of a common purpose among the rebel leaders and because it was
launched in the winter without adequate preparation. But the fact remained
that the arrival in England in May 1568 of the deposed Scottish queen,
Mary Stuart, had encouraged a number of overlapping Catholic-tinged
conspiracies, the proponents of which all wanted to see Mary recognized
as Elizabeth's heir. The rebellion, when it came, took the form of an overtly
Catholic popular revolt. Out came, for example, the 'Five Wounds' ban-
ner which had last appeared in the North during the Pilgrimage of Grace
of 1536.[6]

There had, admittedly, been little enthusiasm among the citizens of York
for the revolt of 1569. Nor did the arrival in 1570 of their new and enthusiastically godly archbishop, Edmund Grindal, lead to any particularly
heavy purge of religious dissidents, at least not during Grindal's first two
years, when only nine Catholic separatists were summoned to attend the
high commission court.[7] There was, however, a zealous, if small, knot of

mislikers who resolutely refused to fall silent or fade away into obscurity. There was now, entrenched in York, a limited number of hard-line separatists who were clearly distinguished from the majority of conservative-minded conformists and also from those whom Aveling calls the 'constant gaggle of feckless, poverty-stricken casual absentees from church'. The source of this stubbornness could be traced to the agitation of Catholics such as the Marian cleric Henry Comberford, people who would not be reconciled to the Elizabethan settlement at any price.[8]

Had things stayed thus, overt Catholic dissent in York would probably have remained the preserve of this group of out-and-out dissenters. The regime would have seen no need to take much cognizance of such people. In fact, in the early 1570s, after the rebellion was suppressed, there was, it seemed, a real reluctance on the part of the regime to deal harshly with Catholic dissent, not least because the queen herself was determined to stand out against the programme of Protestant reform advanced by those who had also wanted, during the parliament of 1572, to make a martyr out of Mary Stuart.

Things, however, did not stay as they were. The earl of Huntingdon arrived in York in late November 1572 to take up his post as the lord president of the council in the North. He and Grindal were from the same ideological stable.[9] Huntingdon's political agenda clearly turned the government of the North upside down.[10] As Claire Cross demonstrates, when Huntingdon got to York, he began to root out those JPs whom he suspected of popery. He was soon involved, with Grindal, in using the high commission to make prominent Catholics conform. In 1573 he was working on a scheme to flush out Mary Stuart's Catholic supporters in the region. Even in March 1574 he was still hunting down rebels who had been involved in the 1569 rising.[11] In other words, after the queen had stubbornly refused to accede to the 1572 parliament's calls to chop off Mary Stuart's head as well as that of the duke of Norfolk, Huntingdon carried on the campaign against the Scottish queen by other, extra-parliamentary means.

Crucially, Huntingdon threw his weight behind the new administration in Scotland, headed by James Douglas, fourth earl of Morton who was determined to eradicate Mary Stuart's remaining influence in the kingdom from which she had fled in 1568. In early 1573 Huntingdon intervened to impound French ships that were carrying aid to Mary's supporters in Edinburgh Castle. Two months later, despite Elizabeth's reluctance, Huntingdon lobbied for and was allowed to send troops to join the siege of Edinburgh Castle, which fell shortly afterwards.[12] The puritan earl in York, according to Cross, saw in Morton 'a Scot he could unreservedly admire' who was also a 'champion of Scottish Protestantism against the gathering might of Rome'. Here Huntingdon was directly implicated in the attempt to protect and secure what some historians have seen as a Protestant and 'British' solution to the difficulties faced by the Elizabethan polity in its relations with Scotland. He did everything he could to hold together the Anglo-Scottish alliance and to retain Morton in power and to keep French influence out of Scotland. Huntingdon seems, however, to have had less than Elizabeth's wholehearted support. He was regularly reduced to petitioning Sir Francis Walsingham, in London, to make her Majesty see sense. As he tried to resolve the July 1575 border incident at Redswire, Huntingdon found himself defending Morton against Elizabeth's determination to humiliate the Scottish regent and to extract a public capitulation and apology from him. Huntingdon was left to whine to the earl of Leicester about what he took to be the queen's complete incomprehension of Anglo-Scottish politics.[13]

In other words, a certain kind of Catholic in York might have dared to hope that, even after the embarrassing fiasco of the northern rebellion of 1569, there was a glimmer of hope for a rapprochement between, on the one hand, the Tudor State and, on the other, the adherents of the old religion who were actual or potential supporters of the Scottish queen. Even in 1572, a notorious pamphlet entitled *A Treatise of Treasons* claimed that the queen's security and authority were being undermined not by Catholics but by those who had bullied and cajoled the queen into becoming an enemy of the Scottish queen, her cousin, heir and, in reality, her political 'best friend'. The same people had railroaded a Protestant reform of religion through the English parliament and Church in order to further their own political interests. In fact, the *Treatise of Treasons* alleged that the real traitors, namely the queen's leading counsellors Sir William Cecil and Sir Nicholas Bacon, planned to divert the succession away from the Tudor line to the house of Suffolk, the members of which had already mounted one coup d'état, i.e. in 1553 when they tried to put Lady Jane Grey on the throne in place of Mary Tudor, Elizabeth's sister. On this account, the Catholics who had opposed all of this Protestant chicanery and double-dealing were the ones who were actually loyal to Elizabeth. They had identified the evil counsellors who crowded around the queen, and they claimed that they, as good Catholics, were her best defence against further plots to undermine and displace her.[14] Elizabeth's absolute refusal to give way to the parliamentary agitation in 1572 for Mary to go to the block may well have been interpreted by Catholics as a sign that Elizabeth was almost persuaded of the truth of their claims, although Catholics in York were undoubtedly not encouraged by the arrival of Huntingdon and may have been distressed by the execution in August 1572 of Thomas Percy, earl of Northumberland, who had been sold to the Elizabethan regime by the Scots.[15]

Grindal travelled south to Canterbury in December 1575, at which point the number of recusants in York suddenly increased. Among those who went explicitly into separation from the Church of England was Margaret Clitherow. She is first cited, in the city's records, as a recusant in June 1576, although, just before her death in 1586 she said that she accounted herself to have been 'within the Catholic faith twelve years', in other words since 1574. The extent of various shades of separatism in York had been revealed when the lord president, early in 1576, demanded from the York corporation a list of Catholic dissenters, both recusants and stubborn noncommunicants.[16]

Significantly, many of them were women; 67 people, at this point, were identified for the first time as separatists. Of them, 55 were women, and 26 of these were, in fact, married to conformist husbands. Approximately half of these 67 separatists were drawn from what Aveling describes as 'the better-off, governing minority of York citizens' and more than 20 were from the relatively affluent families of the sort that engaged in trade in the city and which could be found on the common council. During 1576 and 1577, therefore, Huntingdon started to crack down on these people. The amount which John Clitherow had to fork out on behalf of his dissident wife went up from £7 each year to £20.[17]

Why this sudden ratcheting up of the pressure on York's Catholics? One traditional explanation has pointed to the infiltration into the country of seminarist clergy from Douai, beginning in 1574. Yet, as Aveling points out, until 1578, there is no documentary evidence that seminary priests were in York at all.[18] Local historians such as Aveling would say that Catholic separatism in York after 1569 can be explained by the presence there of Marian priests, books written by exiled Marian clergy who had once staffed the colleges of Oxford and Cambridge, and a sense of malaise created by the new State religion and the inadequate response provided to it by 'survivalist' Catholicism. Among those who reacted against this malaise was Margaret Clitherow. It was during this period, apparently, that she embraced a purer strain of contemporary Catholic belief and practice, although, says Aveling, she might just as easily have been 'converted by the "godly preaching" and catechising' of puritan divines in York. Perhaps, under the guidance of the most godly of York's Protestant pastors, she could still have practiced a 'vigorous kind of household and street apostolate and cultivation of her favourite kind of clergy and spiritual directors' in much the same way as she eventually did after she turned to Catholic priests.[19]

However, we know also that in 1576, the year when Clitherow was first identified as a member of the separated Catholic community, Edmund Grindal, the former archbishop of York and now archbishop of Canterbury, challenged the authority of the queen when she ordered him to suppress the so-called 'prophesyings'. The prophesyings were diocesan meetings in which scriptural texts were worked through by learned clergy for the better instruction of their less adept colleagues. These assemblies were, in some dioceses, attended by lay people. There were suspicions that these meetings were infected by the taint of puritanism and witnessed the public venting of complaints about liturgical conformity and of demands for further reformation of the Church. Those who raised the issue with the queen claimed that the prophesyings were not under proper episcopal supervision and that they permitted those who so wished, in other words puritan clergy and their lay patrons, to foment discord and division.[20]

The queen clearly saw the prophesyings in this way, as did a minority of the episcopate.[21] Grindal, however, refused to obey the queen's order to suppress them and he was, eventually, suspended from office. In summer 1576, however, he conducted a survey of the prophesyings in order to prove that they were not the vehicles of subversion that the queen believed them to be. Grindal's critics in the episcopal hierarchy who provided replies to his survey took the opportunity, nevertheless, to indulge in scathing anti-puritan invective. Their reports of what went on at these sessions served to confirm the suspicions of the queen and others who thought that the prophesyings were dangerous and ought to be put down.[22]

The long-drawn-out process by which Grindal fell from grace stirred up his supporters into direct retaliation against what they took to be popish infiltration of the Church and commonwealth, something which they largely blamed for his troubles. We can see the earl of Huntingdon already doing something like this in November 1576 when he attempted to impose stricter conditions of imprisonment on leading York Catholics such as Henry Comberford. In this month also, Mrs Clitherow's name was certified by the York corporation to the council in the North as a recusant. She was, however, pregnant, and it was claimed that she could not make an appearance to answer for her offence.[23]

Those who were identified as Catholics in York started to be removed from office. This assault on the latent Catholic political tendencies of the York civic elite (particularly the leading men of the corporation such as Dinely and Cripling) may well have provoked resistance from those who had, in all likelihood, welcomed the apparent disgrace of the godly, presaged by the fall of Grindal.[24] No doubt Mrs Clitherow hated Grindal. Though her chaplain and biographer John Mush nowhere mentions her opinions about the former archbishop of York, the almost exact coincidence between Grindal's falling out with the queen and Mrs Clitherow's detection for separation from the national Church does suggest that she, like other Catholics, may have been responding to, and perhaps even celebrating, the apparent reversal of fortune that godly Protestantism seemed to be experiencing at that time.[25]

In 1577, as part of a high-level attempt to save Grindal and to persuade the queen that the real threat to her regality came not from so-called puritanism but from papistry, the privy council procured a diocesan survey of recusancy.[26] Some bishops cooperated more enthusiastically with it than others did. For those who had defended the prophesyings this was the perfect vehicle to prove that the supposed sins of puritanism and, in particular, puritanism's alleged tendency to foment popular political agitation, were much more likely to be found among Catholics. On the recusancy survey return from his own diocese, Grindal appealed to the council 'to be a means for me to her Majesty to receive me again into her gracious favour'.[27] The results of the enquiry are archived in the domestic State Papers series in the National Archives at Kew. Over 1,500 names were returned by the end of the year.[28] Some of the returns were extremely detailed and thorough. The meticulous account sent in by the new archbishop of York, Edwin Sandys, was based upon high commission records. Individual names are, here and there, annotated by reference to a perverse refusal to conform or compromise in any way. The Marian cleric Henry Comberford was 'worth nothing, yet very wilful and a great perverter of others'. The York return lists a fair number of women, some of whom would subsequently emerge as the fiercest opponents of the council in the North. Among them was Margaret Clitherow. On 2 August 1577, shortly before the October survey was hurriedly carried out, she and her husband were summoned by the high commissioners to explain her obstinacy. She was sent off to the castle, while he was briefly imprisoned in the gaol known as the Kidcote. She remained locked up in the castle until February 1578.[29]

Huntingdon's attempts to discipline Catholic separatists in York had, as we saw, anticipated the 1577 survey. He wrote to Burghley from York on 12 September 1576 in order to lament the recent decline in religion. He had already warned the privy council of 'the declination in matters of religion . . . and the obstinacy of many' which 'does shrewdly increase'. He hoped the queen would find ways to reform all this, 'for in truth it is time'. He had heard that some in the North were saying that papists 'were not worse to be liked a little before the last rebellion than at this present'. In other words, some people were muttering that the region was likely to see a surge of Catholic anger and resentment equal to that which had been visible during the rising of 1569. He added that the most stubborn and 'peevish' offenders in York were women and there were quite a lot of them.[30] Here, then, was the Catholic equivalent of the dangers which some had identified at the heart of the prophesyings: lay people below a certain social status who had the temerity to express opinions about the government of the Church and to cast aspersions on the authority of the queen.

In Aveling's account of Catholic recusancy in York, as we have already seen, we have a very full picture of how far the opposition at this point to the civic authorities was coming primarily from women.[31] We find case after case of women who were supposed, in most contemporary patriarchal renderings of the kind of behaviour that was appropriate for females, to be quiescent, if not actually silent, in matters pertaining to the Church, but were becoming a good deal more vocal than many of their menfolk. Some wives remained obstinate while their husbands complied. A substantial number were, as Huntingdon observed, so pig-headed that they were prepared to face long spells of imprisonment.

It is far from clear that this was simply part of a natural division of labour between Catholic-conformist husbands and Catholic-nonconformist wives.[32] Historians of the period have, in fact, frequently taken the combination of a conformist Catholic husband and a recusant wife to have been part of the contemporary economy of religion, and something that was created by the statute law on uniformity. It is virtually axiomatic in studies of this period that Catholicism was able to survive the effects of the law against non-conformity because heads of households conformed and their wives were protected by their married status from the financial and other penalties of the statutes against recusancy.[33]

It is clear, however, that this live-and-let-live approach was not necessarily practised in all households. At least, it is not certain that all conformist husbands actively sympathized with their wives' independence in this respect. If we take the records of the high commission at York for July and August 1577 for example, we find that George Hall declared that, as for his wife's nonconformity, 'he has now and then beaten her for her refusal'. He certainly did not see why he should pay for her recusancy. Ambrose Cooke had 'persuaded' his wife 'all he can'. Although he was not prepared to force her to attend church, he refused to pay the forfeitures levied for her noncompliance. In the 1577 return of recusants for the city it was said that Anne Kitchinman had been in a perfunctory manner to church on the feast of St Simon and St Jude and had been on one other occasion when 'her husband dragged her thither by force'. On 5 October 1580, on the same day as Mrs Clitherow was once again incarcerated in York Castle, 'Mr Alderman Allen, by a special messenger, signified that the lady his wife will not come to church or communicate, nor appear before this court, neither be persuaded by him touching religion in any respect'. Perhaps he did not dare, like Mr Hall, to give her a good thrashing, and perhaps he was not strong enough, like Mr Kitchinman, to drag her along to the parish church. But still, he 'made humble petition that good and speedy order may be taken for her reformation'.[34]

Even those husbands who had an established reputation as (conformist) Catholics could be embarrassed by their wives' determination to flout the law. In July 1577, the lord mayor, John Dinely, was severely discomfited by his inability to make his wife conform; he was left exposed to public ridicule as 'a man who is set to govern a city' and yet 'cannot govern his own household'. He went so far as to 'promise to license a minister to come to say divine service in his house and to his wife'.[35] Edward Besely, a relative of Mr Dinely by marriage, and an MP for Ripon, Thirsk and Scarborough during Mary Tudor's reign, managed to retain his post of clerk to the castle from 1556 to 1588, though he was himself in and out of prison between 1572 and 1590. He was called before the high commission in early July 1577 and said that he had 'travailed' with his wife and could not 'persuade her' and even declared that he himself was a conformist.[36]

Evidently, in some cases, the different courses pursued by husband and wife could put intolerable strain upon the marriage. In the archiepiscopal visitation book for 1586 it is recorded that John Johnson, from Rockliffe, lived apart from his wife. He declared that she was a 'papist' and not conformable and, 'through her frowardness, they live asunder'.[37]

Exactly what John Clitherow's attitude was to his wife's nonconformity was never made entirely clear. If he was as unsympathetic to her conscience as John Mush sometimes makes him seem, it is odd that he should, at least in the early days, for example in August 1577, have been prepared to shoulder the financial penalties levied on him for her refusal to attend church. He was, in fact, churchwarden of his parish when he was compelled to levy the act of uniformity's one-shilling fine on his own goods because of his wife's recusancy.[38] Not long before her final arrest it was John who was hauled before the council of the North to explain the absence of his son, Henry, whom she had recently sent to France, although Mush emphasized that Margaret had dispatched the boy abroad without her husband's knowledge or consent.[39] At her trial, when she was asked whether her husband had been privy to her practice in keeping priests, Mush claims that she answered 'God knows I could never yet get my husband in that good case that he were worthy to know or come in place where they were to serve God'.[40] This was a response that certainly implied that Mr Clitherow had been kept in the dark about the precise nature of his wife's religious activities. So, equally, did the stories which Mush told in his 'True Report' about her dissembling social engagements and visits to women in childbirth to cover her gadding to priests.[41] Arranging her chaplains' room in her neighbour's house might also be taken as a way to avoid direct confrontation with her husband's authority over the household, at the very least giving him plausible deniability and freeing her from the charge of open defiance of patriarchal authority.

But there are passages in Mush's narrative that hint strongly at the fraught relations in the Clitherow household on the subject of religion. One of Mush's stories tells how John Clitherow reduced his wife to a tearful fit at a dinner party by implying that her religiosity was the sign of a weak mind. 'It chanced upon a time', Mush says, 'that she accompanied her husband to a neighbour's house to [a] banquet'. After they had all finished eating, the assembled company fell to talking 'of the Catholic religion and Catholics'. John Clitherow who, if truth be told, had had too much to drink, 'with an oath or two' said that, for the life of him, he could not tell what a Catholic was. They were quite happy to 'fast, pray, give alms', and even to 'punish themselves' more than everyone else, but the fact was that they were really no better than anyone else. They were of 'as evil disposition in other things' as other people. And he went on cursing them until his wife, 'knowing none to be Catholic but herself in that company', broke down and wept. Her husband told her she was an idiot and, rather too late, said that 'he meant not those words by her, for, indeed, he would ever report he could wish no better wife than she was, except only for two great faults, as he thought, and those were, because she fasted too much and would not go with him to the church'.[42] Whether this helped to calm her down or to improve what was evidently a disastrous social occasion, John Mush does not make clear. (Mrs Clitherow went to him the day after and, evidently under the seal of the confessional, told him how much it grieved her that John Clitherow 'should so heinously offend God by slandering the Catholics and the Catholic Church'.) It is certainly possible, therefore, that Mr and Mrs Clitherow became seriously estranged over her refusal to comply with the York authorities' demands that she should conform herself to the religion established by law. Mush referred darkly to further 'crosses' that 'she suffered by her husband' as well as others.[43]

Thus, even before the confrontation between the Elizabethan regime and the queen's Catholic subjects started to escalate in the 1580s, various women in York, including Clitherow, were using the language and performance of nonconformity in such a way as to allow them an independent voice in these matters, whether their husbands liked it or not.

It is only in April 1580, in the high commission records, that one really starts to see groups of male nonconformists beginning to be summoned for their offences, in other words alongside the regular quotas of women recusants.[44] This crackdown on male separatists seems to have more or less coincided with the arrival in the country in summer 1580 of the Jesuits Edmund Campion and Robert Persons though, in fact, Huntingdon's purge of northern recusancy in mid-1580 started just before the Jesuits arrived. The Jesuits' missionizing and their preaching of recusant separation stirred up a latent culture of Catholic dissent and, it appears, were deliberately designed to antagonize the authorities. In particular, they made extensive tours of the provinces. (Campion was the one who came to visit Yorkshire.) They made explicit demands that Catholics should go into separation. Their declarations, through a range of media which included unlicenced printed tracts, launched what was, in effect, a campaign of civil disobedience.[45] The York records show that large numbers of male Catholics were now proceeded against as the regime started to look more closely at what constituted compliance and disobedience as defined by the statute law on conformity. Many of them may have formerly been conformists. It is quite possible that some of those who were picked up as the high commission swept across the region were prosecuted because of their enthusiastic response to the Jesuits' agitation during the summer of 1580.

We have no way of telling what Mrs Clitherow thought of the two famous Jesuits. But we may well surmise that, as Campion's rural rides around the North brought him very close to where she dwelt, the clarion call to separate from the Church of England would have been welcomed by the already separatist Clitherow, though she could not have met him because, while he was in the county, she was detained in the castle. In October 1580 she had been deprived of her liberty again by the high commission. She was released on 24 April 1581 because she was heavily pregnant and about to give birth.[46]

According to the high commission act books, at and after this point, significant numbers of Catholics started to conform. Among them were, for example, the well-known York physician, Roger Lee and his wife. As Katharine Longley notes, Millicent Calvert, the Clitherows' next-door neighbour in the Shambles, provided evidence to the high commission on 3 October 1580 that she was still conformable. William Tesimond, who was Margaret's friend, relation by marriage and the father of the future Jesuit Oswald Tesimond, eventually (in October 1583 and January 1584), produced evidence of his conformity. In the case of Martin Dawson, a butcher, one warning ('to be of good behaviour in words and deed against the queen and all her people and not willingly to resort in the company of any papists') appears to have been enough. His name does not appear again in the lists of recusant York Catholics.[47]

Others may have secured, or tried to secure, an accommodation with the authorities via negotiation. For example, on 16 January 1581 Brian Palmes certified that he had arranged for the curate of his parish to read divine service to his wife and that she had received the communion. It is not clear that this had happened in public in the parish church. It may in fact have been the result of some sort of compromise between the parish and the family. John Palmes of Naburn, on 3 April 1581, certified the complete conformity of himself and his family, although in mid 1582 he was still being harried by high commission officials. On 19 July 1583, Elizabeth Colson, a maid employed by John Palmes, 'confessed that, by reason of a pain in her side and a cough', she had spat out 'the sacramental bread', 'for which abuse she was sent to the custody of the sheriffs of York'. She may have been trying to adopt a style of half-way-house conformity which was nevertheless a rejection of the kind of full compliance which was now being demanded by the State. A number of Catholics signed legal documents which obliged them to conform but then did not go through with the compliance which they had promised. Yet the proceedings of 1580 distinguished the refusers from the conformers quite sharply. Among the out-and-out noncompliers, predictably enough, was Mrs Clitherow. On 13 April 1582 her husband was allowed to compound for the £40 forfeiture which he had incurred on a bond that he had taken out on behalf of his wife (apparently one that guaranteed she would return to the castle after giving birth).[48]

The council in the North by this stage saw the intransigence of recusants such as Mrs Clitherow as part of a wider political problem. It appeared to them that Catholic dissent was being swept up into the political issues generated by the delicate and deeply unstable relationship between Elizabeth and her northern neighbour and cousin, James VI of Scotland.

In the later 1570s, Scotland was only just beginning to emerge from the civil wars which had followed Mary Stuart's deposition. What the young king eventually decided to do as he sought, even in his minority and still under the sway of the regent Morton, to establish his independence from the court-based factions that tried to control him, would clearly be crucial for Elizabeth's security. Huntingdon's onslaught on recusant separatism was integral to the northern regime's response to the revolution in Scottish politics as James turned to the Valois court, in the shape of Esmé Stuart, sieur d'Aubigny. James created him earl, and subsequently duke, of Lennox after d'Aubigny came from France and arrived in Scotland in autumn 1579. These events north of the border were interpreted by godly English Protestants as a menace to Elizabeth's safety. They were probably welcomed by some Catholics who would also have regarded the queen's own negotiations in 1579–1580 with the Valois court as the potential dawn of a new day for them. As is well known, Elizabeth, in the face of much godly Protestant dismay, tried hard to secure an Anglo-French dynastic treaty which would see her wed the duke of Anjou, the youngest of the sons of Catherine de Médicis. Huntingdon was unable directly to interfere in Scotland though he offered assistance to Scots who had crossed the border into England as the earl of Morton's power declined.[49] When it became clear that Morton's fall was imminent, even Elizabeth contemplated using a military force to intervene in Scotland. This was something that Huntingdon was all too willing to lead. He advised that Elizabeth must do her best to resist Lennox's rise. Huntingdon, waiting at the Anglo-Scottish border, received news from Walsingham of the progress of the 1581 parliament in London and in particular of the passage of the recusancy legislation which was being introduced in the wake of the Campion-Persons agitation and which, temporarily, Walsingham was concerned would not even make it as far as the statute book.[50]

This legislation against Catholics was regarded by Huntingdon, Walsingham and their friends as a crucial means of controlling public opinion in England. The queen's own plans to marry the duke of Anjou, which had evoked a flurry of Protestant complaints, were now effectively dead. Those Catholics in England who had hoped for toleration as a result of this proposed dynastic union had seen all their hopes spectacularly dashed. But the new legislation would allow those like Huntingdon, who had viewed the Anjou match with such trepidation, to make sure that no such ideological slippage of the kind that now seemed to be infecting the Stuart court should recur in Elizabeth's realm. Elizabeth may still have resented what Huntingdon and other of her Protestant internationalist subjects were doing. When Huntingdon tried to manufacture the circumstances that would allow him to lead troops into Scotland, the queen, according to the Spanish ambassador Mendoza in late February 1581, lost her temper with Walsingham. She denounced him as a puritan and said, 'you will never be content until you drive me into war on all sides and bring the king of Spain on to me'.[51]

In these circumstances the use of the high commission against Catholics was clearly, in the North as elsewhere, a means for the queen's representatives to take down any kind of expectation that the composition of the regime or the direction of government policy were about to change. The commissioners demanded conformity from a much greater number of Catholics across the region than had hitherto been the case. Huntingdon was right at the centre of this spate of enforcement. Between 18 July and 7 September 1581, he was personally present at the meetings held by the high commission all over York diocese (at York, Beverley, Malton, Ripon, Skipton, Wakefield and Southwell). Leading Catholic separatists were dealt with directly. As for the rest, local juries were empanelled in order to hunt them down and to send them before the commissioners in the autumn.[52] Aveling shows that, in York, the proceedings of the commissioners in 1580–1581 managed to force a third of those who had been separatist in 1578 to conform (even if some of them subsequently reverted into separation). Forty-five new recusants were flushed out. Thirty-four of them conformed immediately. Most of them were never prosecuted for recusancy again. The number of stubborn separatists dropped back to the levels of 1578.[53]

In Scotland, Morton, who had already been relieved of his regency, fell spectacularly and finally from grace. Charged with complicity in the murder of Mary Stuart's consort, Lord Darnley, back in 1567, Morton was beheaded in June 1581. But Lennox himself was overthrown after the Raid of Ruthven in August 1582 when the young king was seized by Lennox's enemies. For the time being, there seemed to be no chance that foreign intervention would overturn the Protestant assumptions which underwrote the relationship between England and Scotland which had subsisted through much of the 1570s.

In York, Clitherow and a few others were left high and dry, as it were, in their out-and-out nonconformity. They were ministered to by a cadre of seminary priests, many of whom were committed to an attempt to secure the kind of separatist character for the community which had been urged by Campion and Persons. However, those with strong separatist inclinations were now pursuing a very lonely path.

As we have seen, at this time large numbers of York Catholics were shifting backwards and forwards between separation and various degrees of conformity. It has frequently been assumed, not without reason, that this was the rather messy and untidy result of pressure often rather unevenly applied by the State. Conscientious Catholics would show themselves in their true (separatist) colours when the times allowed it. Aveling's entire account of recusant separatism is based on the thesis that Catholicism survived because 'many recusants bent before the storm like the willow, rising again when there was a lull in persecution'.[54] Civic records demonstrate how common this practice was in York. To take just one example, the former MP Edward Beseley was detected as a recusant in 1572, and was taken into custody by York's sheriffs. But in 1573 he conformed, at least in the sense that he went to church. In 1574, however, while physically present at church, he refused to take communion, and was ordered to discuss his difficulties of conscience with Protestant divines. By 1576 he had become obstinate again and was sent away to York Castle's prison accommodation. Within five months he had had enough and was allowed out in order to live with his (none-too-Protestant) brother-in-law, Alderman Dinely, under an easy form of house arrest. In 1577 he conformed again, though he was still noncommunicant. His wife, like so many other women, was refusing to attend church at all, but, as we have already mentioned, he claimed to have tried to persuade her to conform. In 1581 he had, apparently, separated from the national Church. At the end of the 1580s he was still marked down as a separatist, though in subsequent years, and even as late as 1600, he was a conformist again. Finally, in 1604, after the queen's death, he went back into separation.[55] There are many other such cases.

The point is that, while some Catholics separated and some conformed, this did not mean that the Catholic community was clearly and cleanly divided into recusants and church papists. So-called 'conformists' were sometimes recusants, and vice-versa. There was certainly no agreement among Catholics about how and when they should exhibit signs of compliance and how and when they should not. This was something that was made evident in the quite bitter debates between Catholics during the initial stages of the mission of Campion and Persons. The Jesuits were told by some people, for example at the so-called synod of Southwark in July 1580, that their call to separation was not welcome.[56]

What is clear is that some mode of conformist compromise was, in the face of the intransigence and hostility of the local and national State, still the norm for very large numbers of Catholics in York after 1581, as indeed it was elsewhere in Elizabeth's realm. In the period between 1578 and 1580, there were, Aveling writes, many recusants within Margaret Clitherow's 'butcher coterie'. But after 1580 this separatist impulse dwindled away, and, 'in her later days, she had to face a great deal of cold hostility'. Among the butcher families of Weddell, Mudd and Geldard there were several recusants in the years 1576–1578 but almost all of them eventually conformed. At the end of Elizabeth's reign, tradesman recusants were distinguished by their isolation.[57]

It was this complex and volatile series of local negotiations and stand-offs which was further complicated by the arrival in York of seminary clergy in the wake of the execution of Edmund Campion at Tyburn on 1 December 1581. Among the clergy who appeared in the city at this time was a man called Thomas Bell.[58] He was joined by the recently ordained Anthony Tyrrell, William Hart and William Lacey. Bell's most daring exploit took the form of a direct challenge to the authorities in the city. He mounted a Catholic liturgical extravaganza in York Castle itself. According to his friend Tyrrell, as soon as Bell reached York he went straight to the castle's prison block and stayed there undetected for a fortnight. He recited Mass on each day that he was there and he preached to the prisoners as well. Then, on 22 July 1582, Bell and four other priests, including Tyrrell, Hart and Lacey, all went to the prison after it had been arranged for Catholics from the city to join them there. Boats on the river were used to make an entrance at night. On Tyrrell's account

all during the night, the priests were busy hearing confessions. The following morning four Masses were said, and after them a fifth, with great solemnity. It was sung with full music, with a deacon and subdeacon,

which is a very rare sight for our English Catholics, especially for those in
prison. At the same Mass all the Catholics went to communion: there must
have been about fifty of them. There were two sermons during the day.[59]

This seems to have forced the castle administration to break up this
demonstration of Catholic fervour. At any rate, as the priests and others
were attempting to leave the castle, the authorities tried to arrest them.
Only William Lacey, however, was successfully detained. He was indicted on
11 August with Richard Kirkman, in circumstances of some chaos, according
to Henry Cheke. The 'assembly at the arraignment of the priests was very
great, especially of papists'. The assize judges were 'forced to make room
themselves like ushers'. Less than a fortnight later, Kirkman and Lacey were
hanged and disembowelled at the Knavesmire. Tyrrell went off to Rheims.
(By 1584 Tyrrell was in Rome in the company of the future Babington plotter
John Ballard.)[60]

Bell and his friends clearly took what they had done to be an appropriate mode of challenge to the established order in York, though it is quite
possible, in view of Bell's later and publicly expressed opinions about the
extent to which Catholics could and ought to offer temporal obedience to
the queen, that what happened in the castle was not quite as flagrant a defiance of royal authority as Tyrrell's narrative makes it seem.

In late 1583, there arrived in the city Clitherow's future chaplain, John
Mush. At the time Mush got to York, she was in prison. She had been sent
there after arraignment at the quarter sessions in March of that year.[61] Thus
he would have been able to begin his spiritual ministrations to her only when
she was released in May 1584. As Claire Cross comments, Mush could have
'known her intimately' just 'for the last two years of her life'. (At around
the time of Mush's arrival, Bell took himself off to Lancashire.[62]) One of
Huntingdon's informers believed that Mush might have been, at one time, a
servant and apprentice of Dr Vavasour, whose household, in Christ Church
parish, was used to harbour Campion.[63] (Vavasour may himself have been
the agent of Clitherow's conversion to Catholicism.[64])

It seems very likely that the latent differences among York's Catholics
over how far they should refuse compliance to the queen's representatives
were radicalized by the arrival of John Mush and other seminary priests.
In standard accounts of Elizabethan Catholicism, of course, the ministry of
seminarist clergy was merely an extension of the zeal of the laity and their
desire for access to the sacraments which those clergy could provide. Here
was the Church under the cross, retaining its faith and waiting for better
times. These narratives, however, simply do not take into account the fissures and schisms which now occurred within the Catholic community.

These divisions are themselves quite hard to recover. But in the story of Margaret Clitherow it is possible to glimpse them, to integrate them back into our account of the mid- and later Elizabethan period, and to use them to describe the inner workings of the mid-Elizabethan Catholic community in a way that is largely absent from almost all extant versions of what happened in late Tudor England.

3

Mrs Clitherow, Her Catholic Household and Her (both Protestant and Catholic) Enemies

How did Margaret Clitherow's resistance to the will of the regime in York, to statute law and, as we shall see, to the conformist compromises adopted by many of her Catholic co-religionists, express itself? How could a woman such as this, in the midst of a patriarchal society, barred from any kind of political and public office and indeed the exercise of any authority outside her own household, intervene publicly and politically so as to bring down on herself the wrath of both the State and, as it turned out, a substantial section of York's Catholic community as well?

Some of the most aggressive contemporary exponents of the patriarchal order thought they knew exactly how a member of the fairer sex could use religion in order to step out of line and flaunt her independence. Richard Topcliffe remarked, in a memorandum to Lord Burghley written at some point after 1588, on those who ought to be dealt with as a matter of urgency: 'there be . . . ladies, gentlewomen as well married or widows, needful to be shut up . . . as much as men'. Topcliffe said that this was necessary because although these women were not able 'to go to the field and lie in camp (for the sex and shame), yet they want no desire nor malice, every one being furnished of a lusty priest (harboured in her closet), who shall serve as her lieutenant when that holy day of Jesus comes. Or else she is prepared of a lusty Catholic champion, servant, tenant or neighbour . . . for her purpose', to 'command her purse, horses, armour and tenants; and whether she be wife, widow, maid or whatsoever, in this mean season she will harbour, receive and relieve priests and traitorous fugitives, labourers of the common cause (in plain terms, civil rebellion) or else to be ready to assist foreign invasion'. Also, it was well known that 'the fury of a woman once resolved to evil' was 'far greater . . . than the rage of a man'. Topcliffe advised Burghley that 'that sex of women be not overlooked', not least because Gregory Martin, the translator of the Rheims version of the New Testament, had, in a recent pamphlet

31

called *A Treatise of Schisme*, wished that 'amongst all the constant Catholic gentlewomen of England' there could be just one who, like the biblical Judith, would 'cut off Holofernes's head to amaze all the heretics'.[1]

Topcliffe's account of the danger represented by the liaisons between women and priests was central to contemporary anti-popish discourse. As Frances Dolan comments, in the special circumstances of post-Reformation England, married Catholic women may have acquired some degree of 'authority and independence' because Catholicism 'empowered women as custodians of household religion'. As a result, it might be that 'Catholic women did not look to their husbands as their spiritual teachers and leaders, but instead to priests'. The relationships created between clergy and laity in this way were widely lampooned in anti-popish satire along the lines which Topcliffe articulated. It was a theme of John Gee's notorious 1624 tractate denunciation of the Romish clergy that 'the priests and Jesuits in their books pretend that they are servants' to those Catholics 'over whom . . . they lord it'. They claimed that they were forced 'to creep into private houses for fear of persecution' but they then carried 'more dominion over the family than any parish priest . . . in those countries where popish religion' was the dominant faith.[2] When it came to the relationship between Catholic clergy and female patrons there was inevitably a good deal of speculation and suspicion as to the possibility of a dishonest and lascivious attraction of the one to the other.

In the face of these satirical tropes about the bonds established between priests and women, John Mush defended Clitherow's reputation. Indeed, the best source for Clitherow's capacity to stand out against both the patriarchal conventions of her world and the taunts of her Protestant enemies is the account of her household penned by Mush, her chaplain, one of those allegedly lusty, sexually voracious and politically dangerous priests identified by Topcliffe as the natural corrupters of untrustworthy, though apparently malleable and often witless, females.

Throughout Mush's account, Clitherow's uncompromising commitment to a fully recusant Catholicism is presented as creating a separate space for her within her own household, and in her relations with her husband and children and indeed throughout her dealings with local society. This was a space which was often far from conducive to familial and social harmony. Here she was able to act as something like her own mistress. She structured her daily round, her social relations and her public performances of religious zeal according to the demands of her own religious opinions. In the process she accumulated, in some circles at least, a considerable degree of charismatic social power and, in others, an equally considerable notoriety.

Clitherow had, as we saw, not started out as a Catholic. She was converted, Mush tells us, 'two or three years at the most after her marriage' to the York butcher John Clitherow in July 1571. 'About twelve or thirteen years past', relates Mush,

> 'two or three years at the most after her marriage, when she heard first of the Catholic faith and Church (for before she frequented the heretical service, not suspecting there had been any other true way to serve God), she became as desirous to learn the Christian duty in truth and sincerity, as she had learned before to serve only the world vainly; and, after a little consideration, finding no substance, truth, nor Christian comfort in the ministers of the new gospel, nor in their doctrine itself; and hearing also many priests and lay people to suffer for the defence of the ancient Catholic faith (which is known to have been the faith of all England, common with all the Christian world many hundred years since the world was first delivered from idolatry and paganism), she carefully employed herself to know plainly the same, and to become a lively member of the Church, wherein this faith had been taught and preached.

Mush partially excused her by saying that

> in those days neither the heretical fury was so outrageous as it has shamefully increased ever since, and there were then more known Catholics in one town (Catholic times being fresh in the memory of all, which the tempest of violent heretics has destroyed and taken away) than are now to be found almost in a whole country.

Still, he was glad to note that

> she had every day a hearty sorrow and humble repentance for her youth spent out of the Catholic Church of Christ; in vain follies and schism, which daily exercise wrought in her a continual sorrow to recompence those years, with her whole strength, by God's grace, to honour Him as she had dishonoured Him before.[3]

Throughout their marriage, Mr Clitherow remained a Protestant, or at least a conformist. Margaret very soon threw herself into some of the most extreme and dangerous contemporary forms of Catholic belief and practice. 'Even at the first', she fully resolved 'rather to forsake husband, life and all, than to return again to her damnable state'. For her pains, or more precisely for her intransigent refusal to attend the services in her local parish church, she was, Mush tells us, 'divers times separated from her husband and children' when she was bundled off to prison.[4]

While several women such as Clitherow were kept imprisoned in York, sometimes for quite long spells, the council in the North was generally reluctant to resort to this sanction. But rather than come to her senses under the relatively gentle lash of short spells of imprisonment, according to Mush, Clitherow positively revelled in this kind of privation:

> the devil and his hellhounds raged fiercely against her by the terrors of the persecutions to separate her from God and His Catholic Church, and drive her again into the damnable snares of heresy and schism. But the matter fell out quite contrary to their malicious intent and expectation; for the spirit of God wrought so graciously in her, that all troubles, persecutions, and cruelty practised against her for the Catholic religion and her conscience's sake daily increased more and more the constancy of her faith'

and 'strengthened her former weakness with all patience and fortitude to resist and sustain what cruelty soever the heretics could devise and attempt against her'. Thus 'the prison she accounted a most happy and profitable school where the servants of God (as delivered from all worldly cares and business) might learn most commodiously every Christian virtue'. In this way, she 'turned all things to her good, and sucked honey out of the cruelty of her enemies'. Those enemies persecuted her

> and she thereby learned patience; they shut her up into close prison, and she learned thereby to forget and despise the world; they separated her from house, children, and husband, and she thereby became familiar with God; they sought to terrify her, and she thereby increased in most glorious constancy and fortitude, insomuch that her greatest joy was to be assaulted by them.

By contrast, as she saw it, at home she was 'tossed up and down in worldly business'. Mush says that her experience of running John Clitherow's butcher's shop in the Shambles in York (see Plates 1 and 2) persuaded her that her life there was 'the occasion of many waste[d] words, loss of time, and distraction of mind from God' and 'she suffered greater and oftener conflicts in dealing in this worldly trade . . . than in all her other affairs besides'. Her young years had been spent in the sociable locale of a respected York inn. Her life was undoubtedly changed for the worse when she was carried off to the less rarefied atmosphere of a butcher's shop (which doubled as an abattoir). In Katharine Longley's wonderfully and tragically evocative account, 'within and without the shop, in that street rarely touched by the sun, she was constantly obliged to pick her way through sawdust and blood'. In 1585 it appears that she was desperately trying to get her husband to surrender his commercial premises in the Shambles when the lease of the place came up for renewal, but he refused. As Mush related it

> she was in hand often with her husband to give up his shop, and to sell his wares in gross with as much gain and with less unprofitable toil. For riches she desired none, but prayed God that her children might have virtuous and Catholic education, which only she wished to be their portion, and would say that, generally, the more folks grew in wealth the further they were from God, and less disposed to do well.

So disenchanted was she with her lot that, 'in all her husband's losses, she would be exceeding merry and say, "yet he has too much, he cannot lift up his head to God for the weight of his goods; I pray God he may by these casualties know God and serve Him"'. In fact, she added, 'God gave them, and He hath taken them away again; farewell they, for I will not be sorry for the loss of any temporal matters. I pray God we may well use to God's honour the rest we have.' This was not an obvious or particularly appropriate attitude for someone who was supposed to be a local businesswoman, and it was unlikely to have recommended or endeared her to John Clitherow.[5]

Considering her own family's wealth, and the political rise and rise of her stepfather Henry May,[6] eventually to become lord mayor of the city, she might indeed have expected better for herself than immersion in the butchers' trade. Perhaps the distraction of mind from which she periodically suffered was a form of melancholy; nowadays we would probably call it depression. Paradoxically, Mush says, imprisonment brought her liberation from her heaviness of mind. From the tedium of commercial activity and from the economic necessity of carrying on her husband's business, she was free, Mush says, 'only in the times of her imprisonment' during which she even had the leisure to learn 'to read English and written hand'.[7]

Out of gaol, too, Mrs Clitherow had begun to use her religious profession as a means to establish a routine devoted as much to the service of God as to the fulfilment of conventional social and familial duty. Mush describes in some detail her exacting daily spiritual regimen: hours of private prayer and meditation, combined with resort to her spiritual adviser. She

> would not in anywise follow her own fantasy, but committed all wholly to the guiding and direction of her ghostly Father. No prayer seemed sweet unto her, no time convenient, no order straight, unless he had first perused them, and judged them meet for her. Every morning ordinarily, before she took in hand any worldly matter, she continued secretly in her chamber the space of one hour and a half, or most often two hours, praying upon

her knees, and meditating upon the Passion of Christ, the benefits of God bestowed upon her, her own sins and present estate of her soul.

After this, 'if her husband or some importunate business hindered not, she came to her spiritual father's chamber to hear the divine mysteries, and with him to offer to God the Father His dear Son, sacrificed upon the holy altar by His priest for the quick and dead'. Such was her zeal that 'if there had been two fathers to celebrate, she would have been present at both' Masses. After the service was concluded, and 'when she had committed herself and all her works that day to the protection of God, she occupied herself in necessary worldly affairs', the thing, of course, which seems to have caused her so much pain and disillusion, though she endeavoured 'all the day long to have her mind fixed on God'. Thus 'her devotions all the rest of the day were as she could get leisure' only,

> which almost she never had until four of the clock in the afternoon, about which time she would shake off the world and come to evensong, where she, praying about one hour with her children about her, afterwards returned again to her cares of the household until eight or nine of the clock, at which time she used to resort to her ghostly father's chamber to pray a little and ask his blessing.

Twice in the week 'she frequented the holy sacraments of confession and eucharist, if her father had thought it expedient'.[8]

Mush thus went out of his way to emphasize that Mrs Clitherow did not shirk from even rather lowly household tasks, many of which she discharged herself, even while she kept a tight rein over her servants. But, as he described, her religious profession could not be entirely restricted to the margins of the day; rather it invaded and inflected her entire running of the household. In prison she had learned to fast four days a week and this was a spiritual routine which she maintained upon her release into the world.[9] Mush describes in vivid detail the intensity of her devotional experiences: 'in the time of her receiving the Blessed Sacrament of Christ's body, she ever coveted to have the last place, so far as she could do it without trouble or notice of others, for she would not seem to any to have desired it'. And,

> whilst she received, her gracious and lovely countenance was often washed with sweet tears trickling from her eyes. Afterward she would depart for the space of half an hour into some close corner, where she might familiarly enjoy the delights of her God, whom she had brought into the secret parlour of her heart, and all the day after she would be merry and smiling.

She was determined,

> once a week at least, to hear some virtuous exhortation by her ghostly father, and would sometimes make secret motions and signs to him of this secret desire; sometimes also [she] reverently requested him to speak something for such audience as she would provide, which thing she did commonly at those times when strangers, or such as could seldom get opportunity to serve God and be present at these exercises, were assembled.

In addition, she had recourse to sacred texts, among which were the Rheims version of the New Testament, Thomas à Kempis's *Of the Imitation of Christ* and William Perin's *Spiritual Exercises*, which was modelled on Ignatius Loyola's famous spiritual manual. Mush heard her say that '"if that it pleased God so to dispose, and set her at liberty from the world, she would with all her heart take upon her some religious habit, whereby she might ever serve God under obedience". And to this end (not knowing what God would do with her) she learned our Lady's Matins in Latin.'[10]

There were things also which she very much disliked doing and actually tried to avoid. In particular, she hated being 'invited to banquets abroad'. Mrs Clitherow's proclivities thus clashed directly with the preferences of her husband 'who, loving company himself, desired to take her with him'. She was often forced to feign 'some urgent business' to escape the dead hand of social duty. She wished rather to use the time in order 'to feed the soul by prayer and meditations'. In fact, Clitherow was not above using the demands of social obligation and neighbourly sociability as a cover for her own prodigious appetite for religious observance and spiritual exertion. She devised a range of elaborate ruses to get out of attending festive social occasions so that she could spend the time in the company of her favourite chaplain of the moment. Mush described, for example, how, when

> she was invited with her neighbours to some marriage or banquet in the country, she would devise twenty means to serve God that day more than any other at home; for she would take horse with the rest, and after that she had ridden a mile out of the city, one should be there readily provided to go in her stead, and all that day she would remain at some place nigh hand, where she might quietly serve God, and learn of her ghostly father some part of her Christian duty as her heart most desired, and at night return home again with the rest as though she had been a feasting all the day long. This she used even from the beginning of her conversion, at which time also she procured some neighbours to feign the travail of some woman, that she might under that colour have access and abide with her ghostly father the

longer to be instructed in the necessary points of Catholic religion.[11]

As Anne Dillon comments, there is an 'underlying eroticism' here and indeed in several of the central chapters of the 'True Report' one can find what one might call the 'conventions of courtly love'.[12] In Mush's narrative, of course, these conventions were spiritualized. As he remarked, 'in all her actions it evidently appeared that she loved Him whom continually she served, and joyfully served Him whom she loved above all things, and that her industry to keep earnestly in her heart this true and chaste love of God far surpassed the diligence of doting carnal love[r]s in the world to accomplish their foolish and unclean desires'.[13] All of this was designed to serve as a potent rebuke to those who knew, by report, of Clitherow's assignations with these priests and had interpreted them in an entirely unspiritual manner.

There could scarcely be clearer proof, however, of Margaret's iron resolve to retain control of her own domestic routine, social persona and indeed body, in the face of the conventionally supervening claims of social obliga- tion and the preferences, desires and status of her husband. She was quite ready to turn aside the traditional expressions and requirements of patri- archal authority (with the explicit approval of Mush, her ghostly father) by deceit and sleight of hand. In other words, while Mush's long and often graceful and uplifting narration of her personal and interior religious life, aspirations and scruples might be taken as an assertion of the complete compatibility of her Christian and her wifely callings, it can, in fact be read as exactly the reverse; as nothing short of a defence of a conscience-based independence. This was something which threatened a whole series of contemporary commonplaces about the structure of the household and, in particular, about how a number of distinct yet connected male–female roles and divisions of responsibility and labour should interact to maintain the household, seen as both a domestic and an economic unit.

The most spectacular expression of her independence, the most insurgent control of her own circumstances, was her reconfiguration of her own domestic space, altering in explicitly illegal and distinctly dangerous ways the physical shape of the Clitherow household. For the rigours of her chosen style of piety were reliant on almost constant access to both the sacramental and the edificational services of Catholic seminary priests. These services became available to her in the early 1580s, though presumably she had from time to time enjoyed, in the previous decade, the ministrations of York clerics such as Henry Comberford.[14]

A major theme of Mush's account is the almost ruthless avidity with which Clitherow sought out the company of the new Catholic clergy: 'so long as she had with her a ghostly father to serve God, no time seemed wearisome'. Once the tiresomeness of her work in her household was over, 'she would once or twice a day see' her 'spiritual father', and 'no trouble could make her heavy or sorrowful during that time'. Only in 'one thing' did she find it difficult to 'overcome herself', namely 'in the absence of a priest'. In the absence of such a priest, 'she thought herself desolate, and ever suspected that for some fault which God saw in her, she was unworthy of them'. Mush claimed that he never saw her 'cast into any sorrow or heaviness . . . but only for the want of a priest and God's service'. 'What secret sighs', wrote Mush, 'have I heard suddenly burst from her, and what a sorrowful countenance have I spied her to have in the departure of a ghostly father, especially when he was to pass some danger, or to abide long from her; for she ever feared that if anything should happen to him, others afterward would be more unwilling to come to her'. Furthermore, 'if any priest had passed the city and had not seen her, she would not have been a little troubled, and [would] have thought herself to have lost no small benefit'.[15] Here again we have a sense that spiritual counsel from the clergy served to relieve Clitherow's intense feelings of despair at the mode of life which her husband's commercial interests had thrust upon her.

Her reaction to her first stint in gaol was, therefore, not to avoid those furtive Catholic clerical frequenters of the city of York but, quite the reverse, to ensure that she was never short of priestly company and support. She took over a room in her neighbour's house in which priests might safely stay and divine service might be said, and she secured the use of another room, 'a little distant from her own house', for the same purpose. Primarily her intention was, though, to provide 'all things convenient, that God might be served' in her own house.[16]

Nor did she intend merely to make sure that she had access to the bare essentials of Catholic worship. Far from it. She 'spared no cost to maintain her religion'. When she was arrested in March 1586, 'the ravening heretics . . . thought so much good church furniture had not been in a whole county as they found with her'. What was technically a conformist household, or rather one where the head of the house was a conformist, became, as far as was possible in the circumstances, an open house for Catholic clerics and all others who wished to resort to them. In other words she had created what was in effect a known seminarist conventicle. Mush recalled that 'she would ever say: "I will not be afraid to serve God, and do well. This is a war and trial in Christ's Church, and therefore I cannot do my duty without worldly perils and dangers, yet by God's grace I will not be slacker for them. If God's priests dare adventure themselves to do me good, I will never refuse them."' Her determination, said Mush, was to serve God and also 'to teach others their duty therein'. This caused her now and then to adventure more than in these ungracious times might be thought convenient to timorous and worldly wise men; as to admit everyone that desired to her house for spiritual comfort . . . by which great resort they all being not so staunch of tongue as was necessary, her house became more notorious than the whole town besides. Her zeal bewrayed her, for none knew her but they were assured she would not be without a priest, if any could be gotten in the whole country.[17]

She took not only priests into her household but also a Catholic schoolmaster, one 'Mr [Brian] Stapleton, who had escaped a little before out of the castle where he had lain almost seven years for the Catholic faith'. In her house he taught her children and 'two or three boys besides'. And, contrary to the law, as we have seen, she eventually 'sent without the knowledge of her husband . . . her eldest son into France for virtuous education and learning, hoping one day to see him [become] a priest'.[18]

In short, in the years following her conversion and release from her first stint of imprisonment, Clitherow had transformed her household into a centre of Catholic activity. Its rhythms were set according to the demands of a distinctly Tridentine pattern of piety and observance and its physical layout and material resources were deployed to create a place of resort and succour for Catholics both clerical and lay. It was a priest's house, a Mass centre and a Catholic school and all was presided over by the recusant wife of a conforming member of the Church of England.[19]

Mush's account more or less admits that Mrs Clitherow was choosing between her husband's will and her own in her decision to deal with the proscribed seminarists. Though Mush rejected the carping and salacious sneers of those who speculated on why women such as Clitherow should become so attached to seminary priests, he does not seek to deny that, in some respects, the priests' authority was being substituted for that of John Clitherow. Following the passage into law of the statute of 1585 (27 Eliz., c. 2, 'An Act against Jesuits, Seminary Priests and such other like Disobedient Persons'), which made the presence of seminary priests in the realm *ipso facto* treason, and the harbouring of such clergy a felony which could also be punished by death, Clitherow was approached by 'a Catholic man (which sometime before had served God in her house)'. 'In the way and manner of friendly advice', he urged her 'to be more careful for herself'. He suggested to her that she should 'not with such danger receive any priests at all, or else very seldom; and this he added also, that it was no wisdom to admit her children and others to God's service, and that she ought not to adventure upon these things without licence of her husband'. Clitherow was absolutely livid, or, as Mush put it, the man departed 'leaving her in some discontentment'. What was clear was that she was not going to tolerate this. Presumably know-ing the answer in advance, she asked her confessor (Mush), 'may I not . . . receive priests and serve God as I have done, notwithstanding these new laws, without my husband's consent?' His response was to ask her what she herself thought. She replied that she did not understand 'how the rigour of these new statutes may alter my duty in this thing'; but, she said to Mush, if 'you will tell me that I offend God in any point, I will not do it for all the world'. Mush was not of course prepared to deny contemporary patriarchal theory completely. Rather he suggested that 'it is your husband's most safety not to know of these things unless he were resolved to serve God notwithstanding any danger'. But, he added, if the matter were to be left to Mr Clitherow and his 'consent and licence', she would not be able to 'serve God at all'. In this matter, said her chaplain, and in her 'necessary duty to God', she was 'not any whit inferior' to her husband. The 'cruelties of these wicked laws' should not 'change or frustrate' her 'duty to God'. So whether the temporal law forbade it or not, if it had been morally good and right to 'receive God's priests and continually to serve Him in the Catholic manner' before these new laws were made, then it remained praiseworthy and godly now. In fact, it was 'now more meritorious in God's sight than ever before'. Besides this, Mush said, 'no man can now refuse to receive' priests 'for fear of these laws, but he must be a partaker in some part and guilty of the wickedness in the law and lawmakers, as by his own deed giving them their intent, scope and effect which is only to banish God's priests from their sheep, and so to abolish the Catholic religion and faith out of the whole realm'.[20]

Here, then, the mere conformist Mr Clitherow was being condemned by his wife's spiritual guide and chaplain as, in some sense, an accomplice of the tyranny of the queen's representatives in York. Mush relieved her of her duty to obey her spouse in matters which touched on her choice in religion. There could scarcely be a clearer example than this of the impact of changes in national policy on the most local, indeed domestic, of politics, as the increased risk attached to Clitherow's Catholic activism raised doubts about her right to unilateral action within the household. This was a right exercised without her husband's explicit consent, indeed, if he knew about it, almost certainly against his wishes. Nor could there be a clearer example of the way in which Clitherow's disobedience to the patriarchal authority of both the Protestant State and her conformist husband was legitimated by the deployment of the spiritual authority of the Catholic priesthood, given local embodiment in her ghostly father of the moment. Mush's narrative went to great lengths to emphasize the extent of her obedience to the authority of the priesthood:

[F]rom the deep foundation of her perfect humility, and forth of the fruitful root of her burning charity to God, did rise up and spring a goodly edifice and great plenty of virtues: for being timorous to offend God, and only desirous to obey His will in everything, and withal suspicious of her own doings that they were not so perfect in God's sight, as both He required, and of duty they should be, she found out the only sure and safe way to do well, which she might ever follow without offence, and exercise with greatest gain. This golden way was utterly to forsake her own judgement and will in all her actions, to submit herself to the judgement, will and direction of her ghostly father . . . to the which persuasion she was much induced (as I remember she . . . said) by this motive, that since God of His infinite mercy had sent His priests already to call her to His grace, by delivering her from error in faith and ungracious affections of the will, He would also with like goodness that by their helps she should continue in the same; and as she might offend God in every of her actions, so it seemed to her the only safe way to please God, humbly to submit herself in all things to follow the advice and direction of His priests.

For she was certain that in following the directions of her chaplains she was in fact obeying God Himself.[21]

Thus was the disobedience to prince, magistrate and husband of a (relatively) humble and (formerly) unlettered butcher's wife redescribed (and hence legitimated) as obedience to the equally patriarchal, but inherently superior, spiritual authority wielded in God's name by the Catholic Church and priesthood. We might, therefore, see Mrs Clitherow's relations with her priests as a rather complicated exchange of spiritual and material goods and services. Here was an intricate set of power relations, in which, in return for her material support, they offered her their spiritual services. In return for her devotion and obedience to their spiritual authority as priests, they used that same authority to underpin and legitimate her disobedience both to her husband and indeed the wider authority structures of the Protestant State. Also in return, they could market her exemplary piety, her status as a 'pattern of virtues given' to Mush and to others to follow 'who are so slack in imitating the virtues of our Saviour and His other saints'.[22] Thus was the efficacy of their ministry and rightness of their style of Catholic Christianity confirmed by the charismatic example of Mrs Clitherow's saint's life and martyr's death. In the process, of course, the formal distinctions and hierarchies, the power relations that usually pertained between clerical mentor and lay adept, confessor and confessand, between the lay patron and the clerical client, were not merely mixed and miscegenated but, in the end, entirely reversed.

Clitherow's insistence on complete obedience to the authority of the priesthood had, however, a significance which was much wider than the gendered politics of the household. Or rather, her assertion of the primacy of her conscience was not confined to the domestic sphere. Mush was quite clear about the nature of her activities as a proselytizer for the Catholic cause as she understood it. On his account, her charitable activities were concentrated first and foremost on such of 'her fellow members and citizens or, as she used much to call them, her brethren and sisters of the Catholic Church, if they were in prison, or other furnace of trial', and she tried, 'by all comforts and means she could devise, to make their burden light, and Christ's yoke to savour sweet to them'. 'If they were Catholics abroad, and yet not void of tribulation (for that the heretics, as the natural whelps of the devouring lion that seeks everywhere whom he may destroy, permits none peaceably to enjoy either spiritual consolation or bodily quietness)' then she sought to 'procure them help and comfort both of soul and body'. Mush swore to himself that he would 'ever witness the same, how carefully she cast her charitable eye into every corner' where God's 'secret servants lay desolate and afflicted, to get them fed' with God's 'heavenly food in due season, lest', for want of it 'they might haply faint or fall'. He recalled how she 'looked to their bodily needs, and procured for everyone relief with discretion' and 'with how much gladness' she had 'gathered together twelve' of God's 'poor Catholic people at once' and had ensured that they were 'purified and fed with' his 'gracious sacraments and then with some virtuous exhortation instructed and lastly' had 'their bodies refreshed with sufficient meat and drink'. She herself also provided 'money for every one according to their need'. These people 'now lament the unjust spoil and loss' of God's 'handmaid, their common mother, and accurse, no doubt, with sorrowful hearts all the heretical cruelty that has so impiously bereft them of so careful a steward'.

However, her efforts were never limited to such people alone. They also encompassed 'heretics, schismatics and lukewarm Catholics', as Mush termed them. When faced with 'schismatics', in other words conformists, she was always anxious 'to reduce' them to 'Catholic unity'. Even 'heretics', if 'she had any hope of their conversion' or if she, 'through some familiar acquaintance with them, doubted not of their secrecy', fell within her evangelical and admonitory purview. She sought to instruct them 'in the true faith'. As for 'malefactors or persecutors of God's people', while they, perforce, remained outside her pastoral range, they still figured in her prayers 'for amendment and pardon of their malice'.[23]

Nor did Mush think that this was merely wasted labour. He could honestly say that 'not only Catholics, but also schismatics, yea, and well-natured heretics would both be glad of her company, and also be most ready to do what she desired them. Some heretics, suspecting the truth indeed [that] she used daily to have God served Catholicly in her house, would be . . . careful to conceal her doings and give intelligence when they learned of any danger likely to befall' her. In fact, though evidently with a good deal of hyperbole, Mush declared that 'everyone loved her, and would have ventured for her more than for themselves'. He described how they would 'run to her for help, comfort and counsel in their distresses', and he remembered 'how familiarly' she would 'use them, and with all courtesy and friendship relieve them'. There were those who clearly had their reservations about what she did and thought, but her powers of persuasion could bring some of them round. Mush knew 'some myself to whom she has used some matters of weight' and they 'after a few words, would yield to her, and say, "For God's sake do what you will, and I am content"'.[24]

But her zeal did not allow her to compromise and give way, even if some of these her unnamed interlocutors were occasionally prepared to do so. Mush observed 'how she lamented and misliked and loathed the state and company of worldlings and lukewarm Catholics which would not give themselves to virtue, neither by the examples of good Catholics, nor the often calls and admonitions of God's messengers'. She was profoundly upset, and uttered 'deep sighs . . . when any loose Catholic lived in folly or fell from the unity of Christ's Church, or when any heretics or schismatics departed this world to the terrible and just judgement of God', even though such things profitably reminded her of her 'own weakness, that might easily slide to the like follies' and, in fact, the 'woeful deaths' of the wicked prompted her to recall 'in what danger she had been herself, and how mercifully God had delivered her'. When she learned of Catholics who shrank from 'persecution', she would, however, 'lament and sorrow'. Publicly she would wonder why it was that Catholics did not glory in their status as the suffering servants of Christ. As Mush explained, whenever she heard of Catholic prisoners who 'behaved themselves' in a disorderly fashion, and gave themselves over to 'idleness, impatience, covetousness, murmuration, dissension, or frowardness, self-love or greedy desire of liberty, inordinate worldly pleasure, or any other thing inconvenient to their calling', she would 'greatly lament their case' and murmur 'fie upon it, that this thing should be heard of, or be at all among Catholics imprisoned for their conscience'. Indeed, Mush said, she wished, during those periods when she was out of gaol, that she might go back, with more than a hint that, once there, she might set about reforming what she took to be the lax standards among the Catholic internees. He had heard her 'many times wish heartily that, if it were God's will, she might be in prison all her life, to ease the griefs of such as were there discontented, to suffer by any painstaking for them. Finally, although she exceeded in compassion', yet Mush never saw her 'heavy or sorrowful for the poverty, tribulation, or persecution which fell to any so long as they showed their patience and gladness to suffer for God's sake; whereas, if she had seen any contrary disposition or behaviour in them, she would have sighed and lamented, and earnestly have prayed for them'.[25]

Phrased like that, of course, Margaret Clitherow's concern for other Catholics' lives and reputations looks like a unifying force, an attempt to keep all York's Catholics together, both in social harmony and some kind of Catholic religious uniformity. Mush felt able to describe all these activities and comments as expressions of Clitherow's charity, indeed, of her humility. 'All her inward contentions and outward behaviours proceeded from singular charity', he claimed. However great the provocation, she, as we saw above, continually 'sucked honey out of the cruelty of her enemies', and marked 'in what virtue everyone did most excel' for the 'beautifying of her own soul'. She was so uncomfortable with praise that she deliberately sought out the company 'of any such as she understood to judge hardly of her'.[26]

To Mush all this looked like the signs of sanctity, the tell-tale marks of the final transformation of Margaret Clitherow, the butcher's wife, into the martyr and incipient saint which she had so conspicuously become by the end of his narrative. Thus he commented,

> as then I admired her, so do I still more and more, hoping by her blessed intercession to emulate some little part of that virtue and purity which I partly knew to be in her; for, if her graces were in her frailty of such efficacy and force that she never came to confession to me but before her departure I was cast into some extraordinary joy of mind and a most comfortable remorse for my own sins, verily I doubt not but now in her secure glory she will be mindful of me and procure me those graces which she knows me to want.

Mush exclaimed:

> You, O my God! the searcher of all secrets, have seen how often your plentiful graces, wherewith you had beautified her, did stir up my soul to you in heavy remembrance of my own miseries, whereby I saw myself far off from you and wished but to be so gracious in your favour as she your servant was, whom here your goodness did adorn with so rare jewels and did prepare as your loving spouse to so glorious a marriage day, that she might so victoriously enter your triumphant city in her bloody scarlet robe.[27]

But it is clear even from Mush's account that her mode of Catholic activism was anything but unifying in its effects. It did not stop her speaking her mind. He insisted that 'this charity so enkindled, and rather inflamed her in such marvellous sort, that it overruled all worldly fears and natural inclination in her; that to serve God she neither feared the world, neither the flesh, nor the devil, neither yet all the cruelty that hell gates, heretics, or other creatures could work against her'. It was this charity which was translated into 'a vehement desire that all others, both heretics, schismatics, and luke-warm Catholics, might know God and His truth, be made the children of His Catholic Church, serve and love Him above all things, and obtain no less grace than she wished for herself, that so God might be glorified in all His people'. Furthermore, 'in this her perfect charity toward God, she let no occasion slip, no opportunity escape, to draw all with whom she might safely deal to their dutiful and sincere obedience toward God'.[28]

Her Catholic zeal served to set her apart not merely from Protestants, both hot and lukewarm, but also from the general run of other Catholics, her sup-posedly charitable relations with whom were almost certainly composed of a good proportion of admonition and rebuke. In short, implied Mush, Mrs Clitherow could be sharp and uncompromising in her comments about vari-ous people, and particularly about Catholics who failed to live up to her own exaltedly rigorous standards of religious observance and ethical exertion. At the same time, her religious profession, both inside her household and with-out, served to create and legitimate a greatly expanded realm of social action and moral comment for this mere woman, the wife of a York butcher.

Mush tells us that many of her contemporaries and neighbours did not regard this elaborate acting out of the norms and forms of an assertive and socially disruptive Catholicism in quite the same admiring light. Perhaps not surprisingly, some Protestants were quite rude about her, but so were some Catholics as well. Indeed, on Mush's account, Mrs Clitherow received short shrift from 'the slanderous tongues' of 'some foolish Catholics'. 'Almost continually after her first conversion', he said, 'she suffered persecution, not only for her invincible constancy in the Catholic faith by heretics, but also for her true virtue by some one or other emulous Catholic'. If 'the heretics had perhaps ceased their rage, as they did seldom, and given her a short calm, forthwith some Catholic raised a storm against her, and often, at the same time, she did bear the assaults of them both together'.[29]

In the sixteenth chapter of the 'True Report' (to which he gave the rather chilling title – 'Of the Persecution that She Suffered among the Good'), Mush described in detail how those who should have been with her were sometimes against her, and he allows us to eavesdrop on their whispered words. 'What ungracious surmises and false judgements', lamented Mush, 'have some in their secret hearts conceived against her; what unjust detractions and untrue reports has malicious envy vomited; what disdainful and crooked looks has cankered emulation procured against her'. Clitherow, 'with exceeding desire and joy, suffered all that heretics could devise against her, accounting them as the enemies of God and of all goodness'. Yet it deeply depressed and upset her when 'Catholics, which professed virtue, would move themselves without cause against her'. Mush related, without even the merest hint of irony, that 'when this chanced, she would sit down with great humility, and bewail her own state, fearing that she were the cause of their offence, and that something lay secret in her which might be the cause of their unquietness'. With absolute and staggering nonchalance, Mush wrote that 'yet she would not by all means cease to pacify them, and humbly to let them see wherein they were deceived; and still she kept a most pure and hearty love to them, imputing all the fault either to herself or to the illusions of the enemy, saying it is but the enemy that seeks to weaken charity amongst us and to hinder us of well doing'.[30]

Though she had, to her own way of thinking, never given the slightest cause or provocation, she found that she was 'assaulted, not indifferently by every Catholic (for with the most and best, she was rightly esteemed of an especial virtue and good life) but by such as were bound to her by many and singular benefits, themselves of no good desert for the same, and also nothing comparable to her in any degree of virtuous life, although externally they might be thought of no small perfection'. As he commented further, 'many in externals show right well, and seem to want nothing necessary to a virtuous life, yet their imperfections are betrayed in some spice of envious emulation to such as are no less virtuous than themselves, or are preferred above them'. There were others too who had 'indeed ascended to some degrees of good-ness', and were 'not enviously grudging to see and have companions in the same way'. But they also showed 'their imperfections' because they were 'void of all joy and alacrity when some others (especially if they be of their own state and calling)' were 'said to be equal with them, or preferred before them; insomuch as every word spoken in commendations of the other' cru-cified their hearts 'with wearisome grief; which kind of gross imperfections were far off from the virtues of this glorious martyr'.[31]

Called upon to explain the adverse reaction of some of Mrs Clitherow's fellow Catholics in York to her exemplary virtue, Mush attributed it, as we saw, to 'emulation', in other words to envy. 'Imperfect virtue, and yet perfect self love, in this kind of adversary ungratefully imagined her chiefest virtues to be their most hindrance; her praise to be their discredit; her joy and con-tinual gladness to be their sorrow and discomforts.' Her detractors 'peevishly gathered to themselves most bitter and hurtful poison out of her sweet and gracious flowers'.[32] Certainly, such a reaction to her intense and insistent dis-plays of moral superiority and more-in-sorrow-than-in-anger Christian love and charity or, as we might see it, her spiritual one-upmanship, might seem natural enough to a modern observer. Indeed, there are obvious parallels with the emergent dynamics of contemporary anti-puritanism which saw a similar reaction against the comparable claims to moral and spiritual superiority and social power being advanced among Protestants by the prodigious piety of the puritans. Mush's account of John Clitherow's critique of Catholics as people who claimed greater sanctity and virtue than their neighbours but who were, in reality, no better than the rest of us, echoes exactly the complaints about puritan hypocrisy being registered at just about this time against the godly by their less self-consciously or assertively pious contemporaries.

As we have already remarked, the way in which Catholics in York responded to the increasingly insistent and ultimately draconian enforcement of the statute law governing conformity to the established Church was extremely complex. Aveling's work on York clearly demonstrates that, for most Catholics, conformity was not a simple category to be absolutely embraced or entirely rejected. What Mush was attempting to present as a simple binary opposition between, on the one hand, good (indeed exemplary) Catholic sanctity – exemplified, of course, by Mrs Clitherow and her clerical handlers – and, on the other, a series of unnamed bad Catholics and schismatics, was, therefore, nothing short of a struggle between different local claimants to or versions of what English Catholicism should be like. This was a struggle conducted in terms of a range of different responses to, on the one hand, the regime's demands for conformity and, on the other, to the no less totalizing calls of certain priests and lay people for a completely separatist form of recusant Catholicism.

We can pick up echoes of these disputes in the terms of opprobrium that Mush used about Mrs Clitherow's Catholic enemies and detractors. Indeed his remarks about them allow us to listen in to the kind of remarks that were being made on the streets of York. These people were the 'worldling and lukewarm Catholics' and 'loose Catholics' who 'lived in folly or fell from the unity of Christ's Church'. Mush spoke more than once of their 'schismatical dissembling'.[33] These were Catholics who murmured, bent or broke down under the lash of persecution. They included the man who had once served at Mass in Clitherow's own household but who, as we saw, later came to persuade her, in the name of obedience to her husband and loyalty to the worldly interests of her family, to give over her rigorously reckless and all-too-public recusancy and harbouring of priests. In short, what we can see coming through the flattened and universalized martyrological lineaments of Mush's account are the traces of an intense local intra-Catholic debate about conformity, or, to put the matter into the argot of modern scholarly commentary, about recusancy and church papistry.

In the chapter that follows, we will try to show how Mrs Clitherow's and her friends' view of the world and of the Church was shaped and inflected by this deep-rooted disagreement among contemporary Catholics about the way in which they should respond to the State's increasingly insistent demands for conformity.

4

The Quarrels of the English Catholic Community

Recusancy and its Discontents

Since the Elizabethan settlement of religion in 1559, Catholics had asked themselves how far was it necessary for good Catholics to prove their zeal for true religion by rejecting the standards of compliance and obedience laid down in the parliamentary statutes which defined what constituted conformity within and to the national Church. There had never been a consensus on this issue within the Catholic community. In the years immediately after the settlement, very few Catholics went into complete separation from the Church of England although a number of Marian clergy did refuse in whole or part to accept the new order.[1]

As we have seen, the call to English Catholics to separate from the national Church was met with a mixed response. The question had been raised in print by the notable Douai divine Gregory Martin in his *Treatise of Schisme* of 1578. The polemical and emotional temperature had then been very considerably raised in 1580 by the mission of Edmund Campion and Robert Persons, in the course of which, both in person and in print, they demanded from Catholics a purer observance of what they said was the traditional command and law of the Church that the faithful should not associate and worship with heretics.[2] This, as we have suggested, was something to which Margaret Clitherow was likely to have paid close attention.

Campion's and Persons's mission can only properly be understood when set in the immediate political and polemical context which produced it and to which it was addressed; a context provided, as we saw above, by the prospect of a marriage between Elizabeth Tudor and a French Catholic prince of the blood, the duke of Anjou. The two Jesuits' intervention in mid-Elizabethan politics might well be thought to have been, among other things, an attempt to maximize the return for Catholics of any such marital alliance. They insisted that only uncompromising recusancy, that is to say, complete and absolute separation from the rites and observances of the national Church, would suffice as a marker of English Catholic identity and zeal. If effective, their campaign would push more and more Catholics into open defiance of the Elizabethan regime. This, in turn, would serve to emphasize both the numerical strength and the ideological backbone of English Catholicism, and it would do this at precisely the point at which the queen was considering marriage to a prince of the house of Valois. Such an overt demonstration of Catholic strength and resolve would amount to a major exercise in civil disobedience as the full extent of English Catholic sentiment was expressed in outward gestures of defiance and refusal. Partial conformists, intermittent members of the national Church, 'church papists' as they were coming to be called, would be converted overnight into conviction Catholics. They were persons whose alienation from the heretical State Church and whose identity as Catholics would now be a matter of public record, performed on almost a daily basis, before a number of Protestant and Catholic, English and foreign, audiences. And they would do this, or so they said, in a spirit of loyalty to their queen who, after all, wanted to marry a Catholic and whose wishes, in this respect, were being hindered and criticized by many 'puritans'.

Thus, on the one hand, what we might regard as a political point of some power was being made through the refusal to attend church. On the other, precisely that same refusal to attend church was being represented as an entirely religious issue, a question of conscience, an outward sign of an inward spiritual impulse and obligation. As such, it had nothing whatsoever to do with 'politics', that is to say, with questions of temporal allegiance or obedience. Robert Persons addressed this issue in his tract of 1580, which bore the title *A Brief Discours containing Certayne Reasons why Catholiques Refuse to Goe to Church*. This pamphlet was designed to demonstrate that 'the refusal of going to the church of so many thousand Catholics at this day' in England 'is not upon disloyalty or stubborn obstinacy, as their adversaries give it out, but upon conscience and great reason and for the avoidance of manifest peril of eternal damnation which they should incur in yielding to that which is demanded at their hands'. For to give way to the demands of the authorities for external compliance when such an act went against the dictates of conscience was to commit the gravest and most damnable of sins.[3]

Thus the punctiliousness with which Catholics responded here to the promptings of conscience and to the demands of religious principle and identity could be presented as anything but a sign of political disloyalty. Rather, it was an expression of the precision and promptitude with which they responded to the imperatives of conscience. This sensitivity to the demands of conscience, Persons claimed, was anything but a source of threat to the regime. In fact, Catholics' very conscientiousness would lead them to recognize and obey the secular authority of the queen with precisely the same zeal and exactitude with which they observed their religious duty to avoid the liturgical pollution on offer in the now heretical national Church. For Persons, the witness maintained by English Catholic recusants must be 'a source of comfort to all men and can justly grieve none, except the common enemy, the Devil himself'. Foreigners would be 'edified' and Englishmen would be 'encouraged', while the queen could not but 'be comforted therein'. She would be able to assure

> herself that if these men do stick so firmly unto their consciences and faith, sworn unto God in their oath of baptism, then will they as firmly, for the same conscience, stick unto her Majesty, if occasion should serve, in keeping their secondary faith and allegiance sworn unto her highness as the substitute of God.[4]

Two conclusions would follow from all this. The first was that English Catholics simply could not be ignored or crushed by the regime. More particularly, the assumption that, over time, Catholicism, if it were denied the oxygen of regular access to Catholic clergy and sacraments, would simply wither away and disappear into an amorphous style of conformist practice and belief, would be definitively shown to be groundless. The second was that, unlike, say, the puritans, who were strenuously opposing the royal will and determination to marry the duke of Anjou, English Catholics were politically loyal enough to be trusted with something like religious toleration.

The position adopted by Persons and Campion on the issue of recusancy thus constituted a direct assault on the principal claim of the regime: namely that it never punished the queen's Catholic subjects for religion but only for politics; or, rather, that Catholics never fell foul of the penalties of the law because of their religious beliefs but rather for their defiance of the authority, and disobedience in the face of the entirely lawful commands, of their queen. By thus starkly redrawing the lines between 'politics' and 'religion', between, on the one hand, the demands of secular allegiance and obedience and, on the other, those of conscience, Persons and Campion were seeking not merely to refute such claims once and for all but also to galvanize English Catholic opinion and to reposition the Catholic cause inside the English polity, which was itself in the process of being remade by the queen's proposed marriage to a French Catholic prince.

But, as we have remarked already, the two Jesuits' claim to be the conscience of Catholic England did not lead them into conflict only with the regime. It also called into radical question a series of compromises worked out, in the period since 1559, by a range of English Catholics. These were compromises and trade-offs made between themselves and their own consciences, with the consciences of other Catholics, and indeed with the legal demands placed upon them by the regime and its representatives. As we have seen, these had involved a range of different gestures made in the face of the conformist norms imposed by the ecclesiastical settlement of 1559. All of those gestures were designed both to maintain the identity of the gesture-makers as Catholics and also to avoid the full rigours of the law. These expedients and trade-offs Campion and Persons now declared to be entirely illicit. They were serious sins which, when committed out of 'frailty' or 'ignorance', were bad enough. But, if they were committed 'wilfully against' the sinner's 'own conscience', 'choosing to sin, although they know it to be sin' – which, after the consciences of English Catholics had been informed on the subject of church attendance by the waves of admonitory instruction now being doled out by the likes of Persons and Campion, would almost certainly be the case – then such acts were likely to damn the sinner's soul to Hell.[5]

As the Jesuit Henry Garnet observed later on, in 1593, to go to the parish church because one was afraid, or because one had not thought about it sufficiently, or even in the knowledge that it was wrong but also with the hope of God's mercy – all this was mortally sinful. If, however, a man who was 'known to be in mind and resolution a Catholic' chose to go to church, and then publicly justified what he did, this was worse still, and exponentially worse if it led others to commit the same sin.[6]

Campion's and Persons's strategy, even though laced with professions of spiritual zeal and political loyalty to the queen, was extremely perilous. It was framed by the Anjou match, the likelihood of which had narrowed almost to nothing even before they reached England. The two Jesuits' mission, both in its underlying message and motivation and in the forms that it took, represented a fundamental challenge to the legitimacy and authority of the regime. That challenge was made and spread by a variety of media – circulating rumour, manuscript, illicit print and semi-public meetings. This virtually forced the regime to defend itself against them, which it did at every available level of action and expression. It hunted down the two priests; it poured out a mass of both elite and popular, theologically sophisticated and entirely scurrilous, printed propaganda; it staged (rigged) disputations between Campion and a raft of interlocutors in the Tower. Crucially, it sought to turn Campion – in other words to make him renounce the Church of Rome. When he refused, the regime put him on trial, condemned him and then publicly executed him as a traitor to the queen. It also pursued all those who had given him aid and succour. The onslaught culminated in a range of new statutes aimed at making the lives of English Catholics altogether more difficult. The result was that Persons's exhortation to his co-religionists finally and definitively to remove themselves from the taint of attendance at heretical worship virtually coincided with, if it did not actually call down, a bout of official repression on the Catholic community. Persons's appeal was, therefore, in part a response to, and in part an anticipation of, the regime's decision to use the authority of parliament and the high commission, as well as the power of the privy council, to attack the resolve of those Catholic gentlemen who had been willing to extend their patronage to the Jesuits. As Persons no doubt anticipated, the onslaught in 1580–1581, by a variety of government agencies, compelled widespread conformity among those Catholics who had for a time been willing to go into separation. Starting out as an act of polemical aggression, Persons's pitch thus became also an exercise in damage limitation.[7] But, if so, it only succeeded in raising the polemical and political stakes even further and in sharpening the antagonism between the regime and the queen's Catholic subjects. There was, of course, for Persons, no contradiction or even irony here, since the intensity of what he now took to be persecution merely served to render the necessity of a coherently recusant witness the more pressingly apparent.

What might seem obvious to Persons was, however, by no means so clear to all English Catholics. From the outset, the Jesuits' insistence that recusancy was the only means whereby true Catholicism could be maintained in England had not met with unanimous approval or assent. Many Catholics regarded such a stance as both a needless provocation of the authorities and an entirely unhelpful subversion of a settled body of assumption and practice that had hitherto preserved the English Catholic community from the depredations of the State. Indeed, as we remarked above, at the semi-public meeting at Southwark in July 1580, at which the two Jesuits had confronted many of the leading English Catholics, some had pressed the two men simply to shut up and/or leave, lest their presence incite the regime to new heights of repression.[8] That initial anxious, indeed, in some quarters, frankly antagonistic, response was only likely to be heightened, and the consequent divisions among English Catholics exacerbated, by the State's campaign of intimidation provoked by Campion's and Persons's insurgently missionary endeavours.

There followed a series of arguments and debates, of formal and semi-formal exchanges, between the proponents of recusancy and the defenders of various sorts of 'church popery'. These were conducted both in person and in manuscript, and, on the recusant side of the issue at least, in print. After the meeting at Southwark, a dispute took place between Persons himself and the former archdeacon of Chichester, Alban Langdale. Other Catholic priests, notably James Bosgrave and Thomas Langdale (Alban Langdale's nephew), were also prepared to say out loud that they did not regard recusancy as an absolute necessity for a Catholic.[9] Persons's *Brief Discours contayning Certayne Reasons why Catholiques Refuse to Goe to Church*, printed secretly at Greenstreet House, East Ham in 1580, took the form of a reply to a manuscript tract allegedly written by Alban Langdale and was thus explicitly directed as much against Catholic defenders of certain styles of conformity as it was at the regime's claims to be punishing Catholics only for their secular disobedience rather than for their religious beliefs.

At this point we need to examine in further detail the nature of the arguments made on both sides of this question. In so doing we will primarily be using Persons's *Brief Discours* augmented by a range of other both printed and manuscript tractate testimony, notably by Henry Garnet and also, as it happens, by Clitherow's spiritual guide and mentor, John Mush. These pamphlets also allow us to reconstruct a good many of the arguments used in favour of conformity. These were arguments which, in the absence of surviving tracts by the likes of Langdale or later of Thomas Bell, would otherwise be lost to history. Much of this debate is, if taken in a vacuum, apparently rather hypothetical. To modern eyes, much of it appears to be crushingly dull. But it was the product of an intense and all-too-real conflict between mid-Elizabethan Catholics, threatened as they were by vengeful agents of the State. Those agents were determined to root out what they saw as a quasi-republican and anti-monarchical style of public agitation launched by rogue Catholic clergy.

Like Gregory Martin before him, Persons argued that Catholic compliance with the statute law on conformity would be taken as 'consent' to everything that the heretics did.[10] He declared that going to church was never 'mere' conformity, as Alban Langdale had claimed it could be. For 'it has always some such thing annexed to it as is prohibited *jure naturali vel divino*', such as 'peril of infection, scandal, dissembling in faith, hearing of God dishonoured, [and] yielding to his adversaries in religion'. Persons took it as axiomatic that what was at stake was the sin of schism: 'going to the Protestants' churches and prayers' was no less than a 'schismatical act' and the effect of it was to cut off the man who sinned thus 'from the unity of the Church'.

Here one of the crucial questions was the social status and significance of attendance or non-attendance at church. Was it (always) a 'sign distinctive', in other words something which would differentiate infallibly a true Catholic from a heretic? Persons argued that it must be so because the Protestant authorities 'ask ordinarily no more when men come before them but when they were at church last, offering unto them . . . that if they will promise to go to church, they shall have liberty'. If someone did promise to go to church, 'commonly they account him a sufficient conformable man'.[11]

In a move that equated attendance at Protestant churches with attendance at pagan Roman sacrifice, Persons quoted St Cyprian to the effect that 'if a man did live never so virtuously otherwise, nay if he should give his life or shed his blood for Christ, yet if he were out of the unity of the Church he could not be saved'.[12]

Elsewhere Persons quoted St Augustine in order to claim that 'the contemnor of visible sacraments can by no means invisibly be sanctified'.[13] But since going to the Protestants' service did indeed constitute contempt for the visible sacraments of the Catholic Church this put the conforming Catholic in the most perilous of spiritual conditions. After all, the Church of England acknowledged only two of the seven sacraments and so badly mangled one of those – the Mass – that it could be said in fact only to acknowledge and practise one (that is, baptism). In the absence of 'the blessed sacrifice of the Christ his body and blood . . . offered up every day for thanksgiving to God for obtaining of grace and avoiding of all evil and for the remission of sin', there could be no true 'Christian service' or priesthood, as indeed was the case in the now heretical Church of England.[14]

On the one hand, such claims allowed Persons to turn aside a whole range of arguments advanced in favour of conformity. What, some conformist Catholics were asking, was so bad about going to the local parish church? Did not the churches really belong to the (in some sense) largely Catholic population of many of these parishes anyway? And, after all, was not the service, passively witnessed as it was by the Catholics who went there, for the most part composed of passages of Scripture? Surely the service was all but identical to the Catholic one, save that it was in English? It had been argued, in fact, that mere attendance at heretical services was not a 'sign distinctive', separating Catholic from Protestant, and heretic from true believer, but merely, as the government claimed, a matter of temporal obedience, an outward act required by the State. This had enabled some to claim, Persons declared, 'that a man may, without offence, keep his conscience to himself', not only holding his peace but also doing against his conscience 'whatsoever is commanded'. Such people might then licitly say that 'all which is done amiss shall not be laid upon them at the day of judgement but upon the prince and the magistrates which compel them to do the same against their wills'.[15] In posing and answering such questions, Persons allows us to eavesdrop on what had presumably become the conventional defences for certain modes of Catholic conformity.

But all such cavils simply collapsed in the face of Persons's description of the practices of the national Church as an anti-religion, the pure negation of true Christian worship, mere contact with which would quite cut off the

person so offending from the universal Catholic Church and from all the
spiritual benefits consequent upon membership of that Church. As Henry
Garnet put it in 1593, 'whilst your body is with Calvin, your soul cannot
be with the Catholic Church'.[16] However much, in *de jure* terms, the parish
churches might still belong to the Catholics, in practice, as Persons pointed
out, they had been taken over by the Catholics' enemies whose service and
sermons, attacking the religion of Rome, contained prayers full of hatred
for the papacy.[17] As Garnet phrased it, while 'the churches are ours indeed',
'the heretics' service and company is not'. Mere contact with the worship of
heretics polluted the one who associated with them; touching pitch inevitably
led to defilement. Thus 'a layman going thither for fear and in offering up
such prayers as he can afford almighty God in that place', and finding that
he was 'touched with remorse of conscience of his unlawful presence' was
'bound, under pain of the same sin', to 'follow immediately the counsel of
the prophet and of the apostle: "get ye hence, get ye hence, go forth from
hence, touch not that which is polluted, go forth of the midst of your congregation"'. It was not good enough for him merely to resolve in his heart
that he 'would go no more; for, so long as he stayed there, so long should he
continue in the act of a mortal sin'. It was not sufficient to protest that 'the
love of the walls possessed you' and that 'you reverence the Church of God
in houses and buildings'. For, Garnet argued, 'the going to the church howsoever does always betoken . . . devotion and religion, in Catholic churches, to
the true faith', but in heretical churches it signified devotion to 'their detest-
able synagogues'.[18] Persons insisted that the authorities bullied Catholics
into attending churches so that 'they, by going, should pray with' Protestants,
'allow of their service and, by their presence, honour it'.[19]

Despite the claims made by some conformists that they were forced to go
to church and that the sin involved in their attendance redounded not to their
spiritual detriment but rather to that of the heretical magistrates who drove
them there, Persons insisted that they could not escape the moral consequences of what they did. Threatened by punishment for noncompliance they
may well have been, but they had not thereby been denied free will. Rather
they had been offered a choice: obey or be punished.[20] Garnet concurred,
arguing that 'whatsoever is done for fear' is nevertheless 'voluntary'. Only
main force – 'violence' – could take away the voluntary status of such acts,
since 'the will' could not 'be constrained'. On this basis, Garnet proceeded
to threaten conformist Catholics with the direst of consequences: 'because
every action voluntary in a matter which of itself is a mortal sin deserves
everlasting damnation, although it be done for fear', it was imperative that
all church papists should 'acknowledge' their sin so that they might the
'sooner obtain remission'; without which, of course, the offending schismatic

would certainly be going to Hell.[21]

What was at stake here was the appearance of compliance with, indeed of approval of, what Persons called a 'contrary religion' and what Garnet was to call 'the Church of Calvin' or 'of the Calvinists'. The resulting society was 'not now a piece of Christ his coat, which is altogether undivided, but a ragged clout raked out of the sink of Hell, although presumptuously arrogating to itself the name and title of a Church of Christ'. For Garnet, as for Persons, the choices were stark: 'either you think them to be the Church and, whereas there cannot be two Churches, us to be schismatics or, if it be manifest that the true Church is in the apostolical seas, then know you that . . . they are divided from unity'. For both Jesuits, the conclusion was as clear as the day: 'we cannot profess any union' with schismatics 'but by disuniting ourselves from the one only dove and spouse of Christ'.[22]

For Garnet, since schism was any act that implied separation from communion with the true Church, to commit any such act was to become, *ipso facto*, a schismatic. Here, at least, there was no meaningful distinction to be drawn between the internal and the external: 'schism requires nothing but a consent of the will to division from the Church and therefore every outward schismatic is also an inward schismatic'.[23] On this basis, Persons felt able to set the bar of recusant purity very high indeed. Anyone tainted with the least hint of conformity, guilty of the smallest gesture towards compliance with the State's demands about church attendance, was also guilty of the sin of schism and hence in the most extreme spiritual danger: 'seeing [that] this going to church is so forbidden by God's law as it is and has so many great inconveniences in it . . . a man may not yield in any one little point in the same, as, for example, to come to church once a year, to have service in his house, to show himself present at a piece of the service or the like'.[24]

For Persons, all such concessions (for example by 'causing a man to yield a little against his conscience to go once to church, to stay but a little there, to have service in his own house or the like') were but the start of a slippery slope that led first to schism and thence to heresy. Some might say that 'a little will do but a little hurt', but it was no different from drinking poison, 'where every little dram will be your bane'.[25] Henry Garnet used precisely the same remorselessly binary logic to exhort his conformist interlocutor that 'the loss of charity is the way to the loss of faith' and so any 'entrance into schism' is 'an entrance unto heresy'.[26] All of which served, of course, to rule quite out of court all of the expedients and compromises that, as John Aveling has shown, many of the Catholics of York (and, of course, elsewhere) had used to protect themselves from the depredations of the Elizabethan State while still maintaining a Catholic identity for themselves.

But there was more at stake here than the spiritual condition and potentially tragic fate of those who actually practised church popery, a group to whom Persons contemptuously referred as 'the cold Catholics' of England. For their practice, and still more the arguments they used to justify those practices, endangered the salvation of many other potentially Catholic souls. Here the question was what, as we have already briefly mentioned above, Persons called 'scandal' – the deliberate leading of others into sin. This, according to Persons, was a 'sin more mentioned, more forewarned, more forbidden, more detested, more threatened in the Scripture, than any sin else mentioned in the same, except it be idolatry'. There were three reasons why a Catholic who attended church caused scandal 'in the highest degree'. First, 'if he be a man of any calling, his example shall induce some other, as wife, children, friends, servants, or the like, to do the same. And howsoever he escape himself, they may be infected and so damned'; and it would be even worse if 'he should exhort or constrain any man to do the same . . . as commonly many schismatics do use'. Secondly, he could not but 'offend many men's consciences'. People would think that he did what he did out of conscience. And, thirdly, all those who were not Catholics would 'both think and speak the worse of the said religion'.[27]

Of course, the decision of some Catholics to attend their parish churches had always been, in some sense, a cause of 'scandal'. But in the context of the State's decision in and after 1580 to go after those who were visibly separatist, there was now absolutely no room to argue, as did some of the defenders of conformity, that attendance at church was not, or under the right circumstances did not have to be, a 'sign distinctive' of religious allegiance and belief and hence a cause of outrage to the true Catholic religion. Garnet, like Persons, went so far as to claim that a Catholic who attended Protestant services was 'an exterior heretic' and 'a favourer of heretics' because he 'increases their number and adds . . . unto the credit of their congregation and so makes heresy to spread itself'.[28]

There was something rather self-serving about such claims. After all, things had only reached the current pass because of the public stir about these issues which had been quite deliberately fomented by Campion and Persons themselves. Indeed those, both Protestants and Catholics, who looked askance at what they had done, could argue that they had brought things to a head precisely in order to impose their view of the matter on the main body of English Catholic opinion and to make a set of ideological and political claims in the face of the demands of the State that Catholics should not transgress the line between conformity and separation.

Thomas Bell and his Critics

As we have seen, from at least the late 1570s, the hard-line recusant position was eliciting a contrary case from proponents of a more dove-ish approach to the issue of conformity. The exchanges and debates provoked and prosecuted by Campion and Persons accelerated this process in which, from the early 1580s, a leading role was played by the seminary priest Thomas Bell. Bell was to emerge in the coming years as the principal proponent of the so-called church-papist position. He was, one might say, Alban Langdale's intellectual and ideological heir. But he was no shrinking violet. Still less was he some pliant conformist or natural moderate. He had, in fact, thrown off his allegiance to the established Church around the time of the rebellion of the northern earls in 1569.[29] As William Hutton remembered in late 1594, Bell had been 'committed twenty-four years since to Ouse Bridge, where he lay all one cold winter . . . in the stocks' and 'divers preachers' came 'to confer with him'. Subsequently he was 'removed to the castle'.[30] His missionary activities in the early 1580s in York look like an attempt to replicate the style of Campion's ministry although, as we have remarked, it is not clear that his exploits in York Castle in 1582 were phrased in quite the same confrontational way as, for example, those of Persons and Campion.[31] Indeed, according to Katharine Longley, as late as 1587, Richard Verstegan, with considerable irony, included an image of Bell suspended for days on end by his feet in York Castle as part of the background to a tableau centred on the image of Mrs Clitherow's macabre fate. This was one of a series of tableaux which described visually the suffering of English Catholics under Elizabeth Tudor's tyranny.[32] All of this renders entirely explicable Bell's determination to be seen, just as much as his opponents, as a suffering servant of Christ.

In theory, then, Bell came from the same Catholic rigorist stable as Campion and Persons and he had a track record of religious defiance and missionary daring to equal almost anyone's. Accordingly, his attempts to justify a certain style of Catholic conformity as the most appropriate way to maintain the cause of Catholicism in Protestant England were not conceived as some soft option. They were not, at best, a mere buffing up and polishing, a bolstering with his own clerical learning and charisma, of existing arguments for a quiet life of the sort which had been catalogued, ridiculed and refuted by Persons in his *Brief Discours*. Rather, Bell's position represented an attempt to redraw the line between religion and politics laid down by Persons and others in such a way as to render it possible for Catholics to defer to the secular authority of their prince, indeed, in some sense, to conform, while still rendering crystal clear their conscience-based and entirely spiritual commitment to the truths of orthodox Catholic religion.

Essentially, Bell asserted that it was at all times necessary to demonstrate the purity and truth of the Catholic faith in the face of the Protestants, but that it was not required to do this explicitly or always by disobeying the act of uniformity and spitting in the eye of the queen. In making this claim Bell was drawing on earlier conformist thought, and in particular that of Alban Langdale. In one of his early exchanges with Langdale, Persons had dismissed a series of gestures which Langdale had suggested might strip attendance at church of its status as a 'sign distinctive' of a man's religious profession or identity: 'you say, that if a man go to their churches, yet there are *signa distinctiva* enough besides', as for example 'not to pray with them' or to 'sit or stand when they kneel', or not 'to receive their communion'. But, said Persons, this was no good at all. For, 'touching the first, no man can tell whether you pray with them or no except he watch your mouth'; for the second, 'many Protestants may do the like if they have the colic'; and, third, the act of refusing the Protestant communion was not a distinctive sign because 'the use of it comes very seldom' and there were other reasons for not receiving it – for example being out of charity with one's neighbour. Even standing there and protesting that one came to church because the queen commanded it was not sufficient because it was unlikely that an appropriate 'protestation' – in other words, a verbal declaration of the true motives of the conformist – could be made on each and every occasion when it should be required. Indeed, such a protestation might well be taken by anyone who heard it as the mark of a bad conscience.[33]

Likewise, in his *Brief Discours*, Persons discussed the well-known, in fact almost commonplace, scriptural case of Namaan the Syrian. Despite his status as a recent convert to the worship of the one true God, Naaman had asked the prophet Elijah's permission to go into the temple of a pagan God in the course of the discharge of his secular duty towards his prince, who was also an idolator. Persons had approved such a practice but only under the strictest of conditions. The business being transacted in the church must be wholly secular in nature and have a very particular purpose. The physical act of going into the temple (or church) could not be attended by 'any sign of reverence or honour' to the service conducted there. Clearly there were some Catholics who wanted to combine the example of Namaan with a variety of outward gestures of religious disaffection and political obedience in order to provide a mode of church attendance which was supposedly devoid of religious content but was designed solely to demonstrate secular allegiance.[34]

It was just such an attempt to square the circle that lay at the centre of Thomas Bell's justification of a certain sort of entirely un-religious, 'secular' or 'political' Catholic conformity. *Pace* Persons's dismissive treatment of the subject, Bell claimed that it was licit to go to church if, through some such verbal protest, the conformist in question made it vocally and even obstreperously clear that he or she was there only to obey the queen and not to commend or endorse the service as it was there being recited and celebrated. The protestation which Bell recommended, according to John Mush, ran as follows: 'Good people, I am come hither not for any liking I have of any sacraments, service or sermons accustomably used in this place but only to give a sign of my allegiance and due loyalty to my prince'. Indeed, Bell said, this device of a vocal protestation or speech made you a better Catholic than if you simply absented yourself and gave no such explanation of your actions, for then you were in much the same case as, and could hardly be distinguished by your neighbours from, puritan separatists who likewise absented themselves from divine service in the Church of England.[35]

Bell and Persons were therefore in competition for essentially the same ideological terrain. Pursuing the same ends, they were appealing to the same political and religious constituencies with precisely the same sorts of arguments. On this basis, it should be no surprise just how close to one another the two sides often came on even some of the central issues. Both insisted that recusancy was indeed a spiritual good. Neither of them allowed that conformity was in any sense spiritually beneficial. Bell's opponents often taunted him with his admission that recusancy was the more spiritually perfect option, indeed the ideal to which all Catholics should technically aspire. Both saw recusancy as necessary in certain circumstances. And both admitted (though phrasing it differently) that recusancy was not *always* necessary at all times, and in the same degree, from all people. In fact, as we have seen, the opponents of church papistry sometimes came close to conceding that certain kinds of occasional conformity were licit as long as they did not give scandal.[36]

In many of the tracts which either allowed or condemned occasional conformity, the issue was not merely the action itself but the intentions which lay behind it. The intentions of the person who was physically making himself present at his parish church were crucial. Both parties to the intra-Catholic debate admitted, in effect, that, if someone went to church in such a way as actually to challenge the Protestants' claims to doctrinal orthodoxy and purity, then this was not conformity in the bad and schismatical sense that the true Church had always condemned. Even Henry Garnet cited a hypothetical example of a man who intended to go to a heretical church to 'preach Catholicly' there. As long as people knew of his intention, he would be justified in his going to church, even if, when he got there, he was prevented from preaching.[37]

Perhaps even more important, however, was what might be deduced about the motives and intentions of the authorities who ordered Catholics to conform. From the time of Persons's debate with Alban Langdale, in fact, the central and underlying argument in all the works urging Catholic separation from the national Church was that the demand for conformity must be evaluated by reference to the presumed will of those who tried to force Catholics to attend divine service against their conscience. This in turn could be measured only against an index of the more general malice which Protestants visibly harboured towards the true (Catholic) religion. Even more than Persons in 1580, Mush was able, when he set pen to paper in 1588, to cite the Elizabethan State's tyrannical treatment of its Catholic subjects – and here the examples of Campion and Mrs Clitherow bulked large – as proof positive of the regime's entirely malign intent in requiring attendance at church from its Catholic subjects. If left to themselves, good Catholics would not go near the parish churches at all. The fact was that the Protestants ordered them to go there 'in *odium religionis*, for hatred of Catholic religion'. The Protestants intended that, 'by that external action', Catholic conformists should be 'partakers with them, approve their ecclesiastical authority and at least seem to give consent to their whole religion, all which is sin of itself'.[38] In the face of such evidence, in the face, that is, of the rampant persecution to which Catholics were being subjected, writers such as Persons declared that the arguments for conformity simply collapsed.

Bell's opponents went out of their way to portray his position as, in effect, a surrender in the face of the renewed persecution that had followed Campion's and Persons's mission. Bell's casuistical justification of conformity was, so Bell's enemies said, a mere front for the spiritual laziness and material self-interest of Catholics who were desperate to save themselves and their estates from the toils of the law while they retained a plausible (but in fact deeply flawed and fallacious) claim to be regarded as good Catholics. Bell, of course, denied this. He averred that what was at stake here was a perfectly viable way to do just what Persons and the others had said that they themselves were doing; that is to say, to establish both the spiritual *bona fides* and the political loyalty of English Catholics by drawing, or rather redrawing, the line that separated 'religion' from 'politics'. This was a line which, as presently defined and policed by the authorities, enabled and justified the official line first that Catholics were only ever punished for politics and not for religion, and secondly that any Catholic who refused to go to church was *ipso facto* guilty of disobedience and was thus either actually or potentially disloyal to the queen.

On the present view, both the hard line on recusancy pushed by Persons, Campion and Garnet and the church-papist position, at least as it was theorized and legitimated by the likes of Langdale and Bell, represented different pitches made to the regime. All the parties to this debate claimed that they had established a way for the conscientious religious scruples and the political loyalism of English Catholics to be expressed publicly. Of course, if they were successfully to ameliorate the situation of English Catholics both positions required, albeit to different extents, a sympathetic response from the State. In the absence of such a response, indeed in the face of renewed and intensified repression, the case for out-and-out separatism slotted perfectly into a discourse of passive disobedience. If and when repressive push came to overtly persecutory shove, it was compatible with a discourse of martyrdom, a discourse that could then be used aggressively to condemn Thomas Bell and all like-minded people of falling sadly short of what both true Catholic principle and the witness and example of the martyrs in this and former ages demanded.

The fact was, however, that Bell was not simply arguing for a soft option. He was not the spineless collaborator that his Catholic opponents, both clerical and lay, made him out to be. However much his enemies wanted to deny it, Bell took very seriously his own prescription about attending church with an overt, formal and angry verbal protest of both political allegiance to the queen and real religious distaste at the Protestant form of worship employed there.

Nevertheless, Bell's claims to be morally consistent and casuistically orthodox cut absolutely no ice with his critics. Mush declared that Bell's natural constituency was the 'many weaklings' to be found in the Catholic community. These were persons who were desperate to find 'plausible advice and doctrine' on the basis of which they could 'yield to the extremity of the time' and thereby escape the 'trouble, the worldly dangers and temporal harms' which 'the heretics' loaded onto them. By making Bell's public protestation, said Mush, such people would 'be in greater danger of her Majesty's laws than they were in only for recusancy'. Specifically, they would, he claimed, be contravening the legislation which assigned fines and punishments for 'despising, depraving or derogation' of the 1559 prayer book far in excess of those consequent upon recusancy. Citing Campion's experience at the hands of the authorities – when he had been indicted under a statute of Edward III's reign that could not possibly have any real application to his case – Mush argued that the heretics had a long history of 'violently wresting' the law against the Catholics. And why would they not now do the same, applying even the relevant recusancy statute against the makers of Bell's protestation, since that statute enjoined not merely attendance at church but also demanded that the queen's subjects should 'abide there orderly and soberly'? Bell expressly forbade 'his protesters' to sit 'otherwise quietly reverently and conformably' through the service. This course might well appeal to weak and cold Catholics and to those who were 'so wearied with suffering these evil and intolerable vexations wherewith the heretics continually oppress them'. But in practice, said Mush, Bell's protestation could only make matters worse. It would call down the fury of the State upon those who actually tried to practise it while, at the same time, it would endanger their souls and fatally compromise the witness maintained by other and truer Catholics who (unlike Bell's followers) were suffering under the cross of persecution with their religious principles intact.[39]

The mid 1580s were, then, a period in which conformity, church popery and the necessity of separation were all topics which were subject not only to almost continuous contest between the claims of the regime and the response thereto of English Catholics but also to very considerable internal debate among and between English Catholics themselves. In practice, if not in theory, the line between 'recusants' and 'conformists' or 'church papists' remained intensely fuzzy and permeable. The ideological terrain denoted by the term 'church popery' was not yet clearly delineated or defined. It was this that generated the polemical activity, the flurry of claim and counter-claim analysed above. The clerical proponents of recusant separation talked as though this was not the case. They presented the issues as a series of clear-cut binary oppositions, either/or ideological choices, when, in fact, many contemporaries were still making up their minds, either oscillating between one stance and the other, or trying rather hard not to have to make any such definitive decisions at all. The resulting tergiversations and doubts afflicted even some of those who came subsequently to be viewed or marketed as paragons of ideological purity and commitment. As her Protestant tormentors were to remind her in gaol, one of Mrs Clitherow's chaplains, the martyr William Hart had been in two minds upon this issue. Back in 1582, Hart had been an associate of Thomas Bell himself when Bell entered York Castle to celebrate Mass for the Catholic prisoners there. It was known that Hart had not always been absolutely set against the partial conformity option.[40]

It was, therefore, surely no accident that, as Alexandra Walsham has shown, it was at precisely this point, during the early to mid 1580s, that the term 'church papist' started to come into currency among both Catholics and Protestants. Among Catholics it served as a term of opprobrium for various sorts of conformist, in other words those who, on this view, prevaricated between a properly coherent espousal of Catholic principle and something more or less like schism. As such it was used by rigorist proponents of recusancy as a means to promote themselves as the only true Catholics in Elizabeth's realm and to defend their line on conformity as the only truly Catholic response to the stresses and strains of life under a heretical regime. Among hot Protestants the term could cover a rather wider range of opinion, serving to encompass almost everyone (save out-and-out recusants) who did not share the definitions of true religion and Protestant zeal being internalized and pushed by the godly themselves. In both cases the term was being designed and deployed by rigorist minorities – crudely, by recusant Catholics and puritans (of various stripes) – in order to confer the palm of ideological purity, of true religious zeal and principle, on themselves, by assimilating other, rival claimants to the 'out' group of choice; on the Catholic side, to so-called schismatics and, on the Protestant side, to so-called papists. Rather than either a stable religious identity, a precisely delineated ideological position, or, still less, a stable middle, located somewhere near the centre of the spectrum of religious opinion, on this view, 'church popery' was a term of art. Indeed it was a term of abuse, developed and deployed, on both sides of the confessional divide, to confer order and stable meaning on what was, in fact, an intensely unstable, even febrile, religious environment. It was developed, moreover, in the interests, and to further the purposes, of two very different, indeed mutually antagonistic, groups of religious *engagés*.

But for all that the 'recusant' and 'church-papist' positions at times seemed to overlap, and for all that the divisions between the contending parties were by no means as clear-cut as the polemical literature tried to make it appear, there remained a great deal up for grabs in these disputes. As we have seen, Persons and Campion had, during their agitation of 1580–1581, very significantly raised the stakes. An unlooked-for consequence of their having done so was that, in the course of the resulting exchanges over the issue of conformity, what had previously operated as a series of assumptions, piecemeal legitimations and arguments, a body of *de facto* compromise, a series of implicit trade-offs, of nudges and winks, exchanged between certain Catholics, their neighbours and the State, now became hardened into something rather more like an ideology. Their rigorism had resulted in the emergence of a coherent body of doctrine and argument designed to justify the practice of certain styles of conformity against the totalizing case for recusancy as the only mark of true Catholicism being made with such confidence and aggression by the two English Jesuits and their allies and followers. As we have seen, from the perspective of those who argued for absolute separation from the filth of heretical Protestantism, the casuistical systematization of arguments in favour of church popery, advanced to and discussed with other Catholics, made a bad situation worse. It was wicked enough, said Henry Garnet, to flaunt one's sin in public, but it was 'more abominable to defend' the sin and even worse to lead others to commit it as well.[41]

Nor was the damage wrought by such active canvassing of the church-papist position merely spiritual or religious. It had very serious consequences for the political and polemical position outlined by Campion and Persons and subsequently asserted and defended by their clerical allies such as Mush and Garnet. It was, after all, central to Persons's and Campion's wider political and polemical purposes vis-à-vis the regime that it was both true and sincerely believed by all the Catholics of England that, if a person conformed, he would lose 'all the benefit of his own religion'. Persons explained that it was the duty of Catholics to make this clear to the queen. For then, opined Persons, she would inevitably pity the 'many thousands of her loving subjects' who were 'Catholics in heart' but 'by going to Protestants' churches' would inevitably 'be brought either to flat atheism, that is to leave off all conscience and to care for no religion at all (as many thousands seem to be resolved to do) or else to live in continual torment of mind and almost desperation, considering that, by their going to these churches, they lose utterly all use and practise of their own religion, being held as schismatics and excommunicate persons of the same'. Were they to die in this miserable state, they would be in the same woeful case as Protestants.[42]

However, such claims were unlikely to be believed by the Protestant authorities if many, indeed perhaps even a majority of, English Catholics continued to act, and even worse to talk, as though their Catholicism was compatible with some sort of outward compliance with (what the likes of Persons insisted were) the regime's (inherently ir/religious) demands for attendance at church. If that happened, the regime would only be encouraged to continue its efforts to reduce Catholics at first to outward conformity and then to conduct them down the slippery slope that led from partial to full conformity, and thence from what the likes of Persons and Garnet termed schism into fully fledged heresy. Not only that, but if many Catholics did indeed continue to go to church, claiming that they did so only for obedience's sake and to demonstrate their allegiance to the queen, then the regime's contention that those who refused to do so were not conscientious Christians concerned for the condition of their souls but, instead, bad, disobedient and potentially disloyal subjects who were being punished not for their religious beliefs but for their political disobedience, would be confirmed. Perhaps even more serious, the unity of Catholics in the face of the persecution of the State would be fractured and the witness of the martyrs, indeed their status as martyrs at all, would be undermined.

Thus it was that both John Mush and Henry Garnet would later accuse Bell and his ilk of effectively selling the pass to the authorities. According to Mush, writing in 1588, it was a 'shameful assertion' on Bell's part to say that the queen demanded that Catholics should be present at their parish churches only 'as a badge of temporal subjection rather than a sign of spiritual profession'. This was, in effect, to deny that the State was persecuting

Catholics, which, said Mush, it palpably was. It was also a refusal to concede that Catholics suffered for their religion alone. It was inevitable that Elizabeth was 'greatly beholden' to Thomas Bell whose words could not but be taken to 'acquit and justify her and all her murders and persecutions of Catholics'. Bell had sold himself to the most tyrannical and heretical of the queen's servants. Mush compared Bell's weasel words with the performance of that sanctimonious hypocrite Lord Burghley at Mary Stuart's trial at Fotheringhay in late 1586. The Scottish queen declared to the lord treasurer 'with weeping eyes: "my lord it is well known that you have sought my blood . . . [for] many years, but I would to God that my blood might purchase peace and liberty of conscience . . . [for] the Catholics of this realm, [and] I would give it most gladly for redeeming their troubles"'. But Burghley 'answered: "Madam, you are wrongly informed, for there is not one Catholic in this realm troubled for his conscience and religion but only for disobedience to her Majesty's laws and for that they be enemies to the State"'.[43] And this, Mush argued, was tantamount to Bell's position. Or, rather, anyone who took Bell's line made Burghley's entirely fallacious arguments seem a good deal more plausible than they actually were. Garnet insisted, in a similar vein, that Bell's style of church popery did not merely cheapen or debase but actually inverted the claims to true martyrdom which could be advanced in the cases of so many Catholics who had suffered for their refusal to recant and conform. On Bell's account, they had refused the lawful decrees and orders of their sovereign: 'see, I pray you', wrote Garnet, 'how many priests, martyrs, men and women and children you condemn to Hell'.[44]

Christianity *sans Eglise*: The Religion of the Heart among Catholics and Puritans

Elizabethan Catholics who separated from the national Church were, therefore, confronted with the dilemma of what kind of Church they now belonged to. As we have seen, one of the major arguments made by certain proponents of church popery was that since the parish churches of England still in effect belonged to the Catholics, or at least to those who were of a Catholic persuasion, there could be nothing wrong in their continuing to attend worship therein. The strength of this argument or impulse was compounded by the fact that if the English Catholics followed the advice of Persons and his friends and denied themselves all contact with the parish churches of their ancestors, they would be devoid of any sort of organized corporate worship or institutional religious life. Protestants who were anxious to push church papists into full conformity took advantage of this

dilemma by arguing that, even assuming that recusant Catholics were acting in accordance with their consciences in separating from the Church of
England, they were still cutting themselves off from the only institutional
Church available, because in England they had no Church to go to other
than the national one.[45]

It was as an attempt to address precisely this dilemma that Robert Persons,
who had so substantially contributed to the creation of this dilemma in the
first place, wrote his *Christian Directory* of 1582. Heavily rooted in the
spirituality and the exercises of Ignatius of Loyola, this was something of
a hitchhiker's guide for the spiritually homeless Christian soul.[46] Indeed,
the volume should almost certainly be viewed as a companion volume to
Persons's *Brief Discours* of 1580, in other words as a piece of practical divin-
ity to complement, indeed to compensate for, the necessary aridities and
rigidities of polemical works such as his own tract on recusancy. As Persons
himself put it, in the course of the introduction to the *Christian Directory*,
'these books of controversy are necessary for defence of our faith against so
many seditious innovations as now are attempted'; but they also risked filling
'the heads of men with a spirit of contradiction and contention that, for the
most, hinders devotion'. This 'devotion is nothing else but the quiet and
peaceable state of the soul, endued with a joyful promptness to the diligent
execution of all things that appertain to the honour of God'. Thus, while
'our forefathers' were lucky enough to receive 'the ground of faith peaceably
and without quarrelling from their mother the Church' and so tried to 'build
upon the same, good works and Christian life, as their vocation required',
unfortunate Catholics now spent 'all the time in jangling about the foundation' and had 'no leisure to think upon the building'. And so, said Persons,
'we weary out our spirits without commodity' and 'we die with much ado
and little profit, great disquiet and small reward'.[47]

Persons's book presented itself as the antidote to this tendency. As
such, it would serve as the means for believers to achieve what he termed
'Christian resolution'. As we have seen, in the *Brief Discours* Persons had
talked the binary, either/or talk of division and contention. He had presented
Catholicism and Protestantism as two religions. English Catholics had a
choice. On the one hand, they had the one true Church, and, on the other,
a form of spiritual pollution, consequent upon attendance at the services
of an institution that did not even really deserve the name of a Church at
all. But now, in the *Christian Directory*, he got to talk the talk of Christian
unity and true piety. The book was most obviously addressed to 'Catholics'.
But, in 'the epistle to the Christian reader', he also made a pitch to those 'of
another religion than I am'. He exhorted these people to lay aside 'all hatred
malice and wrathful contention' and to 'join together in amendment of our

lives, and praying for one another'.[48]

The *Christian Directory* thus fulfilled two tasks for Persons. First, vis-à-vis the Protestants, it enabled him to occupy the moral high ground of amendment of life, of Christian charity and spiritual resolution. But at the same time it made a deeply polemical point about the inadequacies of the Protestant insistence on salvation by faith alone. 'Albeit true faith', Persons conceded, 'be the ground of Christianity, without which nothing of itself can be meritorious before God, yet that one principal mean to come to this true faith and right knowledge, and to end all these our infinite contentions in religion' was for 'each man to betake himself to a good and virtuous life, for that God could not of his unspeakable mercy suffer such a man to err long in religion'.[49] This was, by implication, to overthrow the Protestant insistence on salvation *sola fide* and to reorientate the relationship between faith and works, and faith and charity, in the salvation of Christian souls and the conduct of the Christian life. But secondly, vis-à-vis an English Catholic audience, the tract enabled Persons to explain just how it was that such a properly Christian life, indeed what he presented in the book as the highest state of 'Christian resolution', could be both pursued and attained in the absence of quotidian contact with the rites and observances of the institutional Church. This, of course, as any number of Protestant polemicists were only too anxious to point out, was precisely what recusants were giving up when they cut themselves off so absolutely from the national Church.

Persons's book was concerned almost entirely with the internal spiritual life of the Christian. It dealt with the spiritual blockages and obstacles that stood between the Christian believer and a true 'Christian resolution' and with the mental and spiritual means either to remove or to overcome those obstacles. In this, Persons's *Christian Directory* was perhaps the archetypal example of English Catholics using books as 'dumb preachers'. In other words, it was a means to compensate for the lack of regular contact with a Catholic clergy and the absence of a public or collective Church life, absences visited upon English Catholics by their status as an oppressed minority within a heretical State.[50] In the face of Protestant conformist arguments that Catholics were thereby cutting themselves off from the sacraments and the life of faith, Persons was proffering a way in which such a life of faith could be lived in the absence of formal ecclesiastical structures and, in fact, of any institutional Church at all. As such, the *Christian Directory* provided the second and pastoral half of a one-two punch. This was one aspect or side of a both polemical and pastoral strategy of which his *Brief Discours* had been but the opening pitch. The overall strategy was designed to convert the mass of partially conforming, 'church papist' and (in Brad Gregory's somewhat judgemental but nevertheless authentically Personsian phrase) 'spiritually lukewarm' English Catholics into fully recusant devotees of a 'vigorous Jesuit version of post-Tridentine religiosity'.[51]

On this view, therefore, for all its appearance as a purely pastoral work, an expression of timelessly irenic and pious Christian verities and values, the *Christian Directory* was also a profoundly polemical book, intended to provide a religious rationale and a spiritual method for sustaining an intensely Catholic and recusant piety in the midst of Protestant England. As such, it was a means of persuading church papists into recusancy. It also made Catholics look like the epitome of Christian moderation, charity and piety in the face of the aggressive, indeed of the persecutory, policies and of the unbalanced and arid sola fideist piety of the Protestants. It was a text pushed at precisely the nexus of issues and conflicts clustered in York around the embattled figure of Margaret Clitherow. It should, therefore, come as no surprise, that it was a noted puritan divine from York, Edmund Bunny, who, in 1584, had published an expurgated edition of Persons's great spiritual masterpiece.

As a number of scholars have pointed out, Bunny's version retains almost all of Persons's book. While Bunny made a number of deletions and alterations in order to get rid of overtly Catholic readings or inflections of certain issues and topics, he retained, in Brad Gregory's words, 'fundamental practical admonitions about the sort of attitude Christians ought to have and the type of life they ought to lead'.[52] In thus appropriating Persons's text, Bunny was endorsing a Protestantized version of Persons's vision of practical Christianity and of the spiritual state which both men described as 'Christian resolution'. He was thus arguing that not only did Protestants have a claim to embody a version of true Christianity that even the likes of Persons could and would recognize and endorse, but also that, for anyone who wanted to become a true Christian, of precisely the sort described by Persons, it was certainly not necessary to go into separation from the Church of England. The life of faith was perfectly possible inside the national Church, at least as that Church was personified and administered by the likes of Edmund Bunny. We can conceive of the situation created by Persons's and Campion's mission of 1580–1581, the situation which was also played out with so much bitterness and venom in Clitherow's and Bunny's York, as a struggle between Jesuits and rigorists such as Persons, Mush and Clitherow on the one hand, and puritans such as Bunny, and their official patrons and sponsors such as Archbishops Grindal and Sandys (the latter was the dedicatee of Bunny's version of the book) on the other. The point of that struggle was to turn church papists either into conviction recusants or into first habitual and then conviction conformists. By producing a version of Persons's book purged of certain key Catholic doctrines and phrases, but in all its main lineaments and key passages entirely recognizable as Persons's original text, Bunny was demonstrating that something essentially the same as Persons's version of true Christianity was available within the Church of England to any Catholic who wanted to own and inhabit it. In other words, he wanted not only to reply to what was evidently a very popular Catholic text but also to make a claim that an intense interior spirituality, of essentially the same, quintessentially Christian, sort as that depicted by Persons, could be found and practised just as well under puritan as under Jesuit auspices; and, crucially, entirely within the structures, forms and practices of the Protestant national Church.

In his book's 'preface to the reader', Bunny was quite explicit about his polemical ends in producing the book. Because 'inordinate contention is not only unseemly for the Church of God but also hurtful to the cause of religion', it was, Bunny claimed, 'a special point of wisdom' when 'God has bestowed any good gift on any of us all' freely to acknowledge it, especially when 'it proceeds from those that, otherwise, are, for diverse points, the greatest adversaries we have in the cause of religion'. This would act, on the one hand, to expose those (such as Persons) that would not 'live peaceably . . . so far as the cause of religion itself doth permit them'. By thus exposing them, the book would give them 'just occasion to be ashamed'. On the other, it might 'somewhat occasion some better agreement among certain of us with such of them', in other words with Catholics who were more 'indifferent' and were 'content to dissent no further from us than of conscience they think that they ought'.[53] Thus, by appropriating and correcting Persons, albeit in a 'quiet manner without any grief against the author', Bunny was using a text written by one of 'the greatest adversaries we have in the cause of religion' in order to drive a wedge between such hard-line Catholics and other more moderate or tractable Catholics, people who would indeed 'gladly live peaceably withal' and were prepared, 'as far as the cause of true religion doth permit them' to unite with the likes of Bunny.[54] Thus Bunny sought to turn the force and energy of Persons's initial assault back against the Jesuit.

Such a reading of the book is surely confirmed by the fact that its second edition, of 1585, came with a *Treatise tending to Pacification* appended to it. This was expressly designed, as the title page proclaimed, to enjoin 'those that are our adversaries in the cause of religion to receive the Gospel and to join with us in the profession thereof'. Without mentioning the fact, this part of Bunny's work engaged systematically with all of the central contentions of Persons's *Brief Discours*. Trumpeting the value of Christian unity, Bunny claimed that while 'it becomes and behoves the Church of God, in many respects, to be at unity in itself . . . yet the case so stands in this matter that we are not able in our profession to yield unto them but they very well may and of duty ought to accord unto us'.[55] Irenicism was, in the best of all possible worlds, desirable and praiseworthy, but it was not to be purchased at the price of pusillanimous weakness in the face of the popish threat.

The arguments about corruption, scandal and offence, adduced by Persons to persuade Catholics that they could not conform, were adopted by Bunny to show that, as things now stood, Protestants could not join with Catholics and hope to be saved. In fact, 'in matters of religion', the danger was that Protestants would themselves 'be much . . . corrupted'.[56] But if the fear of corruption and scandal prevented the Protestants from joining the Catholics, the same did not apply to the Catholics, for there was so much of Catholic Christianity about the Church of England that, Bunny claimed, Catholics might well be able to partake of the general blessedness that God had vouchsafed to England if only they would do 'as other of their fellows' were prepared to do, namely to reserve 'their consciences to themselves' and conform 'their outward demeanour no further than is needful to the common tranquillity of all'. This could be done, Bunny announced cheerfully, without 'impeachment to the substance of their profession'.[57]

At this point, Bunny approached the central contention of Persons's tract, namely the Jesuit's denial that the Church of England was any sort of Church at all and his argument that what was at stake in the confrontation between Catholicism and Protestantism was a cataclysmic showdown between two religions, two mutually exclusive Church-like organizations, one of which was the true Catholic Church indeed and the other a mere synagogue of heretics and deviants. This Bunny set out to deny. It was true, he conceded, that 'our contentions are so apparent and known unto all that all Christendom is witness of them'. But it was absolutely wrong so bitterly to handle them 'as if in religion we were utterly sundered from one another and had no point of faith at all that were common betwixt us', precisely because it drove people, especially the 'simpler sort', out of the national Church.

Here, then, the likes of Persons and Mush were being indicted for abusing the truth of the matter in order to frighten simpler people into recusancy. The likes of Mrs Clitherow were being described as their dupes. Clitherow and others were the unwitting victims of their own simplicity and also of the grossly overblown and self-serving arguments of the rigorist clergy whose aim, Bunny claimed, was to win 'credit' with 'the common multitude'.[58]

Luckily, Bunny was on hand to disabuse the priests' poor and deluded victims by providing a very different account of the relationship between Catholicism, Protestantism and his own definition of the Church. This position he presented, legitimately enough, as but an extrapolation of the well-known Protestant claim that the English Church had not separated from the Catholic Church *tout court* but only over those issues which were in controversy between them. Protestants had not done anything to justify the attempts of other Christians (such as Persons) to eject them from the Church of Christ.

To make the case plain, Bunny proceeded to define what he meant by the Church. He was not referring to the invisible Church, that is to 'the Church in heaven, either in the secret election of God or in the glory whereunto it shall come in the end', for that was unknowable. 'We cannot look', he wrote, 'into the secret purpose of God, nor . . . espy the end before it come'. Instead, Bunny defined the Church simply as all those that professed that Jesus 'was the Christ . . . and that he was the son of the living God'. In this sense, the Church was 'that universal assembly or gathering together of all those, whether congregations or several persons in any part of the world, that believe in Christ or profess the same that we call Christianity or the Christian faith'. All those who 'held together the material and essential points of the Christian religion' and yet were 'very often greatly divided in other matters thereunto pertaining but not of the very substance indeed' remained, Bunny insisted, members of the Catholic Church.[59] On that basis, there could be no truth in Persons's claim that the Church of England was no Church at all, or that the two entities confronting each other under the titles of Catholic and Protestant were in fact two different and contrary religions. It was thus quite possible for Catholics to attend the national Church and still retain their claim to be Catholics. The truth of these assertions would be rendered all the more patent if it were assumed that the style of religion, the forms of piety, affect and conversation, being pushed by the national Church were precisely those defined by Bunny's version of the *Christian Directory* to which, after all, his *Treatise tending to Pacification* served as a mere appendix.

But Bunny, of course, did not let the matter rest there. To do so would have been, at some level, to leave people such as Mrs Clitherow in the clear. Bunny had no intention of doing that. There were, he claimed, even if all professing Christians were members of the Catholic Church, very different ways of being a Christian. It was, in short, possible to be a member of the Catholic Church and yet not to be a Catholic member of the same. For Bunny, 'the substance of the Christian religion', which identified the Church and membership thereof, rested upon 'Christ alone for the whole work of our redemption (in his priesthood for our atonement, in his doctrine for all our wisdom, in his kingdom for our obedience)'. Bunny concluded, on that basis, that 'whosoever they are that hold the same, they hold without question the Catholic faith'.[60] But he then spent a great deal of the rest of his treatise showing just how inadequately and how badly English Catholics attempted to rely on 'Christ alone for the whole work' of their redemption.

Throughout his treatise Bunny came back, time and again, to topics and doctrines that showed that the Catholics habitually diminished the role of Christ in effecting their salvation. They imagined themselves both to need and to enjoy the mediation not only of Christ but 'of angels and saints in heaven and the benefit of their own and other men's merits on earth'. Elsewhere he adverted to the 'heaps of traditions and ceremonies which' Roman Catholics had 'abundantly laid upon all men, calling them the traditions of the Church'. Such ceremonies and traditions had then been imposed on believers by force and their omission punished 'by imprisonment, torments and cruel death'. But 'the substance of Christianity' could easily survive without them. The Catholics' doctrine of the *limbus patrum* undercut the sufficiency of Christ's sacrifice on the cross, as did the unscriptural concept of purgatory. For good measure he also condemned, using conventional Protestant rhetoric, the Catholic doctrines of free will and the merit of good works.[61]

On Bunny's account, if Christianity was defined as a complete reliance on Christ for our salvation, some Christians were distinctly better than others at being properly Christian. Indeed, while their profession of Christ undoubtedly made them members of the Catholic Church, conviction Catholics could not, as things stood, be regarded as properly Catholic members of that Church at all; for 'they do not content themselves only with Christ nor with his word nor with his sacraments or at the least not so fully as we'. There could be no doubt that both Catholics and Protestants were members of the Church, but there could also be no doubt as to who were 'the truer members' thereof. So much was Catholics' salvation in doubt that Protestants could not risk associating with them. Indeed, Bunny concluded, the Catholics had adulterated and undermined their sole reliance on Christ for salvation to such an extent that they had 'suffered themselves to be made members of Antichrist or [the] man of sin that sits in the Church of God and insolently confounds all at his pleasure'.[62]

Nor did Bunny limit himself to a critique of Catholic religious error. For, as he explained, it was not possible to join with the Catholics in their religion without also coming under their government. 'Could their Church and court be sundered, their religion and regiment be parted, the one from the other, then indeed', said Bunny, 'with many . . . much might be done'. But 'when as these go so close together that no man can profess the one but that he must be under the other', religious compromise or convergence was not really possible. First, there were the pope's pretensions to spiritual authority. Although God had 'plentifully . . . left his Church furnished with divers functions to keep all in unity of faith and to bring to perfection the

Church of Christ, so to consummate his mystical body', Roman Catholics still believed that there could be no true unity, no spiritual perfection in the Church, unless it was ruled by a single human head. Moreover, even if it were to be conceded that the pope was indeed 'the vicar general of Christ on the earth', which he patently was not, that still gave him no more than a spiritual authority over the laity, 'to lay their sin to their charge and utterly exclude them from the hope of salvation'. And that left the small matter of the pope's claims to secular jurisdiction and, in particular, of his altogether too rough way with princes, 'accursing their persons, interdicting their land and arming their own subjects against them'.[63] Here, then, Bunny drew together again the religious and the political and, no doubt to the considerable satisfaction of the secular authorities, showed why the allegedly conscience-based separation of dissenters such as Mrs Clitherow could not but be regarded as an intolerable threat to all social order and ultimately to the monarchical authority of the queen.

All of this meant that Catholic claims that they had been harshly treated ('they account themselves to be straitly handled both in the fining of recusants and that certain of their profession are put to death') were utterly ludicrous. Not only were those who worshipped 'any strange God', or procured others to do the same, 'by God's own mouth accounted to die the death', but many of their other beliefs and activities did indeed amount to the treasons for which some of them had been, and were even now being severely but justly punished. Claims that 'the bishop of Rome' had the authority to depose 'the princes and potentates of the earth and to place in their rooms whomsoever he will', and that 'their subjects ought not to remain' in their allegiance to any whom the pope deposed, represented 'as rank a treason, as wicked a heresy and as open a way to all confusion as any that ever was heard of before'.[64]

We can conclude, then, that Bunny's concession that Catholics were indeed members of the true Church had not been prompted solely or even mainly by any irenic or even particularly moderate impulses on his part. On the contrary, it was a central aspect of a carefully modulated reply to Persons's equally modulated, double-barrelled, conscience-based pitch, made first in his *Brief Discours* and then in his *Christian Directory*. Addressing Persons's attempt to speak for simple norms of Christian godliness, piety, charity and virtue, claims that were themselves part of the Jesuit's case for recusancy as a sustainable position for English Catholics in the face of a heretical regime, Bunny simply appropriated the Jesuit's profession of mere Christianity. He attached it to his own core Protestant theological attitudes and beliefs. He then turned the Jesuit's message to Catholics (that they could aspire to and attain Christian resolution outside the institutional Church) into a claim that they could rather more easily attain it within the national Church, even while they enjoyed all the benefits conferred by conformity to the demands of the State and suffered none of the now rather considerable disincentives attached to nonconformity. In the process, he was able to wrap himself, and indeed the wider conformist position, in the flag of Christian moderation, as he characterized the proponents of recusancy as extremists anxious to unchurch their fellow Christians and to render the already very serious rents in the unity of the Church still wider and deeper. And he was able to do all this while denouncing Catholics as members of Antichrist, castigating the profession of Catholic Christianity as subversive of all salvation and good order in the State, and maintaining that the current levels of punishment being imposed on English Catholics by the State, as both recusants and indeed as traitors, were no more than they deserved; indeed while claiming that, according to Scripture itself, they deserved to die merely for maintaining and seeking to propagate their noxious views.

Bunny's version of Persons's book was clearly directed at a national audience and at issues of the first importance to English Catholics and to those who might be described by their contemporaries as church papists. It certainly achieved a remarkably wide distribution and it was much reprinted. Both it and Persons's own version came to transcend the particular situation which had called them forth. They became classics of English religious writing.[65] But Bunny's book was first published in mid 1584 (the preface is dated 9 July), while the second edition, to which the *Treatise tending to Pacification* was attached, came out in the following year. That is to say, Bunny's book, replying to Persons, appeared right in the middle of the Catholic conformist controversies in York. Bunny's second edition was issued not long before the final stage of the proceedings against Mrs Clitherow. These books had, therefore, both a remarkably wide reach and resonance. Bunny's may have had, in addition, some intensely local and immediate roots and aims. In that context, in York, certainly, even if also more generally, Bunny was surely directing his arguments primarily to those Catholics who were prepared, under certain circumstances, to countenance conformity. Those Catholics were precisely the same audience as the one which had been targeted by Persons himself.

Faint-Hearted Catholics and Real Catholics: Mrs Clitherow and the Local Politics of Conformity

This, then, was the wider political and polemical context which framed and inflected Clitherow's stance on conformity and also the response to that stance of her contemporaries, both Catholic and Protestant. Clitherow's own opinions on recusancy – as we saw, she herself asserted that she had forsaken the national Church in 1574[66] – predated Campion's and Persons's anti-conformity campaign and can be located within a local both priestly and lay coterie which had deep roots in York society. John Mush had come from a recusant household in York. He was an early candidate for ordination at the flagship Catholic seminary in Rome. (Ironically, he had headed there in the same travelling party as none other than Thomas Bell.) Anne Dillon, like Claire Cross, argues that Mush and other seminarists were 'steeped in the ideal of a separation which was intolerant of any compromise in relation to statute Protestantism'.[67] But, as the case of Bell proves, this was not true of every Catholic seminary priest, let alone all those clergy who might disapprove of the 1559 settlement of religion but had retained their benefices in the Church of England or, like Alban Langdale, had separated (or semi-separated) from the national Church but were not prepared to justify out-and-out recusancy. While, as we have already observed, Mush insisted that Mrs Clitherow was deferential to any and every Catholic priest, no matter what the man's personal capacities or proclivities – it was the office not the person that mattered, or so he claimed – it also clearly emerges from his account that it was a certain sort of rigorist seminary priest that was the preferred object of Mrs Clitherow's devoted admiration. In the section of his 'True Report' in which he described her 'diligence in observing other folk's virtues', Mush stressed how she admired priests who had been martyred, such as Bell's associate William Hart, and also Richard Thirkeld and Richard Kirkman; and when she observed those who did not measure up to their standards, 'for that she earnestly desired to see every one decked with spiritual beauty, she would recite for their instruction what good she heard or saw in such a father'.[68] An equivalence was carefully established in Mush's text between their supreme sacrifice and her own recusancy.

Clitherow herself had performed this equivalence in a practice which she (and Mush after her) termed 'her pilgrimage'. After her priestly friends started to be condemned to death, and the bloodletting had begun in earmest at the Knavesmire, the usual site of execution in York, she decided that, since their blood had 'sanctified the reproachful gallows', she would go there 'accompanied with two or three virtuous women'. Longley argues that she first did this between August and November 1582. 'By reason of this wicked time', Mush explained, she had to go at night, for fear of informers; and she could go only when her husband was away on business. Mush himself advised her not to go 'so often . . . as she desired'. But go she would. Indeed, she wanted to process there often,

where so many of her ghostly fathers had shed their blood in witness of the Catholic faith, where they had triumphed over the world, the flesh, and the devil, from whence they had ascended into heaven, where she earnestly wished (if it were God's will) for the same Catholic cause to end her life, and where she hoped God should daily be glorified in the memory of His martyrs.

As Mush fondly remembered, 'she went barefoot to the place and, kneeling . . . even under the gallows, meditated and prayed so long' as her friends would let her.[69]

If this sort of daring semi-public demonstration of reverence in the face of the witness of the martyrs was a gesture of reproach and defiance directed at the persecuting Protestant authorities and their supporters, it doubled as a rebuke to all those Catholics who had failed or were failing to live up to the gloriously recalcitrant example of the martyred priests and their steadfastly recusant lay followers – such as Clitherow herself.

As the work of John Aveling, Katharine Longley and others has made clear, under certain circumstances, and particularly in the context of the hostile and stringent enquiries made of Catholics by the high commission, the conformist response might become the majority option for those in York who regarded themselves as in some sense Catholic. Even Persons conceded in 1580 that 'many a thousand now in England, being as thoroughly persuaded in heart of the truth of the Catholic religion as the apostles and other Christians at that time were of theirs', were 'content notwithstanding' to behave, for the most part, 'contrary to the said religion'; and they genuinely believed that they were justified before God in so doing.[70]

Despite Mush's tactful refusal to name names or even to drop recognizable hints, there were, as we have already seen, many such among York's Catholics. (No doubt to Mrs Clitherow's horror, the families living on either side of her house in the Shambles, both of them related to her husband and at various times themselves disposed to recusancy, conformed during the second of the northern high commission's sweeps in 1580 against Catholic separatism.[71]) Undoubtedly it was against such 'weak and worldly Catholics', such 'schismatics', that Mrs Clitherow directed many of the barbed comments and moral strictures described by Mush.

The sheer venom of this conflict can, therefore, be gauged from Mush's constant sniping, in his commemoration of his patroness, at those who had opted for a different path from her. One wonders whether what he wrote was consciously aimed also at one person who is, of course, never explicitly mentioned in his text – one who, for the promoters of recusancy, became the great enemy – the one priest in the North whom contemporary sources identify as having evolved something approaching a developed thesis of occasional conformity which would square the circle of spiritual independence and temporal loyalty, namely Thomas Bell himself. It is implicit throughout Mush's account that not all those upbraided by Clitherow were persons located consistently at the margins of the Catholic community – the churchiest of church papists, people who were at best mere fellow-travellers. Rather, Mush's occasional references to at least some of Clitherow's Catholic opponents having been imprisoned shows that they must, at certain points, have been close to the centre of the Catholic community. Her neighbours – who, after all, facilitated her priest-harbouring activities by allowing her to use a room in their house for the purpose – were not exactly peripheral either to Clitherow's own social world or to the wider York Catholic scene. Here perhaps the really tell-tale phrase, used by Mush, is that her enemies 'externally . . . might be thought of no small perfection'.[72] In other words, her critics included those who were, on some accounts, no less zealous than her; people who claimed, in fact, to be just as good Catholics as she. They, however, happened to believe that they had evolved a better mode for negotiating the conflict with the State which the practice of Catholicism inevitably caused, principally over how far, to be a good Catholic, it was necessary entirely to eschew and avoid the inside of local parish churches where the service was conducted by the parson according to the book of common prayer and where the State, via the act of uniformity and accompanying legislation (notably in 1581), commanded obedient attendance.

Thus we should not imagine that those doing the conforming were passively accepting their categorization, first by Clitherow and then by Mush, as in some sense bad or lapsed Catholics, inherently inferior to the inflexibly zealous and recusant Mrs Clitherow. That was certainly how the likes of Persons, Mush and Garnet saw things and it is how most modern commentators (siding, as ever, if not with the winners then at least with those whose views achieved most frequently and easily the apotheosis of print) have tended to see them too. But, as we have seen, there is no reason to believe that this was how a good many contemporary Catholics regarded the matter. Despite the claims of his enemies, Thomas Bell was not the only Catholic priest who held such opinions. Indeed, it looks as if he was at the forefront of a possibly quite powerful and influential group of clergymen which had decided to interpret the caveats against associating with heretics differently from other Catholics, especially Jesuit and Jesuit-supporting clergy. Or, rather, Bell and his friends claimed that they were pursuing an orthodox and workable line on the issue of non/conformity while their Catholic critics were not.

Moreover, the development and significance of these intra-Catholic divisions over conformity may well have been determined by other political considerations and events. We do not know exactly what it was, over and above a different casuistical mindset, that caused Bell to part company with other clergy concerning the issue of conformity. We do know, of course, that there were divisions among Catholics at this time on other issues. In the wake of the blood-soaked debacle of Campion's mission, Persons returned to France and plunged up to his neck into schemes for the violent overthrow of Elizabeth, schemes that merged seamlessly into the revival in France of the Guise-dominated Holy League and the rise of radical resistance against the Valois monarchy. A number of Catholics, notably some of the agents and supporters of Mary Stuart, were frozen out of these plots and conspiracies and became alienated from Persons and his friends.[73] Perhaps they disapproved of Persons's proceedings on principle. At any rate they developed a discourse of loyalism in opposition to what came to be identified, by many Catholics as well as by Protestants, as archetypal Jesuited treasons. It is possible that Bell and his friends also began to think along such lines. Perhaps they identified the evolution of anti-conformist thought with suicidal, unwarranted and, in some sense, truly godless disloyalty to the queen. Certainly, the adoption of Bell's line on conformity provided loyalist Catholics with a perfect means of distinguishing themselves from hard-liners such as Persons or Garnet and hence perhaps of attracting a more sympathetic response from the regime than otherwise they might have obtained.

A brief look at Clitherow's immediate clerical and familial circle confirms just how tense and tight the relations between the parties to these disputes in fact were. By tracing the web of connections that stretched out from Clitherow into the Catholic community, we can see why Clitherow herself might have been regarded as a central figure in these debates. We can discern also just how disturbing the political resonances of those same disputes may well have been. For Clitherow was connected, through links of personal affinity and kinship, with some of the major players in these debates. As we saw, Alban Langdale (who served as a chaplain to Viscount Montague) wrote one of the earliest manuscript defences of occasional conformity.[74] The secretary employed to process and produce the tract was none other than William Clitherow, Margaret's own brother-in-law. His part in the campaign in 1580 to prevent the acceptance of Jesuit-led ideas about recusancy was denounced by Persons. Persons implied that William Clitherow was as much the moving spirit in it as Langdale: 'Mr Clitherow also (as was presumed) had imparted a written book of Doctor Langdale (as was after discovered, to show that it was lawful to go to church), whereupon diverse were ready to fall and go back, as some did'.[75] William Clitherow was later taken into the circle around the queen of Scots, at least the part of it which was dominated by Charles Paget and Thomas Morgan and which opposed the too-ready determination, as they saw it, of some of the exiles, notably Robert Persons, to rely completely on the patronage of the Spaniards and their Guisite friends in France.[76]

The fact that Margaret Clitherow, the sister-in-law of the man who was known to have copied out Langdale's tract in favour of church papistry, had so publicly rejected the church-papist option must have been taken by Catholics as a significant slap in the face for those who were urging the moderation of, as some perceived it, an unwise and excessive Catholic rejection of even a token conformity. On this evidence, Clitherow's whole career and fateful end coincided with and indeed, on the argument being pursued here, were fatally shaped by, a wider debate about the relative value of 'recusancy' and 'church popery' that was endemic among the Catholics of the North at precisely this period. Mush, of course, had no wish either to acknowledge this or to give the arguments and claims of the other side any fair airing. But that should not prevent us from seeing his relentless application of the binary opposition between good and bad Catholics to the disputes between Clitherow and her 'schismatic' enemies not as the natural or dominant Catholic position, but, on the contrary, as itself a contribution to an ongoing debate about conformity. This was a debate that Mush was trying to influence through his insistent equation of recusancy with martyrdom and of both with the highest forms of post-Tridentine Catholic sanctity. These were claims which, of course, he saw personified in Margaret Clitherow's life and confirmed by her heroic martyr's death, and which he hoped to clinch and disseminate through his own account of that life and death, an account which was, as Anne Dillon has argued, shaped by the generic requirements of traditional martyrology.

It looks, then, as though Mrs Clitherow's daringly public performances of Catholic zeal and recusant constancy were Janus-faced, directed both at elements and arguments within the local Catholic community and also against the overarching claims, structures and agents of the allegedly persecutory State and heretical national Church. Rather than the dupe or even merely the agent of a cadre of rigorist seminary priests, Clitherow emerges from this analysis as an equal partner with some priests and lay people in a struggle against others.[77] Her activities were, therefore, doubly disruptive. Her transformation of her household into a centre of overt Catholic activity represented an intervention in the public sphere of religious dispute and political disobedience. In the process, what was, in origin, a quite traditional exercise of female control over the private sphere of family religious observance was converted into a calculated and concerted act of defiance directed at the authority of her husband and of the Protestant State. It also became a threateningly divisive interference in the long-standing dispute about conformity which was currently exercising Catholics in York, as indeed elsewhere. Her behaviour could thus be construed (by both Protestants and Catholics) as challenging a whole series of (often heavily gendered) distinctions between the 'private' and the 'public', between 'religion' and 'politics', between the rights of private conscience and the duty of obedience to public authority. In this light, her arrest for harbouring begins to look like the local Protestant establishment's response to, in fact its attempt to exacerbate and exploit, long-standing divisions among the Catholics of York. This was a ploy which, as we shall see, Clitherow's conduct in prison, and then in court when she was put on trial for her life, can be read as a concerted attempt to frustrate.

5

The Reckoning: Arrest, Trial and Execution

Mad, Bad and Dangerous to Know?

It is clear from the foregoing account of the political implications of Margaret Clitherow's separation from the national Church, and from her aggressive response to the conformist conventions adopted by many of her co-religionists, that she was probably courting disaster. It was no secret that those with whom she associated were some of the most radical members of northern society. Among her clerical friends was William Hart, whom the regime had thought fit to execute for treason in March 1583. The identity of the priest whom she would have been tried in March 1586 for harbouring, had she consented to plead to the charge against her, was Francis Ingleby.[1] His uncle, David Ingleby of Ripley, was, during this period, a known political malcontent; he was a son-in-law of the earl of Westmorland, one of the rebel leaders in 1569. Francis Ingleby was, following his arrest in mid 1586, swiftly strung up and disembowelled in York. This was shortly after Clitherow herself had been done to death. We do not, of course, know everything that Clitherow and Ingleby talked about. Perhaps their conversation never wandered as far as Mary Stuart and the ill will that leading members of the Elizabethan regime bore her. But one of the few things that we know Catholics remembered about Ingleby was that when he had been engaged in the study of the law in London in the early 1580s he had commented 'with great discretion, but very fluently, on the frauds practised' by Elizabeth's favourite, Robert Dudley the earl of Leicester, 'in perverting the laws of the country'.[2] In other words, Ingleby had, undoubtedly like many others, taken up and voiced allegations which were soon notoriously disseminated in the scandalous and inflammatory polemic of 1584 popularly known as 'Leicester's Commonwealth'.[3] Of course, one did not have to be a Catholic radical to take an interest in Leicester's alleged misdeeds. But this book, written in part or whole, it seems, by Robert Persons, was a devastating personal and political indictment not just of the earl of Leicester but also, by implication, of the queen's failure as a monarch. Crucially it pointed to Leicester's brother-in-law, the earl of Huntingdon, whose Yorkist blood put him in the line of succession to Elizabeth Tudor, as one of the principal threats to the claim and indeed the life of Mary Stuart.[4]

Clitherow's closest clerical companion, though, was John Mush himself. Immediately after her arrest, rumours flew around York that she had been betrayed by one of her household and that she had contravened the law by harbouring Mush as well as Ingleby.[5] Mush, too, in the 1580s, was on the radical wing of the Elizabethan seminarist movement, as his writings in favour of recusancy make all too clear.

But if, on the one side, Clitherow was associating with politically dangerous men, men who saw the earl of Huntingdon or the earl of Leicester as would-be tyrant figures, characters straight out of the infamous 'Leicester's Commonwealth', she was also related, on the other, to adherents of Huntingdon who were as anxious to refer approvingly to the earl's potential claim to the throne as Catholics and Marians were to deride and denounce it. Clitherow had several relatives within the secretariat which served the council in the North.[6] Her stepfather was Henry May, the *arriviste* southerner and a prominent man in the York corporation. He would become lord mayor shortly before her trial, probably due at least in part to his standing as a follower of Huntingdon. This was an attachment which he displayed publicly in September 1586, when, along with the aldermen, May attended on Huntingdon for the reading and renewal of the earl's commission as lord lieutenant. At the crucial point in the ceremony, May personally delivered the ceremonial sword of the city to the earl with the point downwards. In doing this he broke with precedent. The city's charter, granted by Richard II, stated that the ceremonial sword should be lowered only in the presence of the sovereign and his heirs. In so doing, May might well have been taken to have publicly affirmed both the earl's status as a potential successor to Elizabeth and his own personal attachment to the earl's cause.[7]

On the one hand, Clitherow's social connections perhaps at one time served to protect her from the full consequences of her increasingly flagrant and publicly Catholic rigorism. A mere woman, she could hide, at least to an extent, behind her conformist husband; and, behind him, she could rely for protection on the rising fortunes and the clout of her mother's husband, Henry May. On the other hand, May's rise in the York elite rendered his notoriously recusant, priest-harbouring, martyr-worshipping stepdaughter a public embarrassment.

A number of events, in both the 'public' political and 'private' familial spheres, now seem to have brought things to a head. First, in June 1585, Henry May's wife Jane (Margaret Clitherow's mother) died.[8] This seems to have removed a crucial personal restraint on May's capacity to act against his recalcitrant and embarrassing stepdaughter. In September of the same year, Huntingdon started yet another push against recusancy which filled the gaols. Quite soon after, a young Catholic who had acted as a school-master in the house of a church-papist gentleman, one Marmaduke Bowes, was arrested and, allegedly under torture, accused Bowes of harbouring the priest Hugh Taylor. Taylor was executed on 26 November and was followed the next day by Bowes himself – the first lay Catholic to fall foul of the new statutory penalty for harbouring separatist Catholic clergy. These trials and executions are the first events in Mush's 'True Report' and they set the scene for Clitherow's sufferings. Mush described Bowes as 'an honest substantial gentleman or yeoman' who was nevertheless an occasional conformist. In other words, technically, he was guilty of the same sin for which Clitherow and her friends denounced so many other York Catholics. He feared 'as infinite do, the extremity of those late monstrous laws and statutes which oppress and violate the natural liberty of man's conscience by forcing them by excessive penalties to do and yield to that which is both against all truth and their own infallible knowledge; he chose rather some times to accompany the ministers and to go into their church than he would fall to the unmerciful handling of heretics, and lose both goods and liberty'. Yet Mush was able to distinguish between, on the one side, those who were fundamentally good and whose weakness could be casuistically excused and, on the other, those whose hearts were really not in the right place. Bowes was tormented by his conscience for his halting between the two religions and he detested 'all their heresies in his heart'. While he feared 'in his bodily actions to show himself a Catholic', he believed 'inwardly the Catholic faith in every point'. The proof of his disposition lay in the fact that he, like Clitherow, refused to 'shut up his hospitality from priests, whom he knew well to be the messengers of God, sent not to commit treasons (as the heretics slanderously pretend, and would falsely persuade the world to believe) but to bring God's grace and salvation to all men'. But this left him open to betrayal by his own employee, the unre-liable schoolmaster. Before Bowes was hanged 'he was made a member of the Catholic Church'. Under the gallows, he proclaimed this fact 'with great alacrity of mind', and said that he regretted that 'he had lived in schism so long'. Now, as he faced the prospect of meeting his maker, he said he had no fear of death and, indeed 'desired not to live any longer'. Rather he hoped that his death might serve to make reparation for his 'schismatical dissembling' past life. As the life was choked out of him, Catholics might be certain, or so Mush concluded, that Bowes had done just that.[9]

This was virtually a dress rehearsal for the proceedings which would, six months later, be conducted against Clitherow. The lord president of the council was himself absent when Bowes was tried. But William, Lord Eure, who had been responsible for the arrest of the priest Taylor, sat in his capacity as vice-president of the council. With him were Lawrence Meares, Ralph Hurlestone, Henry Cheke and others.[10] The authorities' 'malice was so great against' Bowes, wrote Mush, and 'they so vehemently thirsted for his blood, that no insufficiency in the witness' could serve to prevent Bowes's conviction. The authorities were determined to 'have the gentleman's life, judging it to be convenient and necessary for the politic maintaining of their tyrannical state that now and then they murder some, though unjustly, for the terrifying of the country. Yet this cruel fact was loathsome and horrible to the country', with 'most men murmuring that this honest gentleman's life should be thus shamefully taken away' because of the 'testimony of one infamous person', one who was a 'faithless apostate'.[11]

Arrest

The cases of the unfortunate Taylor and Bowes were evidently meant to be a warning to those Catholics in the region who decided to endorse and adopt the programme of a certain sort of clergy, in other words those Catholic priests whose enmity towards, and attacks on, the mid-Elizabethan regime were now becoming more sharp and unrestrained. The parliament of 1585, which had made the harbouring of seminary priests a felony, had also made it an offence to send one's children to be educated abroad in Catholic seminaries. As we have seen, Margaret had sent her eldest son Henry to France for precisely that purpose. According to the 'True Report', the council of the North 'after a while, had intelligence' of Margaret's action and 'greatly stormed thereat, yet lingered to deal in the matter'.[12]

All this coincided with the advancement of May to the mayoralty in January 1586. On 10 March, John Clitherow was called, and appeared, before the council of the North, to answer (as he thought) for the absence of his son on the Continent. In fact this was a ruse to remove him from his own house. On the afternoon of the same day it was searched for priests. His wife was arrested while he was safely off the premises. As noted in Chapter 1, Katharine Longley's painstaking reconstruction of these events demonstrates that the search of the house was in fact timed so as to make sure that none of Clitherow's clergy friends was celebrating Mass when the sheriffs and their servants arrived. The intention was to find evidence 'but not too much'.[13]

As the 'True Report' described it, when they burst in, she was there 'occupied in her household business'. Her priest (who is not identified as such, but must have been Mush) was in his 'chamber, which was in the next neighbour's house', and there were 'some other persons with him'. But, 'being certified of the searchers', they were all immediately spirited away. Her schoolmaster Brian Stapleton, who was 'in a low chamber of her own house', also managed to escape. The searchers 'raged like madmen' and 'took all the children, the servants' and Clitherow herself away with them. They also turned the whole place upside down, ransacking chests and coffers but initially they 'found nothing of any importance', in other words the kind of liturgical paraphernalia which would incriminate Clitherow. Then 'they stripped' a young Flemish boy, one of those who had been taken in the house, and threatened him with a birch, and told him what he could expect if he did not confess what he knew. The child was terrified and soon led them to the priest's room in Clitherow's neighbour's house 'wherein was a conveyance for books and church stuff'.

Those who had been arrested were dispersed to different gaols in the city. Mrs Clitherow was immediately taken before the council. In the face of the awesome grandeur of the supreme legal and administrative authority in the North, she was, the 'True Report' claimed, 'merry and stout for the Catholic cause'. Confronted with her insouciant defiance, her interrogators went berserk. She 'moved their fury vehemently against her, especially by her smiling cheerful countenance and the small esteem she made of their cruel threats and railing'. At seven o'clock in the evening she was sent off to the castle and, about an hour later, her husband was sent after her. The confessions of the Flemish boy led also to the arrest of Mrs Clitherow's friend Anne Tesh.[14]

The final confrontation between the regime and Mrs Clitherow, who is referred to hereafter in the 'True Report' not by name but simply as 'the martyr', had begun.[15] At this point a number of vectors of ideological tension and political conflict were converging on the person, indeed, as it turned out, on the body, of the butcher's wife. Now Margaret Clitherow, the disorderly woman, disobedient wife, embarrassing stepdaughter and harbourer of politically threatening and religiously recalcitrant priests was to be made a public example of. And no wonder. For one of the most significant aspects of the account given by Mush of Clitherow's Catholicism was the strikingly public nature of its outward expression: the establishment of her household as a model of Counter-Reformation piety, a priest's house, a Mass centre and Catholic school; her own repeated and defiant recusancy; her frequent appearances in court and stints in prison; her well-known rebukes of the laxity, as she saw it, of her fellow Catholics both in prison and out in the world; and her nocturnal pilgrimages to the Knavesmire. Taken together, all these actions, performed by the wife of a prominent citizen and the step-daughter of that coming man Henry May, represented the repeated and aggressive performance of religious dissent on the very public stage provided by the tight society and gossip networks, and by the equally tightly packed streets, of York.

Now, when the regime decided to strike back, their response was to be an equally public shaming and silencing of Clitherow's dissentient voice. Either through her execution, or, as the regime in York more likely at first intended, through a publicly humiliating gesture of conformity on her part, this symbol of resurgent and recalcitrant recusant Catholicism would be forced, at last, to do obeisance before the patriarchal, Protestant and royal authorities vested in her husband, her stepfather and in the local representatives of the Protestant regime in Church and State. Clitherow's arrest was followed by what was clearly meant to be a show trial. This would, if it worked as the authorities intended, serve to draw a line in the sand for York's Catholics. It would be a public demonstration of the limits on dissent and the public and semi-public expression of Catholic opinions and attitudes, even by a woman as well connected and protected as Clitherow was or, rather, had once been.

The shaming rituals may well have started at the very outset of Clitherow's ordeal. The 'True Report' tells us that she arrived in prison soaking wet: 'though the day was fair, and without any rain, yet' Clitherow 'came to prison in so wet a bath that she was glad to borrow all kind of apparel to shift her with'. Longley has plausibly suggested that this was due to an impromptu ducking, inflicted upon her as a quintessentially unruly woman and scold, en route to the prison.[16] Then, as we saw, rumours started to go round York that that the Flemish boy from her household had accused her of harbouring and maintaining divers priests, but 'especially two by name . . . Mr Francis Ingleby of Rheims and Mr John Mush of Rome. It was reported . . . that she should suffer for it according to the new law and statute.'[17]

Trial

Her arraignment took place before the assize judges on 14 March 1586. She 'was brought from the castle to the common hall', i.e. the Guildhall (see Plate 11).[18] There were two common law judges, John Clench and John Rhodes. Various members of the council sat with them on the bench, notably the vice-president Lord Eure, Meares, Hurlestone and Cheke, who had all been present at Bowes's trial. Also present in his capacity as lord mayor was Henry May. The indictment was read out. It stated that 'she had harboured and maintained Jesuit[s] and seminary priests, traitors to the queen's Majesty and her laws, and that she had [heard] Mass'. Clench ordered her to answer whether she pleaded guilty or not guilty. With 'a bold and smiling countenance' she replied 'I know no offence whereof I should confess myself guilty'. The judge said: 'yes, you have harboured and maintained Jesuits and priests, enemies to her Majesty'. She answered, somewhat equivocally, 'I never knew nor have harboured any such persons, or maintained those which are not the queen's friends. God defend I should.' Clench demanded, 'how will you be tried?' Clitherow insisted that, 'having made no offence, I need no trial'. The response from the bench was, 'you have offended the statutes, and therefore you must be tried'. But she would not cooperate beyond saying that she would 'be tried by none but by God and your own consciences', which the bench told her, of course, was impossible.[19]

Faced with her staggering intransigence, the opportunity was taken to put on a contemptuous public dumb show using the religious paraphernalia found in her neighbour's house. Out came 'two chalices' and 'diverse pictures'. In 'mockery', they dressed up two 'lewd fellows' in the vestments which had been confiscated during the raid. One of these men then began to 'pull and dally' with the other, 'scoffing on the bench before the judges and, holding up singing breads', i.e. unconsecrated wafers, 'said to the martyr: "behold thy gods in whom thou believe"'. Rather pointlessly she was asked what she thought of the vestments and she snapped back that she liked 'them well, if they were on their backs that know to use them to God's glory and honour, for which they were made'.[20]

Judge Clench, apparently confused by her stubbornness, asked her about her religious beliefs. She, at this point, wrong-footed the court by proclaiming her entirely orthodox and standard faith in the Trinity and her opinion that only 'by the passion, death, and merits of Christ Jesus' could she be saved, to which Clench could answer no more than 'you say well'. She was again asked whether she was 'content to be tried by God and the country'. Still she refused to reply. Clench now took it upon himself to warn her: 'good woman, consider well what you do; if you refuse to be tried by the country, you make yourself guilty and accessory to your own death, for we cannot try you'. It was impossible for the court to deal with her except 'by order of law'. He told her that she did not need to 'fear this kind of trial'. In his opinion, the jury could not find her guilty 'upon the slender evidence of one child'. Still she would not comply, and, for good measure, when asked 'if her husband were not privy to her doings in keeping priests', denied that John Clitherow had had any awareness of what she was doing. Clench warned again that the court would have to 'proceed by law' against her, and the inevitable result would be that she would suffer 'a sharp death for want of trial'. As we have seen, some commentators have taken this as a nuanced offer of an acquittal if only she would comply with standard procedure. But comply she would not.[21] Confronted by her joyful serenity in the face of these tirades 'some of them said, seeing her joy, that she was mad, and possessed with a smiling spirit'.[22]

We are told that, during these exchanges, while John Rhodes led the others in mocking her Catholic faith, Ralph Hurlestone picked up on the circulating rumours about her relationship with Catholic clergy and 'said openly before them all: "it is not for religion that you harbour priests, but for whoredom"'. Henry Cheke and Lawrence Meares, two more of her severest critics, had reported, immediately 'after she was taken, that priests resorted to none but such as were comely and beautiful young women to satisfy their lusts'.[23] In the face of her noncompliance, the authorities turned their proceedings against her into a public demonstration of her alleged ignorance, superstition and adulterous sexual looseness.

In retaliation, Clitherow started to adopt the pose of a martyr, which she did by identifying with those who had been convicted of the treasons recently created by statute. This was something which she had already discussed with her spiritual director, Mush. In the first of two striking, if rather disturbing, vignettes in his 'True Report', he tells her to prepare her 'neck for the rope' if she will not desist from her current courses of action.[24] The second indicates how far she had already mentally planned ahead for what might happen. At the time when she was about to appear in front of the bench, she 'said "yet, before I go, I will make all my brethren and sisters on the other side of the [prison] hall merry", and looking forth at her window toward them – they were five-and-thirty, and might easily behold her from thence – she made a pair of gallows on her fingers and pleasantly laughed at them'.[25]

Her performances of the inner peace and outward *sang froid* of the martyr were, of course, not restricted to Catholic audiences. No matter how public her earlier gestures of defiance against the regime may have been, the stakes had been very considerably raised by the authorities' decision to arrest and arraign her. For her arrest and the intense public interest aroused by it assembled a far wider and more religiously heterogeneous audience before which she could now act out her role as a bride of Christ, prepared and preparing to go to the 'marriage', as she called it, of her martyrdom. She turned her journeys through the streets to and from the court and the prison into public demonstrations of her Christian charity by doling out alms.[26]

On the morning of 15 March 1586, at eight o'clock, she was brought to the common hall again and was told she had been given respite in order to think again about her refusal to plead. Would she now do as she was asked? Clench once more made a covert offer of an acquittal. But Clitherow was as stubborn as ever. She now virtually admitted that she had harboured Catholic seminary clergy, and she got into a slanging match with Rhodes, Hurlestone and others about the merits and demerits of her clergymen. As for 'good Catholic priests', she knew 'no cause' why she should 'refuse them' since they came 'only to do . . . good'. Rhodes and Hurlestone snarled that they were 'all traitors, rascals and deceivers of the queen's subjects' and that Clitherow 'would detest them' if she knew 'their treason and wickedness' as well as her judges did.[27] Clench was clearly now more flummoxed than ever. He reiterated, 'what say you? Will you put yourself to the country, yes or no?' But her answer had not changed. Clench was, however unwillingly, being trapped by Clitherow's all too well-thought-out strategy. 'Well', said Clench, 'we must pronounce a sentence against you. Mercy lies in our hands, in the country's also, if you put your trial to them; otherwise you must have the law'.[28]

At this point, a radical puritan minister called Giles Wigginton, who had already visited Clitherow in prison on the night of 14 March, stood up and demanded to be heard. Struggling to make himself audible over the 'murmuring and noise in the hall', he warned the bench to 'take heed' for they, in a 'case . . . touching life and death', ought not, 'either by God's laws or man's, to judge' the accused 'to die upon the slender witness of a boy; nor unless you have two or three sufficient men of very good credit to give evidence'. When told, quite accurately, that, by the queen's law the court could very well do what it did, he answered that they could not 'do it by God's law'.[29]

After this distraction was over, Clench begged her, with yet another covert promise of an acquittal or at least a reprieve, to consider that there was 'no evidence but a boy against you, and whatsoever they do, yet we may show mercy afterward'. Her resolution, though, held firm. At this point, John Rhodes completely lost his temper and shouted, 'why stand we all the day about this naughty, wilful woman? Let us despatch her.' Clench now gave in. With no alternative left to him, he explained to her:

> [I]f you will not put yourself to the country, this must be your judgement: you must return from whence you came, and there, in the lowest part of the prison, be stripped naked, laid down, your back upon the ground, and as much weight laid upon you as you are able to bear, and so to continue three days without meat or drink, except a little barley bread and puddle water, and the third day to be pressed to death, your hands and feet tied to posts, and a sharp stone under your back.

Clench was articulating the medieval sanction of *peine forte et dure*, reserved for those who refused to enter a plea to a felony charge. Whereas, in theory, this procedure was supposed to allow three full days for the accused to change his or her mind, by the sixteenth century it was in effect merely another method of execution, one of the considerable range of horrific punishments available under the law.[30] At the very last Clench begged her: 'consider of it, you have husband and children to care for; cast not yourself away'. She replied that she wished that they all 'might suffer' with her 'for so good a cause', something which allowed the hostile court reporters to say afterwards that 'she would have hanged her husband and children if she could'.[31]

On the journey back from this, her final appearance in court, she deliberately displayed a joyful countenance, 'whereat some said, "it must needs be that she received comfort from the Holy Ghost", for all were astonished to see her of so good cheer'. Others, though, said that 'it was not so, but that she was possessed with a merry devil, and that she sought her own death'.[32]

Awaiting Death in the Prison

Of course, if the authorities' plan to make an example of Mrs Clitherow was to yield its full benefits, they now, more than ever, needed either to turn or break her, thus disrupting the smooth surface of her, up to this point, impeccable performance as a martyr for Christ and his (Catholic) Church. Accordingly, after her initially recalcitrant performances in court, 'none was permitted to speak with her but ministers, and such as were appointed by the council'.[33] As the 'True Report' describes it, despite the malice of the likes of Rhodes and Hurlestone, other members of the council did not necessarily want to see her put to death. 'Two days after', i.e. on 17 March, there 'came to her Mr Meares, Sir Thomas Fairfax and others of the council, and secretly asked her many things, the certainty whereof', said Mush, 'I cannot as yet learn in particular'. It seems that 'they asked her if she would go to the church with them, if it were but to one sermon'. Deploying her sense of humour in a way that was calculated to send them into orbit, she answered that she 'would, if it pleased them to let her choose the preacher, and grant him safe conduct to come and go'. Still searching for an acceptable compromise and way out, they asked her also 'if she thought in her conscience that she were with child'. She said she 'knew not certainly and would not, for all the world, take it on her conscience that she was or she was not, but if she were it was very young and, as she thought, she rather was than not'. They asked her why she would not jump at this chance of a reprieve. This was a perfectly respectable face-saving stratagem which, they clearly thought, would let her seize the chance of life. At the same time they could claim that they had not compromised or twisted the law for her benefit. But, astonishingly, she merely murmured 'I require no favour in this matter'; it was for them to do to her what they thought fit. They turned the encounter back to the question of her clerical contacts and asked her whether 'she knew not Mr Ingleby and Mr Mush'.[34]

Her family and social circle, however, would not give up the last possibility of saving her, which was the contents of her womb. Her 'kinsfolks and friends laboured much all that week to cause her to say directly that she was with child'. But she would not allow it to be thought that she had grasped at this straw out of fear or dissimulation. So she repeated that 'she would not dissemble with God and the world, for that she could not tell certainly whether she was or no'. For the hard-liners this was the green light to proceed with her as the law dictated. Clench, however, was prepared to take her statement about her condition as a positive affirmation that she was pregnant. The senior sheriff of York for that year, Roland Fawcett, came to Clench and asked what he was supposed to do with her. The judge, almost as if he had been infected with the defiance that was driving Clitherow on, instructed Fawcett that she might not be 'executed, for they say she is with child'.

This did not suit her enemies at all. Rhodes, Meares, Hurlestone, Cheke and others 'urged greatly that she might be executed according to judgement and law'. Rhodes warned Clench that he was 'too merciful in these cases' and that, if Mrs Clitherow 'had not the law, she would undo a great many'. Clench stuck to his guns and insisted that, 'if she be with child, I cannot consent that she shall die'. The exasperated sheriff suggested that 'a quest of women' should be summoned to examine her. To resolve the matter, four women were indeed sent off, on 17 March, to examine Clitherow 'and returned answer to the judge that she was with child as far as they could perceive or gather by her own words'. That, however, was not enough for Clitherow's opponents on the council. 'That night, or the next day' (says the 'True Report') Hurlestone and the 'councillors and ministers who most greedily thirsted after her blood' crowded in upon Clench 'in his chamber', determined to intimidate him into submission. 'My lord', they said, 'this woman is not to have the benefit of her belly, for that she has refused to be tried by the country, and the sentence of death is passed against her'. Clench was clearly taken aback and protested to Hurlestone, 'God defend she should die, if she be with child'. Hurlestone frankly did not much care. He 'urged still and said, "she is the only woman in the north parts, and if she be suffered to live, there will be more of her order without any fear of law. And therefore, my lord, consider with yourself . . . and let her have the law according to judgement passed".' The State could not afford to flinch from its duty. If she were with child, Hurlestone said, let the sin of its death be upon him.[35] If, on the other hand, she was allowed to escape the consequences of her flagrant disobedience, who could tell where resistance to the will of the regime and the State might end?

The council and her own social circle were not the only ones still concerned with her fate. Up until the following Monday, 21 March, a procession of godly ministers (among whom were Edmund Bunny and, again, Giles Wigginton) tried to undermine her resolve, though, of course, they came to see her with the licence and at the behest of the council.[36] The ministers who called on her also wanted to get her to conform in some fashion, perhaps only by agreeing to attend Protestant service and sermons. According to William Hutton, while Clitherow was in the Ouse Bridge gaol after her trial and her sentencing, a series of these divines daily resorted to her and tried to persuade her to 'save her life'. But she 'willed them not to trouble her, for she would not hear them'. 'When they saw she made no account of their prating, and would not hear them, they would kneel down before her, shedding out tears, crying out, "The Lord illuminate your heart", reiterating it oftentimes over.'[37]

Why were these people so insistent in their efforts to convert Margaret Clitherow, particularly when it was clear that she had little time for them? Mrs Clitherow, just like her puritan antagonists, took her religion very seriously. If she objected to the enforcement of conformity, this meant that, on some level, she had something in common with the likes of Bunny and certainly of Wigginton. Their attempt to turn her was, therefore, pitched at the level of spiritual enlightenment and godly conversion and their own account of the life of faith. Their pitch to her might then be seen as but the practical application of the approach outlined in Bunny's appropriation of Persons' *Christian Directory*, the second edition of which, with his 'treatise tending to pacification' appended, had only just been published.

Of course, had she weakened before the spiritual blandishments of Bunny and his mates her compliance could not have been construed as 'mere' conformity. Not only would this have been a considerable propaganda coup for the authorities but it would also have provided proof positive of the spiritual potency of the ministers' strain of evangelical Protestant religion. Here, in other words, would have been the evidence that these godly Protestants required in order to demonstrate that their prescription for beating down popery was the correct one. Mere conformity, particularly when enforced through the formal machinery of episcopal jurisdiction – a bureaucratic machine that was just as likely to ensnare godly Protestants as miscreant Catholics – was simply too blunt and unsubtle an instrument to deal with the likes of Mrs Clitherow. We can be sure that both Edmund Bunny (formerly an adherent and client of Edmund Grindal himself) and indeed Wigginton would have been dismayed at the programme for clerical and ceremonial conformity recently instituted, however unsuccessfully, by Grindal's successor at Canterbury, John Whitgift, of which programme Wigginton himself had recently fallen foul.[38] In the opinion of godly Protestants the enforcement of statute conformity was never in itself a sufficient response to the threat of Catholicism.

The puritan ministers first approached her on 'the second day after her condemnation', i.e. also on 17 March. Among them were Bunny, Robert Pease and James Cotterell, all of whom the 'True Report' described as 'arrogant heretics'. They announced that they had been told by the council to find out why she would not agree 'to be tried by the country, according to the order of law', and also to establish whether she was pregnant. To the first question, she said no more than she had in court. As to her condition, she answered, rather more explicitly than before, 'I can neither say that I am nor that I am not, having been deceived heretofore in this, and therefore I cannot directly answer you; but of the two I rather think that I am than otherwise'.[39]

The third issue was her separatism. They asked her: 'why refuse you to come to our church, we having so plain and sure testimonies to show on our side for the truth?' They then tried to drag her onto their own terrain of learned debate. They 'brought forth many texts of Scriptures'. To this she had an obvious defence. She was not, she said, 'aminded to your Church'. She had been 'within the Catholic Church this twelve years'. She would rather die than renounce her faith. Pease challenged her as to her understanding of the nature of the Church. He asked, 'what is the Church? You know it not: you have been led away by blind guides, making you believe in stocks and stones, and tradition of men contrary to the word of the Lord'. 'Answer me', he demanded, 'what is the Church?'

For someone supposedly unlearned she rose to the challenge very well. The Church was, she said, 'that wherein the true Word of God is preached, which Christ taught and left to His apostles, and they to their successors ministering the seven sacraments, which the same Church has always observed, the doctors preached, and martyrs and confessors witnessed. This is the Church which I believe to be true.' Only when 'she alleged anything for the Church of Rome (which in all her talk with them she stood unto)', did they say 'now you go from us'. Perhaps they were taken aback by her self-assured defence of her faith. Bunny, though, would not retreat in the face of her certainty. He began 'to make, as it were, an oration, and allege places of Scripture, God knows to what end'. She told him not to trouble her, since she was 'no divine'. She claimed she could not 'answer . . . to these hard questions'. She was, she said, 'according to the queen's Majesty's laws judged to die'. In her spirit she was willing to do so, though her flesh recoiled from the prospect of it. If she were to die, it would be as a 'member of the Catholic Church'. Her cause was God's own, and she accounted it a 'great comfort . . . to die in His quarrel'.[40]

In one sense, the puritan ministers were doing no more than the council had ordered: acting, as they were supposed to, as the spiritual arm of the godly magistracy. Yet Bunny, for one, clearly had a personal interest in Clitherow's case. Indeed, his confrontation with her in the prison was one of the climaxes, we might think, of his own struggle against the sources of Counter-Reformation activism, which had drawn so many of a conservative bent into separatism. His performance in front of Mrs Clitherow looks very like a continuation of his campaign against the spiritual and ecclesiological activism of the Jesuit Robert Persons. If we put Bunny's confrontation with Clitherow into the context of what appears to have been a sustained effort on his part to roll back the polemico-spiritual inroads made by the prolific Jesuit into the culture of statute-based conformity in the English Church, we can see how Clitherow's personal stand in York against the demands of the State for at least a modicum of conformity provided a platform for this particular puritan minister to confront a prominent separatist with his own account of the relationship between conscience, Church and State.

Here, perhaps, we have the epicentre of the whole Citherow case, and a demonstration of why, for so many, her stand against the combined forces of the council in the North and the massed ranks of the godliest of York's Protestant divines was a playing out of the debates about the relationship between Catholics and the State which had been started, really, by Campion and Persons. (As we have seen, if we want to know what was at stake in the tragedy of Margaret Clitherow we can find it in the print-based confrontation between Edmund Bunny and Robert Persons, the outlines and significance of which were undoubtedly all too familiar to Mrs Clitherow.[41])

In the course of these exchanges with York's puritan divines, she was confronted with the example and authority of the martyr William Hart, one of her erstwhile ghostly fathers. Those who were trying to persuade her to conform told her that she could not possibly be accounted of the same mind as Father Hart for he had said that 'it was lawful for women, that had no learning to defend their cause, to go to church'. But Clitherow did not fall into this rather obvious attempt to open up the fissures within the Catholic community created by the conformist issue. 'Father Hart', she said, 'was not of your opinion, neither would he say any such thing, and, if he had said [it], I would not have believed him. But he answered all your objections by learning, as it was manifest.'[42] William Hart was one of the clergy whom Catholics confidently took to have militated against conformity.[43] Clearly he was sufficiently stubborn for the regime in York to proceed against him for treason. A circulating copy of an original letter by him, anticipating the crown of martyrdom (and perhaps not dissimilar in its purpose to Mush's life of Clitherow) condemns any kind of compliance or association with heretics. The whole manuscript affirms the absolute necessity of separation: 'Fail not, fear not, faint not, nor fall not, from your faith, from your profession, from your calling, if they persuade you to go to the church'. 'Woe be unto those who . . . frequent . . . the conventicles . . . of wicked and heretical Protestants'; 'before God I speak that I had rather be an abject, a scallion, a vile and contemptible person in the house of God than dwell in the tabernacles of our new fangled Protestants'. The letter mocks the crowd of leading northern Protestants, such as William Palmer and Tobias Matthew, who also buzzed around and distracted Catholics such as Clitherow. If such people, or even 'an angel, should come from heaven and preach another doctrine, faith and religion than that which you have received . . . banish him'. This Pauline instruction, which Clitherow also deployed in reply to Bunny, was quite common in contemporary polemic (and had been cited in Gregory Martin's *Treatise of Schisme*), but perhaps she was remembering and repeating what Hart had actually said to her.[44]

While Hart had been personally known to and admired by Clitherow, York's puritans still taunted her that Hart had been a favourer of at least some measure of conformity. He had, as we have already remarked, briefly been a colleague of Thomas Bell. Clitherow was, of course, certain that Hart had been resolutely on the side of the angels. What this suggests is that York puritans were trying to use the range and complexity of opinion within the Catholic community over the question of conformity and separation in an attempt to drive a wedge between those who were, by and large, convinced that statute conformity was unallowable.

On 18 March, Wigginton came back unaccompanied. He took a more emollient tack. He urged her to think for a moment that she might be in error. He resorted to the classic church-papist argument that fear was a justifiable and acceptable motive for offering a limited measure of compliance:

> Mrs Clitherow, I pity your case. I am sent to see if you will be any whit conformable. Cast not yourself away; lose not both body and soul. Possibly you think you shall have martyrdom, but you are foully deceived, for it comes but one way. Not death, but the cause makes the martyr. In the time of Queen Mary were many put to death, and now also in this queen's time, for two several opinions; both these cannot be martyrs. Therefore, good Mistress Clitherow, take pity on yourself. Christ Himself fled His persecutors, so did His Apostles; and why should not you then favour your own life?

She answered, 'God defend I should favour my life in this point. As for my martyrdom; I am not yet assured of it, for that I am yet living; but if I persevere to the end, I verily believe I shall be saved.'[45]

In between the badgering of the godly, she was bothered, on and off, by 'her kinsfolks, both men and women'. Chief among these was the lord mayor,

Henry May, her stepfather. He realized that he had seriously miscalculated in hurrying forward the proceedings against his rebellious stepdaughter. Now he 'persuaded her to yield in something', promising that he would secure her a pardon for her crimes. The 'True Report' describes with disgust how the lord mayor, on his knees 'as they said, with great show of sorrow and affection, by all flattery allured her to do something against her conscience', though without success.[46]

On Saturday 19 March, Bunny came back to preach at her again. For his pains he got a sermon from her touching the nature of the true Christian faith. He swung between, on the one hand, empathetic exhortation that she should avoid the sanction of the law and, on the other, anger at her stubbornness. He even accused her of shifting 'from point to point' and said 'that she was not the same woman she was before, nor so conformable as she had been', implying that even while she had been in prison someone had been counselling her into further stubbornness. Considering how difficult she could be quite without third-party assistance, this was amazing. She politely asked him whether he found her 'since the first time' she was imprisoned 'in any other mind' than she was now.[47]

The saddest of these encounters was with Wigginton on 21 March. He simply refused to accept defeat. There is a sense, even in the 'True Report's' highly partisan narrative, that Wigginton was at one remove from the other godly ministers who taunted and tormented Mrs Clitherow in her last days. This is not to say that Wigginton positively sympathized with her and certainly not with her profession of Roman Catholicism. But in between the lines of this account we can almost sense a kind of fellow feeling between them. Both of them, after all, had fallen foul of the conformity legislation which governed the national Church. He seems to have had more than a grudging respect for her absolute inability to kowtow to authority. Within a few years he himself would find himself under suspicion that he had been involved in the writing and circulation of the inflammatory presbyterian tracts of Martin Marprelate.[48] On her part there was, it appears, not the antagonism for Wigginton which she reserved for the likes of Edmund Bunny. Wigginton announced that he was sent to her yet again by the council to see if she was 'more conformable' than before. Would she not at least listen to a sermon? Apparently, Tobias Matthew was actually there, ready to do the honours, if only she would agree. But she would not. In reply to Clitherow's insistence that she did not need to listen to Matthew because her faith was 'stayed already' and she did not intend to 'seek for a new doctrine', Wigginton said 'I myself . . . have seen Christ once in a vision, and am assured of my salvation'. Clitherow was clearly not convinced but apparently had not the heart to harangue him for it. She merely smiled and 'made but small answer'. Wigginton wanted to engage her in debate on patristic texts, but she pointed out that she did not think he believed them aright. 'Well, Mrs Clitherow', said Wigginton, 'I perceive you will cast yourself willingly away, without regard of husband or children; you follow blind guides. Is there any of them that has any learning, I would fain know that?' Her last words to him were, 'peruse their works, and you shall see'.[49]

It was only when, as William Hutton describes, she decisively rejected the approaches of the godly men of the cloth that her enemies 'saw they could by no means prevail'. It was then that they deployed 'slanderous speeches against her, and said she was reported to be of evil demeanour with priests, using more familiarity with them than with her husband, providing dainty cheer for them and simple cheer for her husband'. They urged her, said Hutton, to 'ask her husband's forgiveness' to which she, as the 'True Report' narrates, retorted that he would not accuse her of offending him 'at any time, unless in such small matters as are commonly incident to man and wife'. She wanted to speak to him before she died but they would not allow it. In fact he had already, by the council, been told to get out of York, a sure sign that no mercy would be shown to her.[50]

Appealing to the Court of Public Opinion

The time for negotiation and procrastination was now truly past. Clitherow was anxious to consummate the 'marriage' of her martyrdom. As the 'True Report' describes it, she reversed and transformed the appeals made to her duties and sentiments as a wife and mother, which her visitors and kin were using to call her back from the brink, into something else. Her stubborn spiritualized determination not to avail herself of any of the escape routes offered to her allowed her to describe and legitimate, in terms of traditional feminine attributes and roles, her new found marriage to Christ.

What we have here is a set of negotiations, of manoeuvres and counter-manoeuvres, in which the nature and meaning of Mrs Clitherow's life and fate were being subjected to a number of contradictory forces and mutually exclusive interpretations. Either she was an obedient wife and mother, or else a disorderly woman who defied her husband and neglected her children, first by diverting the resources of her household to sustain a nest of disruptive and treasonous priests and latterly by abandoning her family altogether for a sui-cidal 'martyr's' death. Either she was inspired by the Holy Spirit to undergo the worst her persecutors could do to her, or else she was possessed by a smiling devil that was intent on driving her, in effect, to suicide. Either she was a saint suffering for religion and conscience, or an ignorant and supersti-tious woman, the dupe of Machiavellian Catholic priests and traitors. Either she was going to her end (gloriously or ignominiously, depending on your point of view), or else she was going to cry off, submitting to the disciplining hand of patriarchal and Protestant authority through some more or less humiliating and explicit gesture of compliance and conformity.

The result was a brutal, and in the context of the circulating salacious rumours about her, and her allegedly carnal relationships with her priests, deeply sick, game of chicken played with Clitherow's reputation and indeed life as the stakes. It is in this context that we should return to her well-known refusal to plead to the charges brought against her, and to her motives for doing so. The 'True Report' says that Clitherow's rationale for this decision was two-fold: 'if I should have put myself to the country, evidence must needs have come against me, which I know none could give but only my children and servants . . .. Secondly . . . I knew well the country', in other words the jury, 'must needs have found me guilty to please the council, which earnestly seek my blood; and then all they had been accessory to my death, and [would have] damnably offended God'.[51] She acted as she did because she did not wish 'to cast her blood into the hands of many'. She intended that, 'by her refusal', the responsibility should 'principally rest in the judge's bosom, although also many more were guilty of it'.[52]

We can, we think, follow Katharine Longley's account of her motives, which we reviewed above, and see this decision as an integral part of the wider struggle between Clitherow and her persecutors over the nature and meaning and, in particular, the local impact of her death.[53] Longley suggests that the jury which, if she had not refused to plead, would have heard her case would almost certainly have contained a number of conformist Catholics, or persons of Catholic sympathies and associations. They would have been constrained by the political realities surrounding these very high-profile proceedings to find Clitherow guilty. One of them, says Longley, might well have been William Tesimond, the prominent York Catholic who had, after years of obstinate noncompliance, conformed in October 1583.[54]

On Longley's account, Mrs Clitherow was simply concerned about the moral dilemma in which these people might find themselves.[55] We would want, however, to go further and to argue that, if the trial had proceeded, the already very bitter divisions and disagreements among local Catholics, and in particular the rift between conformists and separatists, would have been greatly exacerbated. Certainly the meaning of the conformity (occasional or otherwise) of those who would be empanelled on the jury and of their friends and allies would have been transformed by their complicity in Clitherow's destruction, or perhaps merely humiliation (if she subsequently submitted), at the hands of the law. And all this came at the very moment when that destruction or humiliation were likely to be phrased so as to send an awful warning to separatists and to church papists alike about the costs of further Clitherow-style defiance. Under no circumstances was she ever going to allow such people, those who had compromised with the status quo and, perhaps, those who both disapproved of her and had been criticized by her, to pass judgement, both legal and, in some sense, moral, on her.

At a stroke, Clitherow's decision not to plead had deprived the authorities of that putative propaganda victory. Indeed, it did more than that. It reversed the propaganda polarities. Now it was the authorities who were on the back foot, forced to put a weak and pious woman to a cruel and unusual death, with nothing but the coerced evidence of a minor to justify their actions. Not only did this look very bad; it was more than some on the Protestant side could easily stomach. Giles Wigginton, as we mentioned, protested in open court at the judgement, saying that it was against the law of God, even if not against the laws of the queen (laws about which Wigginton, as a leading puritan nonconformist, had more than a few quibbles on his own account).[56]

John Clench seems to have been unsettled and unnerved by the way that local and factional interests were taking over the conduct and processes of the law. He was hardly squeamish about dealing with separatists. He had, after all, passed sentence against several of the Catholic clerics who had recently been condemned to death in York.[57] But it does appear that he thought something had gone seriously wrong in Clitherow's case.

For Mush, as he wrote up, with the help of William Hutton, these exchanges shortly after they took place, here was proof, if any were needed, that the regime in the North, headed by the queen's vicious vice-gerent, was utterly out of step with other officials and representatives of the State. Clench was reckoned to have the confidence of the queen,[58] but he was powerless in the face of the council's intransigence.

In all this, there could scarcely be a clearer indication of the high stakes attached to Clitherow's trial by the authorities. The intra-Catholic and Catholic–Protestant debates and divisions to which the trial was designed to contribute, and which the trial was intended to exploit, had hitherto existed in a semi-public space of gossip and scandal, of circulating manuscripts and rumours, of rifts and rebukes between and among neighbours, punctuated by arrests, imprisonments and the odd execution. It was a space in which, as we have seen, Mrs Clitherow, as a sort of *femme couverte* and Catholic *ouverte*, had become a very skilled participant. By their decision to bring all this shadow-boxing to an end and, through a brutal exercise of legal power, to force Clitherow and, through her, the local Catholic community, to confront the likely consequences of continued defiance, the authorities had dragged those debates even further into the open. But in so doing they had taken a very considerable risk. For, having brought her to trial to make an example of her, they had themselves materially contributed to her standing as 'the only woman in the north parts' (as Ralph Hurlestone described her) and had assembled a large audience to watch the potentially scandalous and certainly dramatic proceedings against her. Mrs Clitherow's refusal to plead and her martyrly mien now mobilized these factors against them. The force and vigour of the authorities' initial onslaught had been deftly turned against them by the aggressive passivity of Clitherow's noncompliance. Now it was they who found themselves off balance. In responding, their room for manoeuvre was small, constrained by a political logic of their own making; it was a logic that ensured that, whatever their scruples, if Mrs Clitherow's nerve held, there really could be no going back. And her nerve did hold. It rapidly became clear that she would not offer even the most perfunctory hint of conformity.

Clitherow's equivocal response to the pleas of her kin and others to say that she was pregnant reveals the extraordinarily finely judged game that she was now playing. She was determined to do nothing that might infringe her claims to ideological purity, or imply that she was trying to save her own skin. As we saw, she would neither confirm nor deny that she was pregnant. This left the authorities a way out, if they chose to use it. (For all the references to her at this point in the 'True Report' as 'the martyr', Clitherow may not quite yet have given up all hope of reprieve.) But the judges would have to decide the matter for themselves. She left them, quite deliberately, impaled on the horns of an ethical and political dilemma of their own making and in the end – probably inevitably – it was the crude realpolitik of Hurlestone's remarks to Clench that won the day.[59]

Throughout the trial, Clitherow's attempts to ritualize and sanctify, to orchestrate and to Catholicize her death, were frustrated by the authorities. As we witnessed above, when it became clear that she would not relent, they reactivated and circulated an already extant series of rumours about her in order to undermine her claims to moral, indeed to sexual, virtue, let alone to spiritual sanctity. As we noted, before and during the trial, Hurlestone, Cheke and Meares had cast aspersions on her alleged sexual misdemeanours with her various chaplains.[60] Indeed, the day after her execution, various York preachers 'railed against her out of their pulpits with most shameful lies and slanders'. Her stepfather, Henry May, lord mayor of York, related, when he was surrounded by his 'heretical brethren', that she 'died desperately, and that she had been an unhonest woman of her body, and that she had hanged the priests' beds with silk curtains, and that priests used to lay her on their knees and give her discipline, and that they used her body when they would'.[61]

We return here, of course, to the image of the lewd and disorderly woman who had very likely been ducked on her way to the prison after her arrest. In such stories, so common in contemporary anti-popish discourse, Clitherow's marriage to Christ, her feeding of the Church with her own substance and potentially her own blood, is being turned into a literal and carnal infidelity to her earthly husband and children. Preferring the company of priests to that of her husband, she is depicted as siphoning off the resources of the household away from its true owner into other hands and mouths. Her addiction to the company of priests, her assignations and the lies she told to enable them are now redescribed in fleshly terms as literal sexual infidelities. Given what the researches of Laura Gowing have revealed about the nature of contemporary moral norms and the ways in which the sexual and social reputation of women was structured, there was a certain internal logic, indeed perhaps even an inherent plausibility, in these charges. Women who diverted the material resources which should have been used to sustain their household to their own uses, and in particular to their own sartorial display, were conventionally enough blackguarded as whores, their typically female pride and sensuality being naturally linked to a presumed sexual licence and promiscuity.[62] In this case, since Mrs Clitherow's spiritual pride had led her to divert her household's resources to other men (the priests) the same connection must have seemed entirely natural and inherently believable, at least to her enemies. In and through these rumours, her enemies were able to redescribe her life of faith by reference to the disordered household which she allegedly ran, where separatist clergymen, themselves outside the law, had greater access to her time, and indeed her body, than did her husband.

It was a standard component of anti-popish disdain for Catholic piety to interpret it as a set of displaced forms of perverted desire. There was, of course, a contemporary Europe-wide debate about the spiritual efficacy of aspects of Counter-Reformation zeal, particularly of the kind which, it was said, led Margaret Clitherow to practise corporal discipline, allegedly inflicted on her by her priests. By reference to this debate, the salacious and unpleasant stories and rumours about her were phrased and spread. Flagellant piety was once, and certainly in early modern Europe, a mainstream practice and only in modern times has it become the preserve of the religious fanatic and the pervert. But the same dichotomy was, of course, present in the attempts to establish Margaret Clitherow's sanctity or to describe her either as a fanatic or harlot. At this point, certain mainstream Counter-Reformation figures, such as Charles Borromeo, enthusiastically endorsed flagellant piety, while others condemned it just as vigorously.[63] The vicious character assassination directed against Clitherow and her priests fits entirely into the standard contemporary accounts of the lascivious perverted fantasy world of the priest-chaplain-controller of misguided and fanatical women who stripped naked in order to allow themselves to be beaten by their clerical masters.[64]

Significantly, for the argument being pursued here, when Mush came to refute these allegations, he retaliated in kind. Far from needing any priest to chastise her, he proudly asserted, she was more than capable of disciplining and whipping herself: 'this also is not a little to your shame, that this glorious martyr in her lifetime did chasten her body and with scourges subdued her body and sensuality to the spirit'.[65] As for Henry May, Clitherow's stepfather, he was a known adulterer: 'let him remember his own notorious incontinency with his two servants in his wife's days, the one whereof is now his lady'. In other words, said Mush, the new lord mayor had been sleeping with Anne Thomson and one of the other servant girls in his own wife's house before his wife (Margaret's mother) died. When it came to carnal knowledge, May was as guilty as sin itself. For, implied Mush, May had unsuccessfully tried to rape Margaret. The lord mayor should remember 'whether he himself had not good proofs of this martyr's constant honesty at all times when she was in her mother's house'.[66]

As we might expect, Mush more or less insisted that the rumours about Clitherow came solely from Protestant sources. We know, however, from the course of the notorious Archpriest Controversy in the later 1590s that such rumour-mongering was not confined to Protestants. Here the traditional tropes and stereotypes of anti-popery were appropriated and adapted for use by Catholics against each other, and then were, as often as not, fed back into the anti-popish canon. We find the Jesuits and their friends and patrons deploying the same sort of rumours about their Catholic clerical opponents (frequently referred to as 'appellants' since they had appealed against the authority of the archpriest George Blackwell) as Protestants habitually used against the Catholic clergy generally. Robert Persons received a dispatch from a correspondent in England which described how Persons's bitter enemy, the allegedly rebellious and disobedient appellant priest William Clarke, had been found 'guilty of open adultery, to which he himself confessed as well as the woman, who admits that at least once she has had a child by him'. Her husband was 'furious' and swore 'that all his children' were 'by this same priest'. Another man, in London, had said that 'in his own house another woman' had 'been put in the family way by this same Clarke'. But Clarke made 'light of it', and continued to agitate against his ecclesiastical superior and Persons's friend, the archpriest Blackwell.[67] Another report, taken to Rome by the pro-Jesuit priest James Standish, recounted that a Catholic gentlewoman had reported to him that she saw John Mush himself, who was by now a stalwart of the appellant party, 'kissing and embracing her daughter upon a bed'.[68]

One suspects, then, that the rumours about Clitherow, even if they did not reach their final format in Catholic circles, must have been generated in part out of what was being said by some Catholics about her. After all, as we have seen, Mush had gone out of his way to emphasize what he termed 'the persecution she suffered among the good', how she had been 'tossed and afflicted' by Catholic rumours of various unspecified sorts.[69] He remained silent on the precise content of these rumours but he made it clear that when conformist Catholics had urged caution upon her they had cited her obligations to her husband and children; precisely the same considerations used by her friends and kin when, at the last, they were trying to persuade her to conform. This raised in general terms the issue of her obedience and fidelity to her husband. And, in this context, her both emotional and physical intimacy with various priests almost begged for lewd (mis)interpretation by anyone wishing to undercut or deny her irritatingly insistent claims to a superior sanctity, as, on Mush's account, her Catholic enemies most certainly did.

We might want to ask, of course, how far any of these rumours in circulation about her were, in a literal sense, actually true. We know that the redoubtable Mary Ward, for a time, had John Mush as a spiritual adviser and confessor.[70] It is virtually impossible that she would have either tolerated or disregarded any kind of behaviour such as Mush's enemies had alleged him to have perpetrated. On the other hand, if it is true, as Mush strongly implies in the 'True Report', that, as we have already noted, Mrs Clitherow's life in the Shambles in York was a misery to this highly spiritual and sensitive individual, it is more than possible that, as Mush's narrative frequently intimates, she became and was known to have become emotionally very close to him.

While she was in prison awaiting execution of sentence, she was told that the Flemish boy who had betrayed her 'had confessed that she had lain with a priest . . . a week together and then she would discipline herself with whipcords'. He had blurted out also 'that the priests and she would have delicate cheer, when she would set her husband to dinner with bread and butter and a red herring'.[71] On this view, the efforts of the authorities to persuade Clitherow 'to confess she had offended her husband', urging her 'to confess some fault against him, thereby to slander herself', take on a more sinister aspect.[72] In the context created by this nexus of pre-existing rumour, even such a general expression of guilt could be made to appear an admission of marital infidelity and sexual impropriety on her part. It is, therefore, highly likely that the Protestant authorities and their clerical allies were simply improving upon a pre-existing set of rumours that had long been circulating among Clitherow's Catholic enemies in the city. Here the Protestant authorities were exploiting divisions within the Catholic community, using an existing nexus of Catholic rumour as an echo-chamber to amplify their own attempts to besmirch the good name of the martyr and proto-saint into which (to her admirers at least) Mrs Clitherow's (both awful and exemplary) death was about to transform her.

Endgame: From Life to Death

The best efforts of Clitherow's enemies to defame her, as with their attempts to evangelize her, served not one whit to deflect her from her purpose. As the 'True Report' narrates it, 'two days before her martyrdom, the sheriffs of York came to her and told her what day was appointed for her death'. Clitherow wanted to 'go to the place where she should suffer half a day or half a night before, and to remain there all that time until she should die', but they would not allow it. (In fact, she had hoped that she would be executed in public at the Knavesmire, on the traditional killing ground where the other Catholic martyrs, several of whom had been her ghostly fathers, had met their end. But the nature of the sentence made that impossible.[73])

As Mush later described it, 'after unjust malice has condemned us, the same still pursues us in death with as much cruelty, violence, hatred, and barbarousness as it did at other times before'. Afraid of the public backlash which their cruelty might cause, 'the time wherein' the persecutors 'intend to murder us is kept as secret and unknown as may be, both from us and the people'. At moments when no one expected it, they sent the 'tormentors to make us away, ever choosing such times as the people . . . can make the smallest concourse to the place of execution'. Just as Hugh Taylor was executed within hours of his condemnation, and the priest Alexander Crow was executed at night, so 'they . . . pressed Mrs Clitherow, upon the feast of the Annunciation of our Blessed Lady, in the morning, in a close house, as obscurely as was possible'.[74]

Clitherow became certain that the sanction of the *peine forte et dure* would soon be carried out because her husband, as we remarked, had been ordered to leave the city. Now she stopped eating, and she spent much of her time in prayer. During the night of 24/25 March she went through a dress rehearsal of her own death. A prisoner who had been incarcerated there for debt, Mrs Yoward, saw her 'rise from her knees and put off all her apparel, putting on a linen habit like to an alb, which she had made with her own hands three days before to suffer martyrdom in'. Then 'she kneeled down again, without anything upon her saving that linen cloth, from twelve of the clock until three, at which time she arose and came to the fireside'. She lay 'down flat upon the stones one quarter of an hour', exactly the length of time that, as it turned out, she would take to expire, under the weight of the stones, on the following morning.[75]

At eight o'clock in the morning the sheriffs arrived, and she 'went cheerfully to her marriage, as she called it; dealing her alms in the street, which was so full of people that she could scarce pass by them. She went barefoot and barelegged, her gown loose about her.' The sheriff Fawcett, her enemy, lost patience at her behaviour but she paid no attention to him.

She was put to death in the Tollbooth, just yards from the prison on the Ouse Bridge where she had been incarcerated. Surrounded by the sheriffs, clergy and executioners, she refused to pray with them. Like many another Catholic martyr of the period she would not pollute herself in this way: 'I will not pray with you, and you shall not pray with me; neither will I say Amen to your prayers, nor shall you to mine'. Faced with imminent death and, furthermore, the humiliation and the pain of execution as a criminal, the majority are reduced to terrified incoherence. Not so with this woman. With quite extraordinary final defiance she recited prayers for the Catholic Church, the pope and his cardinals, and for Christian princes. Then and only then did she pray for the queen, and express the hope that God might turn Elizabeth Tudor 'to the Catholic faith, and that after this mortal life' the queen might 'receive the blessed joys of heaven'. By this point the other, and more junior, sheriff, William Gibson, had become convinced that what he was witnessing was not justice, not even the rough and ready justice so regularly dispensed by the Tudor penal code. He completely broke down, and 'stood weeping at the door'. This left Fawcett and Mrs Clitherow arguing about whether she accepted that she had broken the law. Said Fawcett, 'Mrs Clitherow, you must remember and confess that you die for treason', even though, of course, the offence with which she would have been charged was a felony. She riposted 'No, no, Mr Sheriff, I die for the love of my Lord Jesu', which 'last words she spoke with a loud voice'.[76] Fawcett, a stickler for compliance with established procedures, then told her she must 'put off her apparel', 'for you must die', said he, 'naked, as judgement was given and pronounced against you'. In a moment of some embarrassment and confusion, they refused her request for modesty but they allowed her female attendants to remove 'her clothes, and put upon her the long habit of linen' which she had brought with her. Once she was lying on the ground, her face was 'covered with a handkerchief', and her 'secret parts' with the linen habit, 'all the rest of her body being naked'. The door was laid upon her. At this stage she joined 'her hands . . . towards her face', but they were forced apart and tied to posts 'so that her body and her arms made a perfect cross'. Berating her and demanding that she 'ask the queen's Majesty's forgiveness' and also that of her husband, they 'laid weight upon her, which when she first felt, she said, "Jesu! Jesu! Jesu! have mercy upon me!"'. A 'sharp stone, as much as a man's fist' had been put under her back, and 'there was laid' on top of the door 'to the quantity of seven or eight hundred weight at the least, which, breaking her ribs, caused them to burst forth of the skin'. This happened at 'nine of the clock, and she continued in the press until three at afternoon'.

Thus, concluded the 'True Report', 'most victoriously this gracious martyr overcame all her enemies, passing from this mortal life with marvellous triumph into the peaceable city of God, there to receive a worthy crown of endless immortality and joy'.[77] She undoubtedly forgave those enemies, as a good saint should. Mush, however, did not. The remainder of his narrative is suffused with searing emotional violence and vitriolic hatred which cannot be read as mere rhetoric. In the final section of his 'True Report' he curses, again and again, those who had been responsible for her death. In passages which, for their vehemence, were not printed in their entirety in the nineteenth-century editions of the work, he poured out his loathing of those who had murdered his spiritual child.[78]

1 and 2. Exterior and interior of the dwelling in the Shambles, York, formerly identified as the house of the Clitherow family and now maintained as a shrine. The Clitherows' house is believed to have been at the

3. Portrait of Robert Persons SJ (reproduced by permission of the governors of Stonyhurst College, Lancashire). This illustration and that of Henry Garnet SJ in Plate 19 were originally located in a series of drawings based on original paintings, now lost, which were at one time retained at the English College in Rome and at other locations. They were copied by Charles Weld in the 1850s.

4. Portrait of Henry Hastings, third earl of Huntingdon, by an unknown artist (reproduced with the permission of the National Portrait Gallery, London).

AN APOLOGY

AGAINST THE DE-FENCE OF
ſchiſme.

Lately written by an Engliſh Di-
uine at Doway, for anſwere to a
letter of a lapſed Catholicke in
England his frend: who ha-
uing in the late Cõmiſſion
gone to to the Church,
defended his fall.

wherin is plainly declared, and mani-
feſtlye proued, the generall doctrine of
he Diuines, & of the Church of Chriſt,
which hitherto hath bene taught
and followed in England,
concerning this
pointe.

Prou. 22.
Doe thou not paſſe the auncient bounds
which thy Fathers haue putte.

21. Title page of Henry Garnet, SJ, *An Apology against the Defence of Schisme* (no place of publication [printed secretly in England], 1593), reproduced with the permission of the archives and library of the British Province of the Society of Jesus.

22. Number 10 of the Painted Life of Mary Ward (© Geistliches Zentrum Maria Ward Augsburg, Foto Tanner, Nesselwang, Germany), in which Mary Ward is depicted as contemplating the possibility and prospect of bodily martyrdom until it is revealed to her that Christ desires her to undergo spiritual martyrdom.

23. Number 20 of the Painted Life of Mary Ward (© Geistliches Zentrum Maria Ward Augsburg, Foto Tanner, Nesselwang, Germany), in which Mary Ward undertakes a night of prayer and penance after experiencing the temptation in London offered by the gifts of a noble gentleman.

PART II

With the death of Mrs Clitherow our focus shifts away from her story to the continuing debate about the issues which framed both her life and death. The relevance of that debate to her experience is crucial, because of both the nature of the issues at stake and the people engaged on either side of the argument. We are dealing here with debates about whether recusancy really should be the sign distinctive, the defining mark, of Catholicism under a heretical regime. These were debates in which, as we have seen, Mrs Clitherow had taken a quite uncompromising position. Of course, Clitherow had not died explicitly to defend the recusant cause. However, disputes within the Catholic community in York and between that community and the local Protestant State about conformity had framed the circumstances that had led her to her death and, according to Mush at least, to a martyr's crown.

Those debates did not end with her demise. On the contrary, her death poured fuel on the fire, as Mush tried to use his account of her life and martyr's death to win the argument about conformity for her and his side. That account was not initially directed at the Elizabethan regime or at Protestant opinion. Rather, circulating in manuscript among Catholics, Mush's account of Clitherow was designed to shape Catholic opinion, indeed to clinch the case for recusancy as itself a form of martyrdom and as the only fit response for Catholics confronted by the demands of the Elizabethan State.

It turned out that Mush's great opponent in the ensuing exchanges, the leading clerical defender of a form of conformity, indeed of church popery, was another figure active on the York Catholic scene in the early 1580s, and thus straight from the world of Margaret Clitherow – none other than Thomas Bell. If, as seems very likely, Mush was the main author not only of the 'True Report' but also of a vitriolic manuscript assault on the tyranny of the earl of Huntingdon in the North (the so-called 'Yorkshire Recusant's Relation'), and indeed of a long and bitter manuscript attack on Bell (the 'Answere to a Comfortable Advertisment'), then the links between the Clitherow debacle and these later disputes are very close indeed. But even if Mush was not the (sole) author of all of these texts – and the attributions are not absolutely certain – the connections are plain enough. By tracing them out we get to watch the central questions raised by Margaret Clitherow's grisly fate being given final polemical and casuistical form by seminary-educated ideologues, as they competed for the allegiance of the

Catholic laity and thus for the soul of Elizabethan Catholicism. An analysis both of the arguments involved and of the forms in and through which those arguments were canvassed, and the ensuing debates conducted, enables us to connect the issues and methods at stake in York in the mid 1580s with the later course of the notorious Archpriest Controversy. Here also we can see Jesuits such as Henry Garnet seeking to make casuistical case law out of the extraordinary obstinacy, pertinacity and courage that had brought Mrs Clitherow to a martyr's death in the Tollbooth and made her something of a poster child for the English Catholic community at bay.

All of which is to say that in contemplating the grisly fate of Margaret Clitherow we are not just watching a single and (arguably) refractory or difficult woman coming to a bad or tragic end. Nor are we merely confronting the consequences of a notably dysfunctional family being over determined by a peculiarly vicious outbreak of local faction. Rather, while we are witnessing these things, we are also dealing with a synecdoche for a far wider set of political, religious and ideological pressures: a situation in which the consequences of religious change and geo-political conflict can be watched working themselves out, first, in and through the family and local politics of mid-Elizabethan York and, then, through the wider politics of the English Catholic community as the dreadful fate and example of Mrs Clitherow was deployed to serve the interests of various factions and fractions within English Catholicism. Thus was (Catholic) sanctity achieved and sainthood conferred in post-Reformation England.

6

Mrs Clitherow and the English Catholic Community after 1586

After the Execution

John Mush's 'True Report', a biting contemporary polemic about the spiritual necessity of separation from a heretical Church, also served to turn Margaret Clitherow into a saint when, nearly 400 years after her execution, the Roman Catholic Church formally recognized her heroic sanctity. Long before then the printing of Mush's text had turned her into an icon of wifely virtue. We might imagine, however, that her trial and execution really must have looked, to her contemporaries, like the end of the affair. But, for those contemporaries, it soon became clear that it was nothing of the kind, at least in the sense of the ideological implications and assumptions which run through Mush's narrative of Clitherow's life and death and which rumbled on after her martyrdom. In fact, in some ways, the battles over the issues in which she had so immersed herself were only just beginning, as the representatives and leaders of the Catholic community, in the face of the hostility of the mid- and late Elizabethan State, started to fight to the death over the identity of Catholicism in England. The sufferings of Mrs Clitherow are crucial in alerting us to the practical ramifications and political context of the arguments about recusancy and church popery and the way in which they defined late Tudor Catholicism.

In some very real sense, we can properly construe what Margaret Clitherow's life and death meant politically and polemically for contemporaries only by looking at the period after her execution and by trying to reassemble a narrative of how her friends and enemies struggled over the issues that had informed her passion and death. Those friends and enemies may not always have referred to her directly but there were very distinct echoes, in what they said and did, of her principled stand on the question of separation from the national Church. We can pick up those echoes in a variety of locales and documents.

Clitherow's long struggle against the Elizabethan authorities in York, as we have seen, had been informed by the crisis-ridden conditions of mid-Elizabethan politics. The failure of the queen's preferred foreign policy option in 1579, namely a dynastic alliance with France, had triggered a furious reaction as those Catholics who had expected this policy to alleviate their political difficulties became involved in a series of conspiracies against the regime, notably the notorious Throckmorton plot.[1] The more aggressively Protestant members of that regime then prevailed on the queen to intervene directly in the Netherlands following the assassination of William the Silent in 1584. These same people were also determined to destroy Mary Stuart whose cause had been taken up in France by the revivified Holy League. The League had reassembled following the death of the duke of Anjou, whose demise left the Huguenot Henry of Navarre as the next heir to the last of the Valois, Henry III. Essential to these manoeuvres was the negotiation of a treaty with Scotland in order to secure the northern border and to prevent the possibility of a Spanish invasion force coming across it, should Philip II's troops ever land in Scotland. The earl of Huntingdon was one of the commissioners appointed in September 1585 to secure this agreement, though the killing of Lord Russell in a border incident delayed the signing of the treaty until July 1586, shortly after Clitherow's execution.[2]

There is, of course, no direct reference in John Mush's 'True Report' to any of these events. But they are the immediate context for what happened to Mrs Clitherow and, indeed, many of the other Catholic victims of the mid-Elizabethan State. Shortly after Clitherow's death, the uncovering of the distinctly weird Babington conspiracy allowed Elizabeth's leading councillors to begin the process of killing the Scottish queen as well.

Up until this point, the Catholic movement in England and its outposts in exile on the Continent had operated mainly in a legitimist political mode, in the sense that Catholics had claimed to support the line of succession in right of blood to Elizabeth, and to stand for the rights of both Elizabeth and her cousin and heir Mary Stuart. However, many Catholics' loyalist support for Elizabeth was far from unconditional. In fact, Catholic polemicists had, during this period, swung between, on the one hand, professing loyalty to the queen and claiming that so-called evil counsellors perverted her government and led her into error, and, on the other, intimating that Elizabeth might be herself tainted and, even if indirectly, responsible for the heretical evils that had afflicted the English nation. These modes of response to the regime were not distributed clearly between, as it were, loyalty and resistance.[3] In other words, claims that Catholics sought only the queen's best interests could be packaged all together inside a treatise such as 'Leicester's Commonwealth', a classic evil-counsellor discourse that combined its protestation of fears for the queen's safety with an excoriating denunciation of the damage which the queen's rule had done to the commonwealth.

But with the travesty of the Scottish queen's trial and her miserable blood-soaked end at Fotheringhay, the logic of the kind of monarchomach resistance theory practised in France by the Holy League became applicable, for some Catholics at least, in England as well. Faced with the candidacy of the Calvinist James VI, following what they viewed as the murder of his Catholic mother, they started to think in terms of a violent overthrow of the murderess, the heretic English queen, if that was what was required to prevent the accession of a heretic king. In Scotland, the apparent subservience of James to Elizabeth set off a series of aristocratic revolts. The rebels appealed to the power of Spain to intervene in their favour, just as Spain was intervening in France against Henry of Navarre. Inevitably, in these circumstances, English Catholic recusants' separation from the Church of England became ideologically compatible with, or even equivalent to, the refusal of the League to tolerate heretical contamination of the line of royal succession in France.

Of course, most English Catholics, we suspect, always remained unwilling to follow a path of direct and violent resistance to the Elizabethan regime. Their opinions on this question were consistent with the outlines of conformist thought as laid out, in part, by Thomas Bell and his friends, those whom we might not inaccurately term *politiques*, even if Bell never located his arguments specifically in the context of the debates conducted primarily in late Valois and early Bourbon France over the true extent of monarchical authority and the limitations that ought to be imposed on popular political choice.

All the same, as part of the Catholic movement in England and in exile started to tip from angry and aggressive loyalist rhetoric into the language and ideology of outright opposition both to the queen's monarchical authority and to the concept of indefeasible hereditary succession, it was inevitable that the most oppositional Catholics would be identified and targeted as potential if not actual insurgents and dissidents.

Following Clitherow's death, retribution started to be visited on those known to have been harboured by and associated with her. As Mush narrated it, 'after Whitsunday . . . at the gaol-delivery, Sir Thomas Fairfax, vice-president, Cheke, Hurlestone, and the rest, arraigned' her chaplain 'Mr Francis Ingleby'. They 'condemned and murdered him as a traitor, because he was a priest of Rheims'. They tried to 'entangle him with an oath to disclose in what Catholic men's houses he had been harboured, but they could not deceive him'.[4]

Then 'at Lammas assizes following, for want of priests, they arraigned divers Catholic prisoners'. The authorities were 'determined to murder some of them' as part of a coherent reign of terror to discourage 'the country from the Catholic faith'. They indicted Anne Tesh who had been arrested 'at the same time when they did apprehend Mrs Clitherow', on the accusation of the same Flemish boy who had informed against her. They intended 'in this drift of time to find out some colourable matter against her to make her away; for they often searched her house and straitly imprisoned her servants, to extort anything whereupon they might have show of a just indictment'. The hapless Flemish boy, claimed Henry Cheke, was ready to accuse Tesh 'to have heard Mass in Mrs Clitherow's house, whereupon they sent for her, and in her presence asked the boy if he knew that woman'. This time the boy blenched and would not fully cooperate. The intended fatal prosecution failed. At Tesh's arraignment, Ralph Hurlestone, John Rhodes and others went through a similar performance to the one which had been intended to discredit and soil Clitherow's public reputation. They 'railed shamefully against her with many dishonest speeches, charged her that she had harboured priests, and openly said to the jury (according to their impudent iniquity), "Find her guilty"'. The jury, for whatever reason, refused to deliver up the requisite verdict. Instead, 'upon the boy's words and a little girl's, about twelve years of age, they condemned her in a hundred marks for hearing Mass'. According to Mush this infuriated the judges, and the 'the bench said, "if we live to the next assizes . . . we will have thee found guilty of harbouring priests"'.[5]

The regime's next victim was a young Catholic man called Robert Bickerdike. Mush related that he had been arrested over a year before, though only 'for being seen in company with a priest'. Mush claimed that the real reason for his prosecution was that he had made too many enemies in York's mercantile community. He was, on Mush's account, indicted 'for saying to a heretical apprentice, which with vehement fury railed against him and the Catholics, calling them traitors', that the apprentice might, for the time being, air what opinions he pleased, 'for the sap is . . . with Catholics in the root of the tree, but it may perhaps ascend upwards towards Michaelmas, and then he would use no such railing words'. According to Bickerdike, all this signified no more than that 'in this prosperous time with heretics they might say and do what they listed but, if God should send a Catholic time', then 'heretics' tongues' would be silenced.[6]

To a suspicious mind, however, this suggested something else altogether. William Hutton narrated that there was an 'indictment against him upon certain words he should speak in a figurative manner' but which could, at a pinch, be 'applied to the Spaniards coming in'. Initially he was cleared, though he was immediately re-incarcerated for his recusancy. Then, at a second hearing, in York Castle, where the crown's case was presented by Martin Birkhead, attorney to the council in the North, and the judges were Clench and Rhodes, he was indicted again. He was asked this question: 'if the pope and the Spaniard should come to the field to make wars against the queen's Majesty of England', whose part would he take? He answered, 'even whether as God would put him in mind'. The court 'said he was a traitor and deserved to be hanged'. In the end the jury convicted him. He was taken out to the Knavesmire for execution on 8 October 1586.[7]

After Bickerdike there was the priest Alexander Crow. His case came up at a gaol delivery on 30 November 1586. As they had done with Clitherow, the authorities tried to destroy his reputation after his death. Mush claimed he was so ill 'before his arraignment until his martyrdom' that 'being upon the ladder, he fell from it in a swoon'. Mush said that the authorities spread it about that he had despaired and had tried to commit suicide before the executioner got to work on him. In any case, they 'took him up and hanged him' from the gallows for a short time; then, according to the sentence for treason, they cut him down while he was still conscious, and in a 'most cruel manner ripped him alive'.[8]

Crow had been arrested with Mush when the house of their patron, Richard Langley, was searched. Langley was extremely obstinate and, like Clitherow, refused to make any attempt at compromise, although Huntingdon initially intimated that some sort of leniency might be extended to him. 'The heretics', said Mush, 'much abused this gentleman at the bar, with railing and uncourteous speeches'. When he first entered the hall 'to be arraigned', he knelt down and 'asked Mr Crow the priest, his blessing'. Langley declared that he 'would never repent that he had harboured priests, and that they were the messengers of God'. In fact he was sorry that he had not 'harboured more and oftener than he had done; also that he thanked God that he might die for so good a cause'. His refusal, like Clitherow, to make even the slightest gesture at compliance caused 'the tyrant and his accomplices' to change the jury, 'which was first empanelled of his honest neighbours', because they were afraid that he might be acquitted. The replacement jury was 'such as they knew would work their desire to murder him, as they did'.[9]

During this same period, it is clear that the already violent tensions within York's Catholic community became uncontrollable. Mush's Catholic opponents were unlikely to stand mute while he condemned them by association for what had been done to Mrs Clitherow. On 4 September 1586, only six months after Clitherow was pressed to death, Mush had, it appears, been denounced by Thomas Bell's former friend and associate,

Anthony Tyrrell, who at this time was bombarding the authorities with what he knew, or thought he knew, about the Babington plot.[10] Tyrrell has usually been regarded as a fantasist, and almost mentally unhinged. He claimed to have privileged information about a vast Catholic conspiracy which he, by turns, denounced to the regime and then denied, almost as the fit took him.[11] It seems possible, however, that his denunciations of the Babington conspirators were in part a product of the battles between Catholics during the 1580s over the issue of conformity and separation. Tyrrell probably hated Mush. Perhaps his betrayal of him was by way of revenge for Mush's acid words, in the 'True Report' of Clitherow's life, about those Catholics who had not lived up to her exacting standards. Tyrrell's list of clergy and their harbourers certainly included Mush's name. Mush was described here as 'the chief layer of plots'. The list noted that he was in York. The authorities were, of course, already quite aware of Mush's whereabouts. After all, Clitherow was known to have harboured him. But Mush was traced almost immediately to the house of Richard Langley. Langley, as we saw, with his other chaplain, Crow, was immediately tried and executed.[12]

Mush's 1588 manuscript denunciation of Thomas Bell remembered that Langley's name had been linked, in the court room, with Thomas Howard, duke of Norfolk, who had died for treason in 1572 after the exposure of the Ridolfi plot, a conspiracy the centre-piece of which had been a dynastic union between the duke and the Scottish queen. Mush set down with bitter sarcasm the remark of Ralph Hurlestone, one of Clitherow's principal tormentors, to the 'gracious gentleman Mr Langley': 'Langley, you served the duke who also pleaded law for his defence but as law served not him, no more shall it you'.[13]

Among those whom Tyrrell named to the regime as guilty of the Babington treason was David Ingleby, the brother of Clitherow's chaplain Francis Ingleby.[14] He was one of the Catholic northerners who had co-religionist friends in Scotland and whose political aims and ambitions were clearly underwritten by the expectation in several quarters that the young Scottish king might turn Catholic, or at least appeal for support to the powerful aristocratic leaders of Scottish Catholic opinion.[15] Tyrrell claimed that the moving clerical spirit in the Babington conspiracy, John Ballard, was visited in London by David Ingleby and Edward Windsor. He said that they had discussed a plan to assassinate the privy council.[16] Ingleby and his priest John Boste (whom Huntingdon had been trying to arrest as far back as 1581) had promised Ballard, or so Ballard alleged, that 'if they might be assured that the matter were once in action, and that the strangers were entered, they should have aid enough' in the North.[17] Ballard confessed also that in the summer of 1585 he had been sent by Ingleby and Windsor 'into the North to understand if the [Catholic] lords of Scotland meant to stand out'. Boste had averred that 'if the Scottish lords had not aid, they were not able to hold out, and that the lords of Scotland found great fault with the English Catholics that they did not hold out as they did'; for if they both 'joined together' they could achieve 'liberty of religion'.[18] Huntingdon's agents continued to hunt down Boste. (He was arrested, finally, in September 1593.)[19]

Mush, however, absconded from prison. He was the only one of Clitherow's known clerical companions to escape with his life.[20] This was something which it seems he found hard, in subsequent years, to justify to those who, like Mush himself, argued that martyrdom was the zenith of contemporary witness to the true faith, a fate which he had, in effect, urged on his ghostly child, Clitherow.[21]

The Tyrant and the Quisling

The fury that had provoked Mush's bitter diatribes in his 'True Report' against the enemies of the woman he adored as a saint was conveyed to the world primarily in two manuscript tracts. The first was the scathing denunciation of Huntingdon and his murderous regime, which is the principal source for the accounts of the prosecutions, described above, of Ingleby, Tesh, Bickerdike, Crow and Langley. It is a shortish text but there are similarities in its style and content to the infamous squib known as 'Leicester's Commonwealth', which had been published two years earlier. Had Mush given his work a title (in the nineteenth century it was printed under the heading of 'A Yorkshire Recusant's Relation'), he might well have called it 'Huntingdon's Commonwealth'. It is a natural companion piece to his life of Clitherow. Huntingdon may personally have been absent from York at the time that Clitherow was done to death. But Mush was in no doubt about who was to blame for the sufferings of Catholics in the North. It was Huntingdon, 'the chiefest deviser and contriver of our troubles here', and, of course, the crowd of hangers-on who enforced his tyrannical rule. These parasites, the murderers of Clitherow and her friends, priestly and lay, were the immediate targets of Mush's pen. Meares, the 'tyrant's councillor', was utterly corrupt. He even took bribes from Catholic gentlemen to leave their wives alone. The irony was evidently not lost on Mush, considering what had happened to Mrs Clitherow. In addition to Huntingdon, Meares and Ralph Hurlestone, 'there be also many more which are companions and fellows with them in murdering us' since the passing into law of the recent 'wicked statutes . . . against priests and their harbourers'. Among these people were Lord Eure, Sir Thomas Fairfax and Sir William Mallory, who served on the bench 'at divers gaol-deliveries in the tyrant's absence at the assizes'. There were also John Clench and John Rhodes, and 'at every turn one arrogant heretic', namely Martin Birkhead, attorney to the council in the North. (There was no allowance made now for Judge Clench who, in Mush's 'True Report', had been portrayed as almost sympathetic to Clitherow.) Mush was entirely bereft of sympathy for the 'malicious puritan' Henry Cheke 'who was here secretary to the tyrant and his council' and had recently died, 'smitten with a fit of raging madness', and who thus 'received a just sentence of damnation for his unjust murdering' of 'many virtuous Catholic priests and lay people'.[22]

These petty tyrants were following Huntingdon's orders in what they did, whether he was present or not. Huntingdon may not, as Claire Cross notes, always have been present when Catholics were put on trial, and indeed the proceedings against Clitherow had been conducted principally at the direction of Lord Eure. But Mush remarked that, even if 'the tyrant himself seldom of late has sat on the bench to condemn us', his officials were eager to do his dirty work for him 'according to his will and direction'.[23]

Though less expansive and without the subtlety of the earlier attack on the queen's favourite, Mush's tract reproduces the principal lines of the assault on the earl of Leicester. Huntingdon was, of course, Leicester's brother-in-law, and was named in 'Leicester's Commonwealth' as the means by which Leicester hoped to come to supreme power, in other words via Huntingdon's own Yorkist claim to succeed Elizabeth. Huntingdon, 'though he be', said Mush, 'descended of most noble parentage, and himself the top of the emulous house . . . yet is he basely accounted of and' was held 'in no worthy estimation'. Huntingdon was

degenerated from all true nobility of his ancestors into a most bloody and heretical tyrant, insatiably thirsting for the lives and destruction of all good men, a fit instrument for the Devil to work his will by, of no towardness in natural wit or wisdom to do well, a pestiferous and most irreligious dissembler for his own gain and credit.

Referring, perhaps, to the recent enlargement of Huntingdon's power (as Cross points out, the renewing in 1586 of Huntingdon's commission as lord lieutenant may have been an extension of the authority he held via his commission of 1581), Mush wrote that 'in these parts this monster is god, king, bishop, president, catchpoll and whatsoever else to annoy the Catholics'.[24]

Mush identified him as part of a puritan plot, very similar to the one which Catholics had said that Leicester was fomenting for his own ends. 'Huntingdon', said Mush, 'expects to be supreme head and chief senior of the puritan synagogue, for of that dissembling sect he is already (though covertly) a principal member, fraudulently using this present time and state of the Protestant regiment to his most advantage'. Among his associates was the odious and crawling dean of York, Matthew Hutton.[25] Mush added, 'you will perhaps marvel why, in all this story, I make no mention of Mr Sandys, the old apostate and false archbishop, seeing he is well known to be as furious and unreasonable in all his doings as any other'. Edwin Sandys had no sympathy for Catholic recusants and he had contributed to the 1577 diocesan survey of recusancy; but neither had he any liking for puritans. Huntingdon had quarrelled with Sandys in 1578 for, as he thought, sticking his knife into Edmund Grindal by informing the queen of the prevalence of puritanism in his (Sandys's) archdiocese, though Sandys denied the charge. Mush claimed that Huntingdon had 'taken the persecution of the Catholics into his own hands', partly because he feared that Sandys would 'deal more favourably with us, as also meaning hereby to overthrow him'. The two had been 'at daggers drawing' and there was still 'a continual grudge and hatred between them'. This was because Sandys was merely 'a profane Protestant' while Huntingdon was 'a dissembling puritan'. Huntingdon apparently believed that 'none can persecute us extremely enough but himself and therefore he will do all'. Sandys, however, refused to 'deal where his adversary hath any intermeddling'. In this unseemly squabble, Hutton, who could not 'brook nor patiently bear any superiority' of Sandys over himself, sided with Huntingdon. Thus Hutton, 'being a licentious companion and an irreligious, dissembling atheist, and bearing among the ignorant a name of learning, but in truth very dotish and unlearned', was exploited by Huntingdon. They did not exactly 'close [together] . . . in puritanism', but Hutton simply told Huntingdon what he wanted to hear, and 'framed his talk in religion as he perceives the tyrant's humour to flow'.[26] Huntingdon was himself an arrant and arrogant hypocrite. He 'abhorred the supreme ecclesiastical authority in the queen as much as Catholics, and yet, dissembling this point', persecuted Catholics 'to death for the same'.[27]

Some of the allegations of corruption which Mush makes against Huntingdon are very similar in tone and style to the ones levelled earlier against Leicester, whose puritan hypocrisy was said by the author of 'Leicester's Commonwealth' to go hand in hand with the worst kinds of moral depravity. For example, Mush says that Huntingdon 'was a chief broker of the shameful marriage between' his servant, one Mr Beckwith and 'one of his lady's waiting women, though he knew Beckwith to have one wife at the least at the same time living in England, which yet lives, if he had not besides her one or two more in Ireland, but I am not sure whether this kind of filthy connection be holden lawful in this puritanism, or no'. Huntingdon also persecuted Catholics with an ulterior motive, namely that 'when his expected day' came, there might 'be few or none of them to hinder his ambitious climbing'. Huntingdon was guilty of crimes, actual and attempted, just as shocking of those of his brother-in-law, Leicester. While Catholics in prison were subjected to all sorts of petty cruelties and extortion in order to enrich those in charge of these terrible places, Mush alleged, for example, that Huntingdon had personally conspired to poison the water supplied to Catholic prisoners in Hull. Huntingdon's own mother, a Catholic, feared 'to feel the smart of this her son Nero his knife, whose nature and inclination she knew to be infected with heretical fury'.[28]

As in his 'True Report', Mush insisted here also that Tudor rule in the North had degenerated into tyranny. In effect, the rule of law stood suspended, and the queen's good subjects suffered at the hands of a rabble of criminals. In addition to the 'chief members of the council of iniquity' were joined 'the whole crew and rout of rascality, that is, bailiffs, catchpolls, promoters, summoners, pursuivants and serving-men'. This 'ravenous nest of spend-thrifts continually wait to prey upon us', said Mush. The result was that the 'world never goes well with them that day wherein they catch not a booty by some kind of prowling, most of these being *foex populi*, wallowing in all dishonesty and vicious lives (for such are fittest instruments for the tyrant, as greedy of other men's harms as they are ever pinched with want and beggary through their slothful loitering), pretend great zeal in religion, and busily stir themselves in promoting, spoiling, apprehending and tormenting us'. The tyrant's rule had spread like a cancer as the natural governors of the region bent to his will, but hardly with enthusiasm, for he put 'no affiance or surety in them'. Mush wrote that Huntingdon did not even trust those who normally bore the burden of enforcing public order. The puritan-minded earl 'sometimes . . . commands gentlemen to search, and in the meantime he appoints others to search their [own] houses, that, whilst they are busily troubling their neighbours, their own families do not escape scot free'.[29]

While Mush did not elaborate on the issue of Huntingdon's political ambition in the way that 'Leicester's Commonwealth' did about Robert Dudley's, Huntingdon's dynastic inheritance and prospects were directly alluded to here. Mush recalled the words of a Catholic, subsequently executed, who had remarked on Huntingdon's Yorkist pedigree. 'His visage', wrote Mush 'bewrays him to be a tyrant, for at his first coming to York as president, a most virtuous and learned man beholding him, said, "truly I am greatly deceived if this man prove not as notable a tyrant as was Richard III, for", quoth he, "he bears the very countenance and face of a tyrant"'.[30]

There is, in fact, little evidence that Huntingdon had vaulting ambition of this kind.[31] But this did not prevent Catholics from speculating about how far his known political opinions and his puritanism might push him and his friends into seizing power if the chance was ever to be offered. Mush described how Huntingdon, 'after his first coming into' the North, 'won to him by great flattery divers worshipful gentlemen, and by their means sounded the hearts of the rest, what they would do for him if his desired day should come. Them he made his instruments to prepare and win to him the chiefest in these parts against that day.' Mush was in no doubt that Huntingdon was as guilty as some others had been, notably the earl of Leicester, in trying to thwart the queen's determination to marry the duke of Anjou. Mush claimed, as had 'Leicester's Commonwealth', that Huntingdon 'was a most rebellious malcontent at the arriving of Monsieur', in other words, the duke of Anjou, 'every day ready to stir rebellion and rise to arms with the disgraced sort against the prince herself, for which purpose at the same time he made a new horse race in the forest near to York, that he might know where to have approved coursers if need required'. He also 'sent to his brethren in Leicestershire, when he heard her Majesty to be dangerously sick, to keep his house [at] Ashby, and to make in readiness the armour intending . . . to be the first that should by force make claim and begin civil war'.[32]

Only, said Mush, if one knew of these people's raging, though partially concealed, ambition could one properly understand why they tried so hard to prove that there was a Catholic conspiracy where none, in reality, existed. They needed the appearance of Catholic treason to cover and conceal their own treachery:

> When any priest or Catholic is apprehended and brought before the tyrant or his council, this is the ordinary usage by railing, arrogant and foolish speeches to abuse them. The whole desire, intent, and drift of these bloodsuckers is by some question to entrap him and bring him within danger of their impious statutes that they may murder him.

By manufacturing a chimera of Catholic plotting they were able to crush the righteous indignation which their own actions had created among the general populace, not just among Catholics. Via the weasel-worded rhetoric of the Elizabethan regime's war on a supposed Catholic terrorism, Huntingdon and his friends were able to associate any form of opposition to their misdeeds with Catholicism. And they used statute law in order to justify and carry out their knavery, though they knew that papal political authority was, in the last resort, available to correct the sins of tyrants. And so,

> of late, it is a usual question with them to ask whose part we will take and fight against if the pope should invade this realm; for they vehemently

dread that he will be their bane, and that their most arrogant and shameful apostasy from him their supreme pastor on earth will end miserably and fall out in short time to their destruction.

But they did not bully and persecute only the known leaders of the separated Catholic community. They also wanted 'to entrap within the compass of their treasonable statutes the timorous consciences of the simple, which never intended to offend either queen or pope and, when that occasion should befall, would be most careful and provident to perform the duty of a true Christian subject'.[33]

This was why they made such brutal and obscene use of the theatre of death to which convicted Catholics were dragged. 'At the place of execution', these 'malicious hell-hounds of Satan' barracked Catholics 'with their ignorant railing, slanderous, blasphemous and frivolous questions, disputations, accusations and lies'. They had a puritan rent-a-mob that cried out, on cue, 'that we be traitors, papists, seductors, and [the] queen's enemies'. They did this with spite, 'mocking and slandering us, belying and blaspheming the Catholic faith'. In their efforts to secure propaganda, they spread lies and rumours about their victims. Thus they claimed that Alexander Crow had tried to commit suicide. Such as 'they make traitors they murder ordinarily with horrible cruelty, dismembering them and ripping them alive'. The persecutors' vileness was such that 'they pressed Mrs Clitherow naked'. Furthermore, at the sites of public execution, 'spies are set abroad to mark the countenances and behaviour of the bystanders, and to note if any be there which by word, gesture, or any other way seem favourable to us, lament our unjust deaths, or show any sign of charitable compassion towards us in our agony, or endeavour to get of our blood or other relics, for all such they apprehend as traitors and enemies to the queen'. The agents of State security tried to ensure that nothing 'belonging to the martyr be either unburnt or escape their hands'. The martyrs' 'sacred blood they conculcate and cast into the fire'. The persecutors habitually took the martyrs' clothes and dispersed them, 'the pins, points, buttons, and all, lest Catholics get them and use them for relics'. After the martyrs had been dismembered, as the sentence for treason prescribed, they generally boiled 'the quarters in some filthy mixture, and the heads' they daubed 'with some black matter, to cause them to seem more loathsome and grizzly'. As for Mush's friend Richard Langley, 'they would not suffer him to have a winding-sheet, nor his body to be interred but among the thieves' and they threw his lifeless corpse into the bottom of a pit with 11 others on top. For those unfortunates who died in prison, they would not allow them 'to be buried in churchyards, but in obscure and profane places, as dunghills'. Their malice backfired in the case of Margaret

Clitherow for, when she was buried 'beside a dunghill in the town', her body lay there 'full six weeks without putrefaction, at which time it was secretly taken up by Catholics and carried on horseback a long journey, to a place where it rested six days unbowelled, before necessary preservatives could be gotten, all which time it remained without corruption or evil savour, and after was laid up as a worthy treasure'.[34]

The evidence which Mush amassed to prove that an evil little knot of tyranny had seized control of the State in the North, and was persecuting the queen's loyal subjects, in much the same way that 'Leicester's Commonwealth' had described of Huntingdon's brother-in-law, was crucial in order to convict Bell, Tyrrell and others of being collaborators, in league with the kind of puritanism which was currently being used to justify the perversion of royal authority.

Mush's tractate attack on the Huntingdon regime was written just weeks before Mary Stuart went to the block. His work is right on the cusp between legitimism and its obverse. He insists that Catholics are grossly defamed and persecuted by the queen's representatives in the North who accuse them of treason. Yet he does not shrink to say here that, in effect, the queen's rule has been turned into a heretical tyranny. We know from other sources that manuscript tracts on the topic of recusancy and occasional conformity were circulating in the North at this time. Some of this material was written by Mush as well. By March 1587, Mush was with John Talbot at Mitcham in Surrey and then, probably quite soon after, went to London. In May 1588 Burghley knew that Mush was in the capital. There, it seems almost certain, he put the finishing touches to a massive manuscript indictment of Thomas Bell and his friends which, we may speculate, grew out of and was based on what Mush had already written against him and his sympathizers.[35] The text, entitled 'An Answere to a Comfortable Advertisment' (see Plate 15), was dated 10 May. It was a full-blown reply to Bell's case for conformity.

This tract has traditionally been attributed to John Gerard and has been assigned to 1593; but even a cursory reading of it indicates that it was completed in May 1588 and was almost certainly by Mush or, perhaps, was the product of collaboration between Mush and his friend the Jesuit Henry Garnet. The author describes himself as 'a Catholic priest in the South'. By the date that the manuscript was finished Mush had, of course, fled southwards after breaking prison in York in late 1586. The tract mentions the treatment of Campion and his friends but deals mainly with the cruelties inflicted on northern Catholics, and particularly those living in York, primarily the same individuals as the ones who are listed in the manuscript now known as 'A Yorkshire Recusant's Relation' which, as we saw, was also written by Mush. Later on, during the Archpriest Controversy, Robert Charnock argued that it was ridiculous to affirm, as Robert Persons did, that 'neither

M. Mush nor his fellows have ever written any books concerning devotion, or controversies, for they have written much in both kinds, although they had not that means which F. Persons had to set them forth; and M. Mush in particular put his pen to paper against M. Bell, now an enemy'.[36]

It is not impossible that the manuscript was aimed, in part, also at Anthony Tyrrell, who may have betrayed Mush in late 1586. Tyrrell had agreed, at the end of January 1588, to preach a recantation sermon at Paul's Cross. But he used the event, or so it appears, in a vain attempt to justify the approach of himself and others, notably Bell, in distinguishing their spiritual and temporal loyalties. Tyrrell's performance, which Mush roundly mocked, can be read as a form of protestation of the kind recommended by Bell.[37]

Predictably enough, Mush's tract strongly commends Persons's *Brief Discours* and hews closely to the strict line on church papistry and recusancy laid down by the Jesuit. It quotes and refutes passages from manuscript tracts which Bell had circulated in the North. As in his 'True Report', Mush uses the death of Clitherow to prove that the intentions of the authorities towards the Catholics were thoroughly malign. Any gesture towards conformity on the part of Catholics could function, therefore, only as a mark of approval of, and submission to, the heretical religion that was currently being enforced with such cruelty by the authorities. The argument here was all of a piece with that of 'A Yorkshire Recusant's Relation' where the malice of Huntingdon and his friends was described as being 'so great and deadly that impudently they deny us the small benefit which the statute grants us, neither will they permit that we . . . plead for only just defence their own laws unjustly made against us, for the tyrant has plainly said that no papist in England should have that right at his hands in any matter which law would give him'. This had been plain enough when he verbally abused 'Mr Leonard Babthorpe, the counsellor, and Mr [John] Launder, the attorney, for pleading law in their Catholic wives' behalfs'. Huntingdon gaoled them both and then 'lightened their purses with an unreasonable fine', and 'deprived them of the whole practice in law to their undoings', and finally 'in most villainous manner disgraced one upon the pillory'. It was, Mush claimed, 'the tyrant's nature to be implacable where he has once conceived offence or displeasure, though it be without just cause, and to pursue till death such as he may overrun'. Indeed, 'all the Catholics in these parts, yes, and many schismatical dissemblers also, which have had occasion of suits before him', could 'witness how his heavy malice to them for their Catholic faith at all times' had 'overswayed the equity of their causes to make judgement proceed against them'.[38]

Between Resistance and Compromise?

If, therefore, we read what we take to be Mush's three principal manuscript treatises of the period 1586–1588 against one another, we see the figure of the 'martyr' (Mrs Clitherow) juxtaposed against that of 'the tyrant' (Huntingdon) and between them we find the quisling figure of Thomas Bell, the effect of whose principles and activities, however much he might claim to be acting in the true interests of English Catholics, was, or so Mush argued, to undermine true believers such as Clitherow and to give aid and succour to the persecutors.

Mush's treatise of May 1588 on recusancy and conformity (assuming that the 'Answere to a Comfortable Advertisment' is by him) savaged Bell mercilessly. It was penned, or at least was completed, when the approach of the Spanish Armada could no longer be prevented, and when, for the first and, as it turned out, the last time Catholics might reasonably expect the Elizabethan regime to be toppled by military force. Furious, even desperate, preparations were being made to muster troops in order to take on the Army of Flanders, should it reach the English coast.[39] Of course, nowhere in Mush's account of the need to avoid the heretics' churches does he link the issue to the question of political resistance to the will of the queen or to imminent invasion by the Spaniards. It is a densely argued casuistical version of the substance of what he says about conformity and separation in his 'True Report' of Clitherow's life and death. But it is fairly clear, in the context of the date at which it was completed, what the political implications were of such an explicit recommendation of absolute rejection of the allegedly heretical national Church.

It suggested, in fact, how potentially close together were, on the one hand, the Catholic exhortations to reject the queen's authority when it was used to order Catholics to conform to the religion of the established Church and, on the other, Catholic exhortations to resist the queen's government altogether. As we saw, evil-counsellor literature of the kind which had been circulated in print and manuscript by the likes of Mush and Persons (or whoever was responsible for writing 'Leicester's Commonwealth') could, at a pinch, be regarded as a form of Catholic loyalism, a loyalism which distinguished between the sovereign herself and those who, without her blessing, perverted and corrupted her rule. The claim here was that dark forces were in the process of seizing control of the State. Those forces were trying to annihilate those who were actually loyal to the queen, namely Catholics, who refused religious conformity only out of conscience and who had not withdrawn their political obedience from the queen whose sovereign status they accepted and whom, in secular matters, they were happy to obey.

On this basis, Catholics could argue that, should the queen grant them the religious toleration which they craved, this would be no more than political prudence on her part, since those Catholics would now be able to stand up against those same evil counsellors who sought, for their own nefarious ends, to subvert her rule.

As we have already remarked, it was a lot easier for Catholics to make this case while Mary Stuart was still alive and was Elizabeth's heir in blood and the successor whom Elizabeth herself recognized (or at least did not reject), despite many Protestants' hostility to the Scottish queen. However, as some of the queen's leading councillors stoked the fires of public and parliamentary agitation against Mary, loyalist Catholicism inevitably became a good deal less overtly loyal. As we observed, in Mush's manuscript attack on Huntingdon, penned while the final assault on Mary Stuart's life was actually in train, the distance between Huntingdon's sins and the general tyranny of the regime had diminished to virtually nothing.

As Mary Stuart worked her way towards annihilation, the incentive for Catholics to preserve the loyalist fig leaf was, therefore, greatly reduced. This can be seen, for example, in the evolution of Nicholas Sander's great text, the *De Origine ac Progressu Schismatis Anglicani*, which was published first in 1585 (with a section supposedly written by Edward Rishton, which described Elizabeth's reign) and then, again, with additions by Robert Persons, in 1586.[40] At one level, Sander's work, certainly in its first edition, was like 'Leicester's Commonwealth' in that it claimed to reveal the political machinations of court-based cliques for their own purposes, although Elizabeth is herself implicated in their corruption. Unlike 'Leicester's Commonwealth', Sander's book is an avowedly and overtly Catholic work, at times (and particularly in Persons's version of it) verging on a martyrology. In places, it is rather like Mush's account of the northern tyranny perpetrated by Huntingdon, the queen's viceroy in York. The book emphasized the religious errors of the Tudor State and dwelt on the cruelty used against good Catholics such as Campion. The famous passages in which Sander rakes up the court scandals which had led to the fall of Anne Boleyn themselves quite clearly threw doubt on Elizabeth's legitimacy. Sander's suggestion that her birth was the product of adultery and even of incest (between Henry and Anne) virtually destroyed Elizabeth's right to the crown and intimated strongly that the still-living Mary Stuart had a better claim to it. In Rishton's section of the work, Elizabeth is directly burdened with bringing into being the monstrous settlement of religion of 1559, which had subjected the Church to lay control once again. The conservative aspects of the settlement were retained merely to delude the people.

One of the products of the intrusion of heresy into the Church and of the sinister cleverness of the exercise of royal control over the Church was the kind of pusillanimity that led to the spiritual enslavement of the people, including many of the lower clergy. They remained Catholic by inclination but believed that they were entitled to offer outward obedience to the law and to the will of the queen. Sander's text, or rather Rishton's continuation of it, condemns as the product of heretical tyranny the kind of conformist compromises that Mush's work also condemned.[41]

The line in Sander's book was, as in earlier Catholic texts, that the mission of the seminary clergy was a purely religious one.[42] Nevertheless, whereas 'Leicester's Commonwealth', like Mush's attack on Huntingdon, just about maintained a loyalist stance, Sander's book anticipated direct action against the Elizabethan regime, and signalled, arguably, a move towards, if the circumstances permitted it, outright resistance.

It was a short step, then, from Sander's work to the tirade penned by Cardinal Allen in 1588 directed against the bastard and heretic Elizabeth, and entitled *An Admonition to the Nobility and People of England and Ireland*. The tract was written both to justify and actually to accompany the Spanish Armada, and it located the justification for resistance to the queen's rule squarely in the papal supremacy. Allen's tract declared a war of religion and denounced Elizabeth as a Jezebel who had compelled God's servants into spiritual fornication by eating the 'bread of idolatry in schismatical service'. He condemned her usurpation of 'supreme . . . spiritual sovereignty', and also her 'licentious irreligiosity' and 'Antichristian pride'. He listed all the crimes against religion that she had committed, and he recited the more secular reasons, as they had been laid out in Sander's *De Origine*, for which her title might be regarded as worthless: she was, Allen wrote, 'known for an incestuous bastard, begotten and born in sin of an infamous courtesan, Anne Bullen, afterwards executed for adultery, treason, heresy and incest'. The issue of Henry VIII, via his 'incestuous copulation with Anne Bullen', had been 'justly declared illegitimate and incapable of succession to the crown of England'. It had been the martyred Mary Stuart who had been 'our true, lawful and worthy sovereign'.[43] As we have already mentioned, Richard Verstegan's *Theatrum Crudelitatum* of 1587, which featured an engraving of Clitherow's death (see Plate 12) was a publication which condemned the crime committed by the English queen when she executed her Scottish cousin (see Plate 14). As Anne Dillon points out, Verstegan commenced work on his pamphlet within days of the receipt in France of the news of Mary's execution.[44]

Elizabeth was now as guilty as the worst of her subjects who had formerly led her astray. She was as bad as the loathsome earl of Leicester. Indeed, said Allen, she had, with her favourite 'and divers others . . . abused her body, against God's laws to the disgrace of the princely majesty and the whole nation's reproach, by unspeakable and incredible variety of lust'. Her personal lusts and vices were reproduced publicly in the tyrannies that she inflicted on her people. Her people were subject to intolerable exactions which served to make her minions into overmighty subjects. The money which was extracted by way of taxation was sent abroad to 'set up and sustain rebels and heretics against their natural princes', and particularly, of course, the Dutch against Philip II of Spain. Allen was, in effect, doing here to Elizabeth's reputation what some of Clitherow's critics had tried to do to hers. Elizabeth's sensuality and lust had driven her to 'turn the life and whole weal of our country, once most flourishing, to the feeding of her own disordered delights, being loath, no doubt, that anything should be left after her life that her rage and riot had not overrun'.[45]

After the execution of Mary Stuart, therefore, Catholic ideologues rewrote the Catholic political rule book so as to reinterpret former Catholic 'loyalist' impulses as merely a biding of time before God's providence and the availability of Habsburg military forces made it possible for good Catholics to rise up and destroy the English Jezebel. We can grasp here how the separatism of recusants such as Clitherow, which the regime had long regarded as threatening enough, might potentially become a campaign of civil disobedience, which could quite easily mesh with a Spanish attempt to crush Elizabeth once and for all with the most powerful land army in Europe.

7

Thomas Bell's Revenge and the 1591 Proclamation

Thomas Bell Changes Sides

God, in his wisdom, did not see fit to allow Philip II's Armada fleet to join with the duke of Parma's troops and set them ashore in southern England during August 1588. We might think that, after Philip's ships disappeared along the east coast towards Scotland, most Catholics would have concluded that, whether they had actively hoped for it or not, any reliance on foreign military intervention in Elizabeth's English realm was futile, even though, during much of the 1590s, there were rumours both that the Spaniards would return and also that James VI was prepared to take action to secure the recognition of his title to succeed Elizabeth. Those among the English Catholic exiles who had looked to Philip had ventured everything but they had lost. One might have expected also that the Armada's failure would have seriously diminished the extent or at least the overtness of Catholic separatism among Elizabeth's Catholic subjects. Why would any Catholic want to be tainted with political disloyalty in an apparently defunct cause?

What is clear, however, is that the conflict among Catholics themselves over the question of conformity and separation did not become any less intense. Elizabeth was still at war with Spain. By the early 1590s English soldiers were being sent to assist Henry of Navarre in his struggle against the Holy League and its Spanish friends. A royal proclamation against Catholics, dated 18 October 1591, denounced Elizabeth's traitorous Catholic subjects. It declared that the Spanish king had begun 'a most unjust and a dangerous war' against the new king of France. Philip had procured the election as pope of Niccolò Sfondrati (Gregory XIV), who was a Milanese vassal of his own, so as to appropriate the wealth of the Church for his military campaigns.[1] He also practised 'with certain principal seditious heads, being unnatural subjects of this kingdom (but yet very base of birth) to gather together . . . a multitude of dissolute young men', in other words fugitive Englishmen who had gone abroad to be ordained. Having been ordained, these priests returned into the realm to 'stir up and persuade as many' of the queen's subjects as they could 'to renounce their natural allegiance' to her, and 'upon hope by a Spanish invasion to be enriched and endowed with the possessions and dignities' of the queen's 'other good subjects'. The State had done its best to discipline these people 'by direct execution of laws . . . for mere treasons', and not for 'any points of religion as their fautors would colour falsely their actions'. These traitors had assured the Spanish king that 'though heretofore he had no good success with his great forces' against Elizabeth's realm, should he renew military hostilities in the forthcoming year, there would be 'found ready' inside the realm 'many thousands . . . of able people' that would be willing to assist his soldiers when they came ashore. Robert Persons himself, the proclamation alleged, had shown a list of such men's names to Philip, while William Allen had shown a similar list to the current pope. The seminary priests in the realm were said to be able to guarantee that those Catholics who looked to them for guidance would rise in rebellion to assist invading Spanish forces. The proclamation therefore demanded that the country should be put in an even better state of military preparedness than it currently was. It also stipulated that 'certain commissioners, men of honesty, fidelity and good reputation' would 'inquire by all good means what persons are by their behaviours or otherwise worthy to be suspected' of being seminary priests and also which persons might have been seduced by them into treason.[2]

The 1591 proclamation was a crucial foray by the regime back onto the ideological battlefield. It was fairly obviously the product of Burghley's brain and pen. It was a restatement of much of the substance of Burghley's own *Execution of Justice* of 1583. It was aimed first and foremost at the Spanish monarchy but claimed that, in the context of Spanish aggression, English Catholics were a clear and present danger to the queen and to national security. The instructions issued to the commissions which were set up by the text of the proclamation served to make ideological inroads into the Catholic community, inroads which much of the community had previously sought to avoid.[3] The proclamation made it clear that the regime intended to drill down into the community and to find out how many Catholics, including conformists, actually meant what they said when they claimed that they were loyal. It would not be an easy bar to clear. It was evident that recusancy prosecutions, convictions and resulting property sequestrations were going to rise.[4]

In the wake of the proclamation's release, the hostilities that had been stoked up among Catholics over the previous decade or so turned into open war.[5] While the calls at the beginning of the 1580s by clergy such as Robert Persons that all Catholics should separate themselves from the national

Church forced Persons's Catholic opponents to formulate a coherent conformist position, the lurch into outright political resistance by some Catholics at the end of the 1580s put self-consciously loyalist Catholics under almost intolerable strain. One of these self-styled loyalist Catholics was, undoubtedly, Thomas Bell.

In September 1592, Bell turned himself in to the earl of Derby, the lord lieutenant of Lancashire.[6] Bell must have known that printed attacks on him by Henry Garnet were about to come off the press. According to Garnet, reports that Rome was about to censure Bell's opinions about conformity were what pushed him over the edge into what contemporary Catholics described as 'apostasy'.[7] Ever since the late 1580s, Bell had been fighting a desperate rearguard action against his Catholic critics. According to a government informer in August 1588, he was styling himself 'bishop of Chester'. This may indicate that he was not only claiming a superiority over other Catholic clergy in his region but also that he was starting to appropriate the language of anti-puritanism (somewhat ironically in view of his later friendship with prominent godly Protestants). Though we cannot prove it, it seems that he may have started to accuse his Catholic critics of behaving like puritans, in other words like Protestants who were alleged to harbour a latent separatist mentality and to reject the right of the queen to exercise supremacy over the national Church.[8]

Garnet wrote in mid-March 1593 that, 'within ten days from the promulgation of the decision in the city of Rome, like another Judas or a guilty Cain', Bell

> went forth from the face of the Lord. Hitherto, though he had published that evil doctrine of his, yet he had always professed himself a Catholic; but now, warned by the Devil perhaps of the sentence pronounced in Rome, for it was not possible that he had any inkling that his case was being discussed in Rome, he made himself known to the commissioners, betrayed his friends, and abandoned his faith and his religion.[9]

We may speculate that Bell had changed sides not only because he was threatened with an, in fact non-existent, papal censure but also because his version of how Catholics should reconcile their duty to God and to the queen had been made unworkable by the issuing of the 1591 proclamation. The proclamation was hardly the first official public statement which took the queen's Catholic subjects to task for their lack of obedience. But it does appear to have marked a watershed in the early 1590s in the relationship between Catholics and the State. A number of furious replies to the central claims of the proclamation were issued from presses abroad. The best known is Robert Persons's *Elizabethae Angliae Reginae Haeresim Calvinianam Propugnantis Saevissimum in Catholicos sui Regni Edictum . . . .. Per D. Andream Philopater*. Arguably even more aggressive was Thomas Stapleton's *Apologia pro Rege Catholico Philippo II*.[10] This was a work directed primarily at French Catholics in order to persuade them to resist the heretic Henry of Navarre, but it used evidence of what was happening in England in order to make the case against this Huguenot successor to Henry III. Like Sander, Stapleton claimed that despite the corrupt dominion established by Cecil, the queen was herself personally responsible for and guilty of the sins which her regime had committed. The royal rape of the Church had been accompanied by the setting up, via the royal supremacy, of a crowned idol. Her crimes in her own country, typified by but not limited to the persecution of her Catholic subjects, were matched abroad as, by aiding the Dutch and the Huguenots against their princes, she helped to plunge the Continent into war, while she blamed the virtuous Spanish king for the chaos that her own misdeeds had helped to create. When Philip intervened in the affairs of other European countries, for example in France, it was only for the cause of religion. Stapleton reproduced in his text the arguments adduced by the French Holy League which proved that the leaguers were fighting in a just cause, and that Henry of Navarre was demonstrably an enemy of the Catholic religion. What Navarre, given half a chance, would do in France, if he vanquished his Catholic opponents, Elizabeth was already doing in England. Her persecution of Catholics was as bad as the suffering inflicted on early Christians by imperial Rome. She had redefined purely and inherently religious acts as unlawful and liable to the severest punishment, including the aiding or harbouring of a Catholic priest from the Continent. In reply to those who charged the seminarists with disrupting the peace of the nation, Stapleton said that, if there was peace, it was a *diabolica pax*, and was itself the product of the queen's heretical religion. It was the duty of the priests to disrupt that kind of peace, though only via spiritual means and in the spiritual sphere.

From within the country there were less politically radical replies to the proclamation. The best known was by the Jesuit Robert Southwell, entitled *An Humble Supplication to her Maiestie*.[11] Henry Garnet put out two tracts against Bell, the most direct and aggressive of which was his *Apology against the Defence of Schisme*. For our purposes the crucial point here is that Garnet used Bell, perhaps the best known Catholic conformist ideologue in the North, as the focus of a headline grabbing denunciation of the 1591 proclamation. Garnet went out of his way to condemn outright the conformity which the commissioners who had been appointed under the terms of the proclamation were seeking to enforce.

Bell was prepared to lend his services to the regime when it struck back at Catholics after the proclamation was so violently attacked in print by the Catholic exiles abroad. Indeed, he was prepared to supply information which would facilitate the work of the commissioners who had been instructed to root out the seminarists and their lay harbourers. According to Bell's enemies, this was not the first time that he had informed on Catholics. As far back as 1588, four years before Bell switched sides, Mush had claimed that, with 'indecent terms, slanders and accusations', Bell had been persecuting 'his brethren' and had passed 'their names to heretics'.[12] In September 1592, shortly after he had approached the earl of Derby, Bell had, by order of the council (which was at that point on progress and had not 'convenient leisure to receive the confession of the said Bell'), been sent to Lambeth Palace in order to be interviewed by Archbishop Whitgift. Whitgift was to 'receive such matter from him as he shall voluntarily deliver for her Majesty's service' and, 'upon diligent perusal of his books, papers and writings', to 'examine him of such further matter as by them shall appear worthy of discovery'. He was to be urged to 'reveal his knowledge of any enterprise or practice intended against her Majesty and the State'.[13] Either just before or just after he changed his allegiance, Bell had prepared a dossier of households in Lancashire against which he advised the regime to take action. He even drew up suggestions for the government agents who were ordered to conduct the searches of such houses. Derby was instructed in late October that Bell, who had now been interviewed by Whitgift, should be taken back to Lancashire in order to help to round up the Catholic seminarist clergy and their harbourers.[14]

Here, then, was a denunciation of the double-edgedness of the kind of conformity which Clitherow, her friends and other Catholics had censured. In fact, if anyone needed proof of the evils to which conformist ideology and practice might lead, this was presumably it.

Acting on Information Received

Bell claimed, for example, that, at High-le-Carr, in Thomas Gerard's house, could be found George Blackwell (the future archpriest), who was the 'best furnished with books of all other priests'. His tomes were concealed there, mostly unbound in order to make them more portable. These books should be seized 'before conveyance' could 'be made of them'. Bell's precise knowledge of Blackwell's living arrangements there allowed him to recommend that once inside the house, the regime's hired thugs should 'post . . . with speed through the best and greatest chamber of the little house into a long narrow chamber in fashion of a gallery; beyond that cast your eyes on every side, look roundabout, search diligently, sound the places and measure the same proportionably'. At the end of his lists of Catholic names in the county, Bell actually wrote out general rules for searching and ransacking Catholics' houses.

Bell's information allowed the privy council to vet the 13 gentlemen who had been named as commissioners under the 1591 proclamation's machinery to arrest Catholic separatists in Lancashire.[15] In Burghley's notes for the conduct of proceedings against Lancashire Catholics there is a list of 16 gentlewomen, all of them named by Bell.[16] A letter from the privy council to Whitgift, dated 10 December 1592, dealt with the interrogation of 'certain gentlemen' sent up to London by the earl of Derby. It stated that some bore 'an outward show and countenance to go to the church' and yet were 'accused by Bell secretly to be papists and harbourers of priests and seminaries and by them also [to] have been reconciled to the Church of Rome'.[17]

The authorities were not exclusively reliant on Bell for advice about the best means of hunting down Catholic clergy. There were, after all, at this time several officials in the North who were well practised in the discovering and arresting of Catholic seminarists.[18] But what Bell could reveal was the full structure of Lancashire Catholicism in both its separatist and outwardly conformist manifestations. On 16 November 1592, the earl of Derby issued a detailed warrant to Richard Brereton for the search of Sir John Southworth's property at Samlesbury. Southworth was technically a conformist. He had obtained in 1587 a certificate of his submission from Archbishop Whitgift and, in January 1589, he had attended a sermon at the earl of Derby's house at Lathom. But Bell had denounced Southworth and claimed that he had recently entertained a string of clergy (including Bell himself).[19] The warrant specified that Brereton, accompanied by a 'convenient number of such trusty persons as you think fittest to take with you', should make 'very diligent, exact and careful search in all chambers, lofts, studies, cellars, vaults and all other rooms and secret or suspicious places . . . for any Jesuit, seminary priest, unknown or suspected person that may be found there'.[20]

Bell even advised the use of the rack to get Catholics to talk. He suggested methods to sort out which Catholics could be indicted for treason for having been reconciled to Rome. As for the 1591 proclamation, Bell recommended that, by deploying informers 'near unto suspected places', the authorities might learn which people visited these houses, 'setting down the month, day and hour of such resort and likewise of their departure from thence'. When Derby should discover 'any suspected persons so to resort' to such dwellings, he should 'call upon the owner of the place to give the name of all strangers' who had been in the house. Refusal to comply, said Bell, could be taken as prima facie evidence that any such unknown persons who were subsequently detained on suspicion were indeed seminarist clergy.[21]

All the way through his family-by-family denunciation of Lancashire recusancy, Bell mentions the sums of money given to him by particular individuals. He evidently regarded this as evidence of harbouring, sufficient to convict under the statute for the same offence with which Margaret Clitherow had been charged. Perhaps he imagined that these people might potentially suffer the same fate as Clitherow, or at least finish up at the end of a rope. Indeed, in the margin of the page on which he denounced the crypto-Catholic Sir Richard Molyneux, he wrote that Molyneux must have known that he, Bell, was a priest, and a seminarist as well, and therefore, 'by the statute made Anno 13 cap. 2 et Anno 23 cap. 1 he is guilty for concealing the same'.[22] Subsequently, Catholics accused Bell of actually leading as opposed to merely advising searches of Catholics' houses in Lancashire.[23]

Garnet related how Bell had decided to teach Lancashire Catholics a sharp lesson, and that, shortly after he changed sides, he was allowed 'to sit with the justices, his contempt for whom he openly showed, like some commissioner of lofty standing'. Garnet understood that Bell had 'addressed the Catholics, whom he summoned from all the neighbourhood, after this fashion'. With one of them standing in front of him he shouted 'do you know who I am? No! You say that you do not, you damned accursed rogue! Did not you hear me preach at such and such a place, on such and such a day, at such and such a gathering?' Furthermore, in both Wigan and Standish, he 'mounted a pulpit to preach and, as report has it, was unable to utter a word in either place; except that in one of them he said no more than this: "be good subjects"'.[24] What Garnet portrays as a lamentable and failed attempt at a sermon by a notorious apostate was, we may surmise, an exhortation to loyalty to the queen which was entirely compatible, in Bell's mind, with his own previous record as a Catholic priest who taught that it was wrong to use the issue of conformity to challenge the legitimacy and authority of the regime.

Bell's apostasy, however, had much wider political ramifications. It was used by some of the most powerful men in the late Elizabethan regime for their own purposes at exactly the point when it seemed that many of their own assumptions about the prevailing political culture in the Church of England were under threat. Bell's information was, we are certain, also intended to provide confirmation for Burghley's reading of the balances which ought to be struck by the regime as it tried to deal with Catholic separatism and with radical puritanism. In mid-October 1592, in preparation for a discussion at the council table of how well the 1591 proclamation was being implemented, Burghley had overseen the preparation of a report on the recusancy problem. He was in possession of memoranda from several counties which demonstrated the extent of the Catholic separatism uncovered by the commissioners who had been appointed to guarantee the proclamation's enforcement. But the situation was, he said, especially bad in Lancashire.[25] By that date, of course, he already had the information which Bell had supplied to the earl of Derby about the Lancashire Catholic community. There is, in fact, a set of reports, archived in the State papers and speculatively dated to 1590 and 1591, about the general state of religion in Lancashire. Though it is difficult to date these documents with complete accuracy, it appears that Burghley's well-known map of Lancashire, generally assigned to 1590, was connected with proceedings against Catholics in the county after 1591.[26] We think that Burghley may have brought this material to the same council meeting. One of these reports, clearly penned after the October 1591 proclamation had been issued, describes, evidently for the benefit of the council, how in recent times very 'small reformation' had in fact been made by the ecclesiastical commission. This was all too obvious from the 'emptiness of churches on Sundays and holy days in the time of divine service'. It was directly linked to the recent increase of social disorder, notably the upward trend in drunkenness and bastardy.[27] This, in turn, was traceable to the ignorance of the people and the unlearned state of the ministry. Inadequate candidates were still being ordained and instituted by bishops. These were, of course, standard godly complaints about the slow pace of reform in the Church. However, this document also stated that 'the proclamation lately set for the apprehension of seminaries, Jesuits, Mass priests and for the calling home of children' from abroad was 'not executed'. Furthermore, privy-council letters dispatched to the JPs in Lancashire to do something about the failure to resort to church were 'buried without execution'. The families of these JPs did not frequent the church, and some of those JPs were themselves noncommunicants. The seminary priests swarmed all over the county of Lancashire and had 'offered disputations against the religion settled', while 'diverse gentlemen' gave 'them countenance'. Godly preachers had concluded that it was a waste of time trying to instruct the faithful because of the 'lack of auditories'. In the mean time, seminarists went around conducting baptisms and weddings. The county was on the verge of social as well as religious anarchy. (There are related documents in the State Papers which denounce specific Lancashire JPs for refusing to conform and to enforce the statutes against recusancy.[28])

This information, it seems certain, was based in part on Bell's testimony. Privy councillors were obviously well aware that Lancashire was a county with, in places, a largely unreformed and overtly Catholic social and religious culture. But it was also a region where the Catholic sentiments of so much of the local magistracy had meant that there was also a kind of modus vivendi, based on a conformist Catholicism which, in turn, allowed for a working compromise with the national State. It was precisely Bell's dramatic change of sides, and his decision to kick over the traces, which allowed Burghley to prise open and expose the tidy little consensual arrangements that currently preserved the status quo in Lancashire.

The returns from the 1591/1592 commissions were the evidence needed by those such as Burghley who wanted to steer more stringent legislation against Catholic recusants through parliament.[29] Burghley, however, was becoming isolated in his attitudes to the question of Catholic separation. His hard line against it was in part a response to disagreements with other councillors over the threat from puritanism. There was considerable hostility at this point between puritans of various stripes and the regime as it became clear that the 1593 parliament would consider new legislation against some of them. In fact, two anti-Catholic bills introduced into the parliament in late February 1593 (one into the upper House and one into the lower House) became, in the end, one measure against Protestant separatists and one much watered down anti-Catholic one.[30]

The bill in the Commons excited anxiety among those who thought that its penalties might be extended to puritans; a large number wanted it confined to popish recusants only. In mid March it ran out of steam altogether; it never passed. In its place came down from the Lords another draft bill which had been passed there. This applied one of the treason penalties of the 1581 anti-Catholic act (in the branch which condemned those who reconciled or were reconciled to Rome) to Protestant separatists. John Neale judged that 'the wording of the bill' was so loose that it served potentially to trap 'puritans as well as separatists'. While Burghley spoke for the first recusancy bill introduced into the Lords, he was deeply concerned about the implications of the drafting of other aspects of the session's anti-separatist legislation. At this time, Neale suggested, Burghley was 'outcountenanced in court and council' by Whitgift. When the Commons attacked this new measure at its second reading on 4 April 1593, some of the bill's sponsors took their revenge. Two days later, Henry Barrow and John Greenwood were hanged. They had been indicted and condemned under the 1581 anti-Catholic legislation. Burghley had temporarily secured a reprieve for them, and now he tried again to save them, but without success. After a few weeks more, John Penry was executed as well. Thomas Phelippes reported that Burghley 'spoke sharply to the archbishop of Canterbury, who was very peremptory, and also to the bishop of Worcester, and wished to speak to the queen, but none seconded him'. The executions of these Protestant separatists thus 'proceeded through malice of the bishops to the lower House'.[31]

It appears, then, that this information about Lancashire was garnered by Burghley in order to reinforce the point made in the proclamation of 1591 that the root cause of trouble and disorder in the Church and in society was popery and not the kind of godly Protestantism which some people referred to as puritanism. It could, of course, be put alongside all the other information which was being sent in from the provinces by the recusancy commissioners to Burghley in late 1592 and early 1593 about the extent of recusancy in other counties and the network of seminarist clergy which was underwriting it.[32]

Bell was evidently delighted that his change of religion should be interpreted and exploited in this way. His conversion tract, *Thomas Bels Motives*, was dedicated to the privy council. In the context of the accusations made by him the year before, it was intended to confirm Burghley's reading of the manner in which order and discipline ought to be restored to such a troubled and troublesome shire. Lancashire's ills were likely to infect the whole of the North if they were left untreated.[33]

Reading against the Grain; or What Thomas Bell Had Really Been Doing in Lancashire

Bell's act of betrayal was intended to give the authorities a snapshot of the Catholic community in Lancashire. Through it he was able to take his revenge on those whom he had, for some time, considered his mortal (Catholic) enemies. However, if we read his lengthy and detailed denunciations carefully, we can discern within them clues as to what Bell had really been doing in Lancashire and about the nature of the ideological struggle that he had been conducting for the hearts and minds of Lancashire Catholics.

In the course of these denunciations Bell indicated how, after he had gone into Lancashire, he had remained locked in an ideological brawl with the Catholic clergy who had demanded full separation from the Church of England. In fact, we have here, perfectly preserved in the aspic of surviving manuscript material, an early 1590s case study of exactly the issues that had been thrown up by the Clitherow business in York a few years before. Among those clergy was the ubiquitous John Mush, Mrs Clitherow's former chaplain. Mush had evidently been determined to get back to the North and to carry the war against his conformist enemies across the Pennines. In Bell's remarkably detailed account of who was who in the section of the Catholic community in Lancashire to which he had ministered, we get reference after reference to his having offered spiritual and casuistical advice to his Lancashire patrons, and of his having tried, it is clear, to win over large congregations and audiences at packed sermons. (For example, Bell claimed that he had been at the house of Edward Standish of Standish Hall. A Marian priest called Kinley had reconciled Standish 'after he had heard my sermon'. Moreover, 'great multitudes of people flocked together to hear Masses and sermons', and the Standishes' 'chamber has been full many times while I there did preach'.[34]) Bell had been thwarted, however, by the stinging censures of him which had come from clergy such as Mush.

Entry after entry in Bell's denunciatory account of the Catholic community in Lancashire shows that both he and Mush had been part of a lay-clerical network in which they, along with other clergy, were in competition for the patronage and endorsement of the households where they preached. Of 'Widow Clifton', whom Bell described as 'meretrix Babilonica', he said that her house was 'the common receptacle of all priests . . . and especially of Mush the Jesuit, whose prescript rule she, with such obeisance' followed 'as if every word were *oraculum Apollinis*'.[35] Bell had also been in competition with Mush in the household of Mrs Rogerley of Lathom. Bell had lodged with her 'at odd times', as had Mush and other clergy. In order to posture as a conformist, however, Mrs Rogerley kept 'a minister in [her] house with her', and thus avoided 'all peril'.[36]

Interestingly, here, John Mush, the champion of absolute separation from the Church of England was, apparently, prepared to condone the retention of a Church-of-England cleric in a Catholic household. There was evidently a good deal more flexibility in his casuistical position on the question of conformity than publicly he tended to give out. Indeed, Bell named Mush as a frequenter of several of these partly conformist households. We may specu-late that Bell's hatred of Mush was only compounded by what he took to be the latter's hypocrisy. On the one hand, as we have seen, Mush and his cleri-cal allies were outspoken in their condemnation not merely of church popery but also of Bell's principled protestation-based style of Catholic conformity. On their account, not only was the one position the moral equivalent of the other, but both constituted schism. On the other hand, Bell's account of his rivals' practice on the ground in Lancashire shows them, in Catholic house-holds where they were made welcome, not merely tolerating but conniving at dissimulation and deceit of the most outrageously church-popish sort.

Bell's denunciation of individual Catholic households reveals quite starkly how he had been driven out of the Catholic community when he had ended up on the losing side in the debate over the conformity issue. This was evidently not something that had happened suddenly but rather seems to have taken place over a period of years, as Bell came under attack from those clergy who subscribed, at least in theory, to uncompromising separation from the national Church. Bell gave some graphic instances of how this process of exclusion was achieved. In one of the Houghton family's residences, said Bell, they had ritually incinerated one of his own manuscript tracts on recusancy and conformity. Bell urged the earl of Derby to 'call to mind the burning of my counterdialogue, whereof mention is made in my letter sent unto' Mary Houghton, a letter which had come into Derby's hands. Bell described how a Catholic had 'borrowed a treatise of mine for going to the church, which when he should have . . . read [it] again' his wife told him, much to his irritation, that it was 'burnt at the Lea'.[37] John Bradill of Portfield Hall, Whalley, had a son, Edward, who had been ordained as a priest in May 1587. He was 'one of the first that malapertly wrote against me', said Bell. The younger Bradill and Alexander Gerard had joined together with the 'arrogant Jesuit' John Mush in order to spread manuscript censures of Bell and his teachings. Bell wanted the authorities to arrest Mush so that Bell could humiliate him in a 'public dispute'. Bell reminded Derby that he had 'their foolish letter signed with their own hands at large and sent abroad in the country by Edward Stanley, now beyond the seas'. Bell advised that their letter should 'be well examined for it contains no small treason'.[38]

According to Bell, long before he actually defected to the Church of England, and even while he had been working as a Catholic priest, trying to inculcate his loyalist doctrines into the heads of lay Catholics, he had been burdened with the reputation of a renegade. Thomas Barton, a servant of the Houghton family, had heard many Masses and sermons from seminary priests, not least from Bell himself. When Bell 'began first to write against the Jesuits', i.e. in the 1580s, Barton had claimed that Bell had become a client of the queen's principal secretary, Sir Francis Walsingham.[39]

But even if Bell lost out in the end, it seems clear that he had not been devoid either of clerical or lay allies in his struggle against Mush and the Jesuits. Of course, we find Bell denouncing Catholic clergy with whom he was not on good terms, such as Richard Haydock, Thomas Lister and also George Blackwell. Bell railed against 'young Mr Eccleston and young Mr Tarbock', who 'do converse with seminary priests, Blackwell and Lister above the rest'. (Thomas Lister was the Jesuit who, in the late 1590s, was to accuse the appellants of being schismatics. George Blackwell, of course, was the future archpriest, nominated in 1598 by Rome, whose appointment set off the notorious Archpriest Controversy.[40])

But if Bell denounced some priests it seems likely that others had been his allies. We do not know all of the names of Bell's friends, but we know that, for example, two other clerics, Anthony Major and William Hardesty, followed him across the confessional divide.[41] Hardesty had been censured by the Jesuit Henry Walpole as far back as November 1590. Walpole warned Joseph Creswell that 'Hardesty, who is come to Rome', had 'published articles scarce sound, showing himself a cynic and schismatic'.[42] It is possible that Hardesty was in Rome in order to lobby on behalf of himself and his associates, perhaps in the same way that the priest James Younger may have done in 1593, though Younger was prepared to denounce both Bell and Mush to the authorities in England (ironically at almost exactly the same point that Bell changed sides).[43] During the appellant business, Robert Charnock remembered that Younger, a future theology professor at the seminary in Valladolid, presented a copy of 'the discourse which Bell made in defence of going to the Church with a protestation' to the Jesuits in the English College at Rome.[44]

Remarkably, Bell emerges, from the information that he passed to the authorities, not so much as an enemy of recusancy but rather of the wrong sort of church popery. For, while Bell did not censure those who had practised his protestation-based style of conformity, he certainly did denounce many church papists. Here Bell adopted the rhetoric of godly Protestants who claimed that some conformist Catholics were more dangerous than separatists because, unlike the separatists, they concealed what they really thought behind a mask of conformity, and thus sought to hide from the scrutiny of the authorities within the broad mass of the English Church. Not only was this was likely to cause scandal and offence among the weak in faith, and encourage the Protestants in their view of the Cathlolics as hypocrites and dissemblers (precisely what his opponents accused Bell and his followers of doing). It also provided cover for genuinely seditious and treasonous Catholics to hide their true affections from the prying eyes of the authorities.

Thus, of John Culcheth, a JP, Bell said that he was 'no recusant in fact external, but no less culpable than some that are recusants, if not more, the reason whereof' was that his wife was a recusant and had been so for a long time. So had his daughter, Mary Ormiston. She had heard Bell say Mass and preach at Rixton, and had given him two shillings when he left the house. Culcheth's son and son-in-law were recusants also. Culcheth knew perfectly well what his family's opinions were, and was himself acquainted with seminarists, and yet 'to save them harmless' he had procured 'the meaner sort to be indicted for recusancy'. He permitted 'no priest . . . to come to his house and yet' suffered 'them to resort to other places freely'.[45] Thomas Gerard of High-le-Carr, as we saw, was a patron of George Blackwell. Gerard had 'for many years frequented confession' at the hands of, and had heard Mass celebrated by, Blackwell, whom he had entertained since 1585. But Gerard was 'deemed no recusant because he' dealt 'covertly in such affairs'.[46] Bell named Thomas Brockholes of Claughton Hall who retained 'in his house George Dakins alias Green, a seminary priest'. Brockholes was also the brother-in-law of James Leyburn who had been executed at Lancaster as a traitor. At one time Brockholes had been, 'though not now, a recusant'. He had been 'convicted for 20*li* the month' under the recusancy statute of 1581, but now lay 'dead and buried in the exchequer'; in other words he was getting away with his offence because royal officials at Westminster were doing nothing to sequestrate his property as the act required. Bell said that Dakins was one of those who had written against him for his opinions about church papistry.[47] To Bell's way of thinking this was clear evidence of the hypocrisy of his Catholic critics; a hypocrisy which was apparent in their denunciation of his principled defence of a certain style of severely limited conformity and their own practice of a pusillanimous church popery.

On Bell's account the dangerous deceits practised by church papists were facilitated, at almost every turn, by sympathetic Church-of-England clergy and local magistrates. Bell reminded the earl of Derby that George Hesketh 'the parson of Halsall', was 'a proctor for recusants', for he would not 'stick to say whatsoever' was 'requested at his hands'; and it was 'his politic practice forsooth to go some day from home of purpose and to will the recusants', especially Lawrence Ireland of Lidiate Hall in Halsall parish, 'to be present that day at the church' in order that they might 'avoid the penalty of the statute'.[48] Of Robert Langton of Low Hall, Bell said that he 'deserved worse for disloyal proceedings than many open and plain recusants' did, for he halted 'on both sides'. Bell claimed that Langton could easily arrest George Blackwell if he chose, because he (Langton) was not feared by the papists. Bell declared that Langton had saluted him on the highway, and evidently knew him to be a priest. Langton knew other seminary priests as well. He was aware of an 'infamous libel' published by his brother Edward, and had even promised to bring his brother to book; but he had conspicuously failed to do so. 'Such disloyal and dissembling justices', thought Bell, did 'more harm than hundreds of recusants'. Bell asserted that he himself had written a 'counterblast' to Edward Langton, presumably on the topic of occasional conformity.[49]

In the same vein, Bell asserted that Sir Richard Molyneux of Sefton Hall was – just like Sir Gilbert Gerard, the master of the rolls – a master dissimulator. Molyneux knew that his wife heard 'many a Mass at his house'. He himself sat 'at table with priests' and said they were 'welcome', in that they were 'his wife's friends'. He was 'no small enemy to the State' because, by his direction, nothing could be 'done in that coast without peculiar authority'. Molyneux rebuked 'openly' and favoured 'secretly everywhere'. His servants were notorious recusants. 'This is Sir Richard's policy', Bell proclaimed; namely, to 'have credit on each side, when any strict charge comes out, he gives open charge to all his servants that will not go to the church to depart out of his house, which charge they observe for some few days and, after, return again'. And 'this, forsooth, all the country knows to be so'. At one time, one of Molyneux's servants had approached Bell at Crosby and requested him 'to come in the evening to talk with his master'. Bell did so, at Sefton, 'and lodged there all night'. After Bell had spoken to Molyneux, Molyneux had asked to be reconciled to the Church of Rome, but on condition that Bell would agree to 'dispense with him for going to the church'. Bell claimed that he absolutely refused to do this, and Molyneux mumbled that he 'would consider further of the matter'.[50]

In other words, a number of Catholics had wanted to take advantage of Bell's doctrine about occasional conformity in order to licence their own deceitful and self-serving practice of church popery. But, in several cases, Bell had refused to allow them to have their cake and eat it. To him that would have represented the encouragement of precisely the sort of dissimulation and hypocrisy that his position was designed to avoid.

Whatever his Catholic critics such as Persons and Mush might claim, Bell was far from simply condoning statute conformity. Indeed, he had spent a good part of his Catholic ministry reconciling schismatics to the Church of Rome. Of Bartholomew Hesketh, Bell said that he 'did hear me preach at Westby, by hearing of which sermon he was willing to be reconciled, as his wife told me, and so that proved indeed'. Bell was 'requested to go home with them to accomplish the said matter'. Bell 'lodged with him one night, said Mass in the morning, and reconciled him to the Church of Rome'. This was relatively soon after Bell had come to England, back in the early 1580s. But, 'of latter time, since my conflict with the Jesuits concerning going to the church, he came to me to confession and heard my Mass, receiving the eucharist at my hands, and so did his wife then' and at 'many other times' at Mrs Gerard's house at Aughton. Hesketh's wife and Lucy Stanley were 'still recusants' and they conversed with seminary priests 'wheresoever they come, albeit at some odd times they go unto the church'.[51] Of Lawrence Ireland, Bell recalled that he 'was first reconciled' to Rome and, subsequently, after he was 'fallen by going to the church as they termed it', Bell himself 'reconciled him to the Church of Rome again'. This was not the conduct, and these were not the associates, of someone concerned to push the Catholic laity into simple conformity. Of course, Bell is our only source for these events, but all this suggests that Bell's casuistical advice to Catholics was not intended just to licence and excuse mere compliance.

In other words, on the central casuistical question of how far it was licit to attend Protestant churches, Bell really was, as the confrontation with Mush and others had suggested, much closer to his critics than either he or they would have cared to admit. While the formal points of difference between the two sides were clear enough, it was also clear that in practice Mush and his friends did not look for support solely to those who were out-and-out recusants, just as Bell and his associates did not, in fact, condemn recusancy outright or simply associate with or patronize church papists. Rather both groups associated with recusants, church papists and outright conformists in their efforts both to minister to the needs of the Catholic laity and to win a broadly Catholic public over to their position. Indeed, on this evidence, it appears that what Bell was trying to do was something very similar to what Mush and his allies were attempting; to reconcile schismatics to the church of Rome, that is to say to turn church papists, nominal conformists and other waverers into real Catholics. It was just that under Bell's dispensation the result of such a conversion would not be recusancy pure and simple but rather the principled combination of both Catholicism and loyalism contained, Bell claimed, within his own style of protestation-based conformity. On this basis it should not therefore surprise us that, even after he had gone over to the Church of England, Bell still seems to have regarded himself as the Catholic clergyman who had, at one time, been the most zealous and consistent promoter both of spiritual separation from the Church of England and of true obedience to the secular powers of the English crown.

Bell's rage against his opponents among the Catholic laity and clergy was directed against many of his former associates precisely because of these real and apparent contradictions. While he stuck to what he took to be a principled Catholic loyalist position, his opponents, claiming to occupy the high ground of recusant recalcitrance, characterized him as a turncoat, and at the same time, in practice, connived at the continued hypocrisy and dissimulation of many of the laity. Moreover, Bell seems to imply, it was his opponents' hypocrisy and complaisance in this regard, rather than their apparently unbending recusant principles, that won them the support of so many of the laity. It was very probably this, as much as anything, that drove Bell to the point of what his enemies called apostasy, but to him, no doubt, seemed like a natural response to the duplicity and hypocrisy of his erstwhile Catholic associates, patrons and protectors.

Thus when Bell accused his principal patron, Miles Gerard of Ince, he alleged that Gerard and his wife were 'now no recusants', but had 'in times past received' various priests, namely 'Norden, Blackwell, Gardiner, Forth, Howes, Dakins, Hardwick and all that would come'. Bell said that he had lived in Gerard's house for many years. Gerard conformed as soon as he was brought in. In March 1593 the privy council register recorded that, after being named by Bell, Gerard made 'a very humble submission, acknowledging his fault and offence to her Majesty in receiving of priests in times past, and also in harbouring the said Mr Bell, knowing him to be a seminary priest'. Gerard had 'likewise made a dutiful protestation of his conformity' and now stood 'bound to perform the same hereafter'.[52] We do not know precisely what Gerard may have thought about the crucial issues that divided Bell from his critics. But it appears, rather ironically, that Gerard may have been trying quite hard to follow Bell's prescription for negotiating the toils of the statute law on conformity. Gerard had, or so he claimed, been attending church regularly for the previous seven years, though he would not receive communion.[53] He was viewed quite sympathetically by the authorities. On 10 January 1593, Sir Thomas Egerton, the attorney-general, a friend of Bell, wrote to the lord keeper to tell him that, in his opinion, Miles Gerard was a simple man who had been 'over much misled . . . by his wife', Grace Hesketh, daughter of Gabriel Hesketh of Aughton Hall.[54]

Egerton's mention of the malign influence of Gerard's wife leads us to another Clitherowesque aspect of Bell's position although nowhere in Bell's betrayal of the Lancashire Catholic households which he had frequented does he so much as mention Margaret Clitherow of York. There is a distinct streak of misogyny in his denunciation of Lancashire Catholicism. He was obviously irked by the combination of obstinate female spiritual independence and supine, even distasteful, female reliance on the ministrations of clergy such as Mush. There is no doubt that he was infuriated by households where the male head, even if of a conformist disposition, tolerated the waywardness of his recusant wife whose zeal and ill-informed understanding of religion he either would not or could not control. Of Edward Stanley of Winwick, Bell said that he was 'no recusant . . . but . . . a great favourer of the same'. His wife Lucy kept 'as her chaplain a seminary priest usually'. This man had, however, recently been 'displaced' by the 'Jesuit' Mush and another one, named James Cowper, had been 'put in his place'. Bell understood that none would be refused there who brought 'commendations from Mush or any other Jesuit'.[55]

Bell associated the encroaching dominance of Mush and his Jesuit and Jesuited friends with the Society's success in garnering funds and influence. Typically, such people were not only accused of lording it over their lay hosts but also of enjoying an entirely unsuitable set of relationships with the women in the households where they were entertained. Thus Bell wrote that Ann Barton of Barton Row, the wife of the conformist Catholic JP Thomas Barton, had entertained various priests (including Bell himself). Mr Barton's cousin, Anne Southworth, was 'a sworn sister to the confraternity, whom the Jesuit Mush commanded to pull off his boots in token of humility'.[56] Perhaps the sight of Anne Southworth kneeling in front of John Mush reminded Bell of everything he must have hated about the, to some, undoubtedly infuriating Mrs Clitherow.

Bell saw Mush as the representative of a Jesuitizing tendency in the Church. Mush, though not himself a member of the Society, certainly was, at this time, on very good terms with leading Jesuits such as Henry Garnet. Bell, by contrast, was in effect an appellant 'avant la lettre'. By a rather convoluted logic, Bell was adopting the standard anti-popish stereotype of the Jesuit casuist and compromiser in order to tar those families by whom he had been rejected.

Bell's critique of his opponents was, therefore, based not just on the strict issue of whether it was allowable to come to church but also on the political consequences of certain kinds of conformity. At stake, Bell told the authorities, was not merely hypocrisy, spiritual weakness and duplicity, but also disobedience, subversion and even treason. He evidently thought that those occasional conformists who nevertheless patronized and listened to the likes of Mush were not loyalists at all; certainly not of the sort that Bell was trying to foster. On this view, the widespread adoption by many of his former associates and patrons of a mode of church popery was at least as bad as, and very probably worse than, complete separation from the national Church; if, that is, the occasional conformity in question was used to mask politically subversive beliefs and actions of the sort of which Bell himself disapproved. In that case, the act of conformity, performed without the declaration or protestation, which Bell, like others, had argued should accompany the act of going to church, was not merely dissimulative and reprehensible but also politically dangerous. Of the prominent Catholic conformist Sir John Southworth of Samlesbury, one of those gentlemen who had entertained Edmund Campion back in 1580, Bell wrote that he had, 'for many years . . . ordinarily heard Masses from seminary priests' and resorted to them for confession as well; and this 'he did continually until' his recent 'supposed conformity, or perhaps cloaked hypocrisy. This he did as well at Chester in time of his endurance as at home in time of liberty, for when, upon licence obtained for a few days, he returned out of prison to his own house, he lodged in one night four seminary priests, Dakins, Haydock, Cowpe[r]' and Bell himself, and also the priest John Hardwick, and each of these priests had 'said Mass there'.[57]

In short, the falling out between Bell and his former Catholic associates led him to interpret what he had come to see as their hypocrisy and dissimulation as close to treason. This was a case that Bell sought to clinch by mapping his own doctrines about conformity and separation onto the question of loyalty and disobedience/treason:

whensoever the question is proposed whose part recusants will take, if the king of Spain or the pope invade this realm, be it known for certain that all will answer commonly they will take part with her Majesty and yet mean nothing less indeed, for [they] do but equivocate, no not though they swear . . .. The reason hereof is evident, for recusants are taught by their religion that the pope is supreme head in all causes ecclesiastical, as well in England as in Rome, and consequently they must obey his ordinance, under pain of damnable sin. But they cannot obey him unless they take part with him when he invades this land for religion. Ergo they must and will take part with him, whatsoever they say, by way of equivocation. Hereupon it follows necessarily that many, both captains and trained soldiers, would,

in the time when the Armada was in the English Channel, have 'forsaken their sovereign' and would have 'taken part with the pope'.[58] In the same vein he argued elsewhere, of those who had burnt his manuscript treatise, that 'all such as did consent thereunto', were culpable in high degree 'for, if the sequel' were 'well noted, hardly' could 'any that consented thereunto escape the crime of treason'. Bell inferred this as follows:

> By statute of parliament, that is by uniform consent of the whole realm (a better ground I trow than the bare definition of one only man, the bishop of Rome) it is high treason to deem her sacred Majesty either heretic or schismatic; or religion established to be of like degree, but so it is that if my book be heretical as they in fact reputed it when they burnt the same (because burning by their religion is a peculiar note of heresy) it follows evidently that either her Majesty must be a heretic or her religion heretical, for the contrary cannot be defended.[59]

Thus if we read between the lines of what Bell told the authorities we can trace the outlines of the struggle for the souls of Lancashire Catholics, in which struggle, for years, he had been engaged with the likes of John Mush. While his opponents had sought to convert their flock to overt recusancy, Bell had sought to convert them to his peculiar style of conformity. Despite what his opponents said about him Bell emerges as anything but a proponent of the soft option of church popery or partial conformity as a means of staving off the prying eyes and disciplinary procedures of the Protestant State. Rather than a conflict between rigorists and laxists, then, we have a competition between two different styles of rigorism. For both sides were proponents of a solution to the problem of conformity that was rather more severe in its demands upon the intestinal fortitude and material resources of the laity than many of the laity liked. But since they were priests, whose function was to minister to the spiritual needs of the Catholic laity, no matter how imperfect the laity's profession of Catholicism may have been, and since their aim in so doing was not merely to save souls but to do so by recruiting as many of the laity as possible to their view of the matter, both sides had perforce to associate with lay households and persons with whose conduct they were in anything but agreement. As they did so they clearly both took every opportunity to slag one another off to their hosts, protectors and spiritual charges.

To put it another way, both Bell and Mush had, to some considerable extent, failed; or rather, to continue their pastoral and proselytizing efforts, they had had to accept behaviour in the laity that fell well below their own rather high standards of ideological rectitude. This of course was a structural necessity; an inevitable consequence of their complex, ambiguous and contradictory relationship with the laity, who doubled as erring members of their flock and as the enablers, patrons and protectors of a missionary priesthood that could not subsist without the support of a laity whose conduct and belief they were simultaneously supposed to be monitoring and controlling. Thus both Bell and his clerical opponents had been forced to connive at various levels of church popery. From Bell's perspective, given their formal insistence on recusancy as the necessary mark of true Catholic profession, the willingness of his clerical rivals to do so looked peculiarly egregious; indeed it looked like the rankest hypocrisy. The resultant animosities were considerably heightened when their complaisance in this regard was combined with denunciations of Bell as little better than a renegade or apostate because of his position on conformity.

Not only that, but Bell had come to be disgusted with the pusillanimity of the many lay persons who had misconstrued his position on conformity as a hypocrites' charter. They presumed to take what he said as little more than a clerical sanction for the sort of duplicity, the playing of both sides off against the middle, which his own position was in fact specifically designed to rule out of court. Moreover, the hypocrisy of such people was compounded by their continually keeping company with Bell's clerical adversaries, the ones who claimed that out-and-out recusancy was the only fit means to be a Catholic.

Since Bell clearly thought that his mode of protestation-based conformity was the only legitimate way to maintain a pure religious profession and to demonstrate a proper allegiance to the crown, persons who persisted in these fudged compromises came to look like not merely weaklings and hypocrites but sinister dissemblers. Such people, Bell clearly came to believe, could, and if allowed to, would, pretend to be loyal and obedient subjects till the cows came home, but that would not stop them from harbouring the most sinister beliefs and preferences; beliefs and preferences that would surely reveal themselves in their full enormity if the Spaniards should ever arrive. Hence sprang his disgust at those erstwhile conformist and even nominally

Protestant clergy and justices who continued to connive at such practices.

There was clearly much that was self-serving and revenge-based in Bell's denunciation to the authorities of his former co-religionists, enablers and audiences but beneath the treachery and spleen, the grudge-holding, the pay-backs and the grovelling we can also discern a good deal about his activities in Lancashire over the previous few years. We can see at least the outlines of the ideological struggle over the issue of conformity waged in the many Catholic households that had welcomed both Bell and his opponents; a strug-gle conducted through sermons, rumour, spiritual counsel and advice and indeed the circulation in manuscript of various works of polemic. And we can also see a principled position that had eroded under the pressure exerted on the Catholic community by the authorities, under the efforts of his cleri-cal opponents to attack him as an apostate and a quisling and in the face of the continuing determination of both the Catholic laity and their friends in the local establishment to avoid and elide the hard questions about the relationship between Catholic religion and political loyalty, the promptings of conscience and the demands of secular obedience, that both Bell and his clerical rivals continued to try to make them confront.

8

Mrs Clitherow Vindicated?

The Church under the Cross and the Resort to the Public

If we put Thomas Bell's account of his own and other Catholics' activities in Lancashire next to the intense, albeit fractured and episodic, insights afforded us by the Clitherow affair into the religious situation in York, and then combine the two with certain other asides from the tractate literature discussed above, we can construct a picture of the ways in which, and of the means and media through which, these disputes were conducted. What emerges is something like the operation of an intra-Catholic 'public sphere': the conduct of debates, the canvassing of claim and counter-claim, before a national, indeed at times before an international, Catholic audience. In play were all the contemporary genres of expression through which religio-political polemic could be conducted and the full range of media through which such differently structured messages could be sent. The pulpit, for-mal disputation, and other forms of performance, up to and including the dreadful choreography of execution for treason, were all enlisted for the cause. Oral, manuscript and sometimes even printed accounts of those same performances, public gestures and statements were then sent around the country and even beyond.[1]

The Clitherow affair itself provides us with a wonderful microcosm of how this Catholic public sphere operated. Here intensely local but also intensely public acts – the refusal to go to church and indeed the decision, albeit intermittently, to attend, performed by people otherwise known to be Catholic; Mrs Clitherow's notorious patronage of priests; and her nocturnal pilgrimages to the Knavesmire – provoked rival renditions of what those acts either meant or ought to mean and of the moral and spiritual character of the people committing them. As the representatives of the local State sought both to exacerbate and exploit the resulting divisions in Catholic opinion, Clitherow herself performed the role of martyr before a local audience primed and assembled by the State's own efforts to stage a show trial. Rival versions of the meaning and moral standing of her fate circulated. Was her otherworldly calm in the face of certain death inspired by the Holy Ghost or by a smiling devil? Was she a martyr to be admired or a suicide to be reviled? Was she a model of Christian piety and courage or a heartlessly cruel, fanatical and delinquent wife and mother? Was she, in fact, a whore or a saint? All these rival versions of her actions and their wider significance clearly circulated around the backstreets of York and, undoubtedly, beyond.

But, as we have seen, what this represented was a peculiarly intense local outbreak of more general arguments both between the State and its Catholic subjects and victims and within and between various strands of Catholic opinion and interest. These arguments had been staged and disseminated through a wide variety of media; through face-to-face discussions such as those held at the meeting in Southwark at which Edmund Campion and Robert Persons had first announced the nature and purpose of their mission to an English Catholic audience; through more formal disputations like that subsequently staged between Langdale and Persons; through the exchange of position papers in manuscript; and through the wider circulation of accounts of those disputations, as well as of the position papers themselves. Thomas Bell's retrospective account of his activities in Lancashire affords us a series of insights into the conduct of such arguments, on the local level, from the pulpit, in person and through circulating manuscript, as he and Mush fought over the allegiance of the same Catholic, crypto-Catholic and apparently entirely conformable families and persons. Sometimes these exchanges even achieved the apotheosis of print. Or, rather, they did so on the recusant side of the question since the likes of Persons and Garnet had access either to secret presses in England or to others controlled by the exile community on the Continent, which the likes of Bell did not enjoy. Persons's tract of 1580 took the form of a reply to a manuscript of Langdale; one of Garnet's later polemical effusions – his *Apology against the Defence of Schisme* – presented itself as an open letter to a Catholic in England who had not only conformed in the face of the renewed repression consequent upon the proclamation of 1591, but also had had the temerity, Bell-like, to defend his fall. But even the conformist side of the debate had frequent recourse to formal statements of its own case and equally formal refutations of the arguments of its critics. These circulated in manuscript as Mush's extended reply to Bell of 1588 shows. As well as simply to vindicate and publicize Clitherow's sanctity and witness, it was surely also in order to address these wider disputes and audiences that Mush's account of Clitherow's fate as 'the martyr' had been written and disseminated.

Denied access to the press, it was Bell who most frequently resorted to the circulation of manuscripts in order to submit his arguments to the court of Catholic public opinion. Indeed, the alacrity and assiduousness with which he did so was a central part of the case assembled against him by the advocates of separation. As we have seen, Garnet had made much of the sin involved not merely in going to church but also in refusing either to feel bad about it at the time or to say sorry afterwards. On his account, the sin and scandal involved in church attendance were greatly increased by the spreading of arguments that defended such attendance as both a licit and an appropriate response to the State's demands for conformity. As Mush complained in 1588, Bell had, 'amongst the people . . . published' manuscript books which defended his position. As we have seen, the circulation of such manuscript publications had bulked large in Bell's proselytizing efforts in Lancashire, just as the burning of his writings had allowed certain Catholic households publicly to purge themselves of his errors and, presumably, to indict and shame him in the sight of other Catholics.

Through a close reading of the resulting exchanges we can dimly perceive the central role, in the prosecution of these disputes, of performance and rumour – with rumours often recounting different versions and interpretations of the same performances. Thus Bell bragged that his device of attending the church with a protestation had been successfully put into practice by several of his followers. Mush replied with the story of the Lancashire gentleman who, coming to church during the assizes at Lancaster, had intended to stand up and protest his Catholicism in the face of the world, only to sit quiet as a church mouse through the whole service, listening to the 'sermon as orderly and soberly as any heretic . . . without making any protestation' at all.[2] In Garnet's *Apology* it was made quite clear that the other side had spread the rumour that the pope either had or was about to dispense with the requirement entirely to avoid the heretical services of the English national Church. Garnet devoted several pages to refuting this claim.[3] However, just before Bell finally defected, the wholly erroneous rumour had been spread that he was about to be denounced by name by the pope himself.

What we are seeing here is the attempt formally to expose and refute stories and claims that had presumably circulated throughout the Catholic community by word of mouth. Similarly, Mush's account of Clitherow was itself an attempt to deny, or rather to put a definitive condemnatory gloss upon, a body of rumour circulating about 'the martyr', while producing his own account of her life and fate.

The controversy generated in January 1588 by the recantation sermon required of the turncoat Anthony Tyrrell, which we briefly mentioned in Chapter 6, illustrates these points to perfection. Tyrrell, who had done his best to betray Mush to the authorities in 1586, tried to use his sermon to justify his and Bell's approach by distinguishing sharply between their spiritual and temporal loyalties. A good deal of what he intended to say was a denial of the accusations he had made against those supposedly involved in the Babington conspiracy, though he also meant to declare that he detested heresy and that he would 'live and die in the holy Catholic faith of the Roman apostolic and universal Church'. Anticipating that he would be silenced before he had got out more than a few sentences, Tyrrell composed a manuscript apologia and made 'divers copies . . . to the end that when he should be taken from the place he might cast them among the people'. He did indeed manage to throw some of these papers into the crowd. The presiding justice of the peace, Richard Young, immediately demanded that they should all be returned. But, in the event, 'one copy amongst the rest did fall right between a Catholic priest named Mr Richard Leigh . . . and another Catholic . . . named Ralph Ashley'. It was immediately whisked off to 'a gentleman's chamber' in the Middle Temple, and 'diverse copies' were 'drawn forth' and 'were sent abroad to Catholics for their comfort throughout the realm'. Tyrrell's performance, which Mush vigorously mocked, can be seen as a form of verbal protest of the kind recommended by Bell, though with an overtly political purpose, and not limited simply to the issue of church attendance.[4]

Tyrrell's case was, of course, very sensitive, since the dual question of what precisely he had done while in custody, and why, was of peculiar import for the conduct and outcome of the disputes between Bell and his enemies. Had he really sung like a canary and entirely conformed? Had he completely, that is to say, both politically and spiritually, apostatized, thus confirming the worst fears or most heightened claims about where Bell's position would ultimately and inevitably lead, or had he not? In such cases, achieving narrative fixity came close to achieving polemical victory. The attempts to secure a copy of his manuscript protestation distributed from the pulpit and the subsequent copying and circulation in manuscript of that text among Catholics show how subject to different readings such inherently evanescent events were. They also show how necessary it was to be able to give accurate, received accounts of 'what really happened' not only in order to prevent the circulation of other false accounts by one's opponents but also to fix the meaning of such events firmly within one's own view of the world. Thus might it be possible to recruit the most current recent anecdotes and scandals to the confirmation of one's own case rather than allow them to be recruited to that of one's opponents.

It was, therefore, not the least of the many ironies attendant upon these processes of glossing and reglossing the same texts, events and gestures, that the claim that a group of the best learned priests in England had met in

London and there decided to allow one of their number to stand 'by secretly to hear' Tyrrell was later cited by Bell to show that, under the right circumstances, it was indeed licit for Catholics to be present at heretical services and sermons. Mush's response to this claim was in itself a wonderful example of the dynamics of rumour management. First he denied that all the best learned priests were ever to be found in London. Then he poured cold water on the existence of any such meeting. But Mush did not know for certain what had happened. So he avoided categorical denial – lest, presumably, the subsequent emergence of the 'real truth' of the matter should give him the lie. He settled instead for an icy scepticism, which he then proceeded to pour all over Bell's account of events:

> Again, if all the best learned were at one time there assembled which we never heard of . . . yet he says this gratis, without proof, that they all agreed of this, as he writes, with one uniform consent. Again, suppose they did, as it is not probable for that there was no such meeting, yet they put it not in practice at that time as himself confesses, saying it had been put in practice if Mr Tyrrell had preached there indeed.

We can clearly see here the role of rumour and counter-rumour in these disputes and the difficulty of finding out precisely what had indeed happened, let alone of fixing one's own interpretation on events, as, in this passage, Mush sought to bend this 'uncertain and perhaps feigned report of some good fellow from London' to his own, rather than to Bell's, purposes.[5]

The difficulties inherent in securing certain news which afflicted all contemporaries were, of course, compounded for Catholics, operating, as they were, in secret, under the constant threat of surveillance and arrest and under the impact of the insistent misinformation campaigns both of the authorities and now of at least some of their co-religionists. Garnet was surely obliquely referring to such difficulties when he assured his conformist interlocutor in 1593 that the only reason such a man might cling to Bell's opinions in these matters rather than defer to the collective judgement of the rest of the English priesthood was 'because you dare not, either for the love of your own opinion or for the fear of the penalty of the law, go forth of your doors to confer' with other Catholics.[6] In such circumstances one can easily appreciate through what sorts of dis- or misinformation, of wishful thinking or projection, the rumour that the pope either had dispensed, or was about to dispense, with the obligation not to attend heretical services could have spread, and, once spread, how extremely difficult it would have been definitively to refute. The same, of course, applied to various stories about when and where, by whom and with what effects, Bell's protestation had actually been performed. Hence, when Bell's enemies wanted to sustain and circulate their case among English Catholics they resorted to precisely the methods and media which he himself had used.

It was one of the major claims made by Bell's enemies about him that he was the only person who fashioned and deployed such arguments. He was, in Mush's words, 'an odd and singular person among us all'. Mush claimed that Campion, Persons, another Jesuit called Jasper Heywood and indeed many more had been asked about this issue 'by gentlemen which were desirous by any lawful means to have redeemed their unjust oppressions'; yet none of these priests had answered as Bell was now doing.[7] Garnet agreed. He claimed to his conformist interlocutor of 1593 that he was

> credibly given to understand that there is not one Catholic priest in England who differs from the rest of his brethren (one only excepted) of whom I hear that no good and godly person makes any account at all lest perhaps the ministerial spirit of pride which must needs have been once in him before he was a Catholic should, returning unto his former house, make the last things worse than the former.

This, of course, was a wonderfully self-confirming argument. In Garnet's view, Bell could not be held in any regard by any 'good and godly person' because paying regard to Bell automatically excluded one from the ranks of the good and the godly. The entirely circular logic at work here echoed exactly that which underwrote Mush's claim that Margaret Clitherow always deferred to the authority and counsel of the priesthood, since, as we shall see, on the logic being employed by Mush and Garnet, as schismatics, the likes of Bell scarcely counted as real priests at all.[8]

According to Mush, Bell's 'enterprise in this matter of going to church' was 'strange and never taught or practised in this realm before'.[9] Garnet noted the 'arrogancy of the defenders of schism' and denounced the 'heretical dregs of pride and singularity' in which they remained mired.[10] Bell's whole position, Mush claimed, was therefore based on 'self liking', in other words on his desire to appear the sole comforter of the woes of the Catholic laity. All Catholic priests, Mush explained, were as anxious as Bell to relieve the sufferings and legal burdens of the laity and yet only he had fastened upon conformity as a licit way to do so. This was, in effect, 'to labour so vehemently by the disgracing of all his brethren' so as to 'draw the ignorant after him'. His vainglorious manner gave him away: his humour was to be 'delighted with wrangling, as at all times rather desirous to cavil upon words and to study how to contradict, yea, in most evident points, than to find out the truth'. He was always convinced that he was right and everyone else was wrong. And he dispersed his stupid opinions without consulting other priests or seeking 'dispensation or approbation from our superiors abroad'.[11]

Bell apparently boasted that many priests had refused even to try to refute him. He took this to be a sign that they were unable to do so. But Mush retorted that many could have done so had they felt like it. They did not, however, want to be drawn into endless disputes. Garnet claimed that the superiors at the English College in Rheims issued instructions that they should not feed Bell's pride and singularity by arguing with him. Garnet himself got round these strictures by framing his book as a letter of counsel and admonition to a 'friend' of his who had recently conformed, rather than addressing it directly either to Bell or Bell's arguments, of which, nevertheless, Garnet's tract served as a theologically and casuistically sophisticated refutation.[12]

Of course, had Bell been so personally isolated and his opinions so novel, singular and eccentric as his opponents claimed, insouciant disregard might well have been the best policy. But Mush's and, later, Garnet's own determination to take up the cudgels against Bell, in manuscript and then in print, belied the confidence and, indeed, the truth of such assertions. Mush tried to square this particular circle by claiming that while Bell had no priestly following and no appeal among 'learned and virtuous' Catholics, he did have, and was active in cultivating, such a following among the many 'simple children' and 'weaklings'. As a result, they would be ready, 'with every little puff of persecution, to fall'. They would be (as we have already rehearsed in Chapter 4) glad 'to take any small occasion or appearance of sufficient reason to yield to the extremity of the time thereby to escape trouble, worldly dangers and temporal harms'. On this account, Bell's real aim was to pervert the 'simple and ignorant', who would not see the need even to resort to the fig leaf of a protestation. The scandal of their example would then spread everywhere.[13]

We return here to the topic of 'scandal' and to the notion of the slippery slope that led directly from Bell's position to schism and thence to heresy, a slippery slope down which the Devil was intent on leading as many people as possible. Satan's method in perverting Christians had always been to draw them first to 'omit works of perfection . . . and to observe and exercise only necessary things', and, 'after this, to make them bold in light matters and small imperfections and so by degrees to bring them to be familiar with mortal sins'. All of which, of course, made Bell an instrument of the Devil.[14] Since this was clearly the case, those who denounced Bell did so reluctantly and, in fact, out of a sense of charity, which was the only remedy for the scandal which Bell's example gave.[15] Thus were even the most aggressive of polemical acts justified under the rubric of 'charity'; as, of course, had been Mrs Clitherow's rebukes and admonitions addressed to her lax and lukewarm co-religionists in York.

As Mush's admissions, quoted above, make clear, in taking Bell on directly his critics were running something of risk. They might well declare that he was an isolated figure, devoid of clerical support, motivated simply by pride and vainglory and with a following drawn entirely from the weak of faith and the ignorant, the wavering and the worldly. But in addressing his arguments in formal refutation they were according Bell something like equal status. In so doing not only were they (by implication at least) admitting the strength of both his case and his support; they were also circulating his arguments and those of his followers and allies (as well as their own refutations thereof) throughout the news and gossip networks of Catholic England. It is one of the chief paradoxes of the resulting situation that the best surviving source for the opinions of the defenders of conformity, and our best evidence for the salience and force of Bell's arguments and assertions, can be found in the tracts designed to denounce and refute them.

Moreover, for all their best efforts to marginalize him, it emerges from these tracts, just as it does from Mush's account of Clitherow, that Bell enjoyed considerable lay and even some clerical support. Indeed, the very intensity of these attempts to dismiss him as some eccentric, prideful and self-obsessed loner might well be taken to reveal just how serious a threat Bell represented to the spiritual authority of the hard-line recusant clergy. For these disputes about conformity, and Bell's very public stand on the issue, created a situation in which lay English Catholics got to choose which sort of priest to believe and obey. The result was something like a crisis of clerical authority, the nature and extent of which these tracts did their very best to play down, indeed almost entirely to obscure. Hence the intensity of their efforts to portray Bell as a lone wolf, devoid of clerical support, acting against the collective judgement of the English clergy, the determinations of the universal Catholic Church and the witness of so many martyrs, both ancient and modern. But, in a crucial aside, Mush let slip the realities of the situation, referring to 'these dangerous times wherein we live as sheep without a pasture or pastors, without a head in our country to govern us'.[16] That being the case, it was entirely unclear who Mush's superiors were. In that situation, Mush and his friends had a problem. Bell made claims that the best learned of English Catholics agreed with him; that there were no explicit canonical judgements of the Church that outlawed his position; that the council of Trent had not pronounced on the matter; that the pope either had dispensed or would dispense with the requirement not to attend church; and that whatever ecclesiastical pronouncements did exist were too general to apply to the particular circumstances of English recusants. These claims could all circulate with as much force and credence as their recipients cared to afford them. It was the need to refute such assertions and to scotch such rumours that had forced the likes of Mush and Garnet (as they claimed, against their better judgement) to resort to formal polemic and refutation.

Again, the Clitherow affair gives us telling insights into the interior dynamics of the resulting struggles for clerical authority and priestly charisma. As we have seen, in his account of Clitherow's life and death, Mush had put enormous emphasis on just how obedient Clitherow had been to the authority of Catholic priests and he had done so in large part to legitimate her defiance, as a woman and a wife, of the patriarchal authorities lodged respectively in her husband, her stepfather and indeed in the Elizabethan State. What his tract did not admit, but what we now know, is that there was another sort of priest – in other words, those who endorsed and legitimated certain styles of conformity – to whom she was being anything but obedient or even respectful. Mush's tract was designed, therefore, not merely to praise her 'obedience', but also to use her sufferings, her status as a martyr indeed, to buttress the authority of the priests whose strictures on recusancy she had obeyed, even to the point of death, while blackguarding, as the aiders and abettors of her persecutors, those, such as Bell, and briefly, even William Hart, who had taken a different tack.

In some telling admissions or asides these tracts give us fleeting insights into just how unpopular in certain quarters the hard-liners among the seminary priests were. Thus in his other anti-Bell tract of 1593, *A Treatise of Christian Renunciation*, Garnet ventriloquized the objections raised by some of the laity against the proponents of recusancy as a necessary act for any and every good Catholic: Garnet remarked that 'the question of going to the heretical churches' had been endlessly discussed and everyone knew what 'the general resolution' of the 'learned, resolute and godly priests' was. But 'certain private persons', who were completely 'addicted' to worldly comfort, conformed in the face of the rest of the community. They said that the proponents of separation were youthful and immature priests to whom no one was required to pay any attention. This was something which Garnet, of course, strenuously denied.[17]

Here, then, was proof positive that the laity, or rather some of them, did indeed distinguish between different types of priest, picking and choosing between different clerical opinions on this most crucial of issues and assimilating the rigorist position to 'young priests', newly emerged from the seminaries. These newcomers, with their novel and decidedly un-English notions about the necessity of complete separation, were then contrasted with the 'old priests' who had long kept the Catholic cause alive in England and had at first merely winked at, but, increasingly, since the later 1570s and early

1580s, had come to theorize and legitimate various (more or less) 'conformist' practises designed to spare the Catholic laity from the depredations of the law. One thinks here of the likes of Alban Langdale. And, of course, it was as the natural successor to such men that Bell presented himself.

Garnet, naturally enough, would not go so far as to deny the existence of generational tensions and divisions of opinion among the clergy. But he said that to make such distinctions between and among the clergy was itself schismatic. It implied that some priests were better than others and that God's Church might be 'forsaken of God's spirit' and might lack the 'assistance in latter ages' which it had had in former ones. Just as the universal Catholic Church was all one, so was its clergy 'in manner of government and doctrine' also united. Indeed, he claimed, the English Catholic clergy had never enjoyed such purity, zeal and unity as they did now. Their warrant and licence to do as they did came 'not from any particular bishop or ordinary authority of diocesans' but through 'the immediate delegation or extraordinary commission of the only chief bishop from whose particular knowledge they do not swerve in the resolution and managing of matters of the chiefest moment appertaining unto our religion'.[18]

Here is something very close to confirmation, from the horse's mouth, as it were, that Bell was not alone in taking the line that he did over conformity. Not only did he enjoy considerable support from the laity, his position was also perceived as being based on the teachings of a previous generation of clergy, a generation of English priests whose authority and judgement were frequently compared to those of the young clergy, but much to the latter's detriment. Ordained abroad, and as such scarcely English, the seminarist clergy came back loaded down with new fangled ideas and extremist claims which were of no value or relevance to the experience and needs of English Catholics.

If this was part of the case being made for Bell, then it is far easier to interpret the claims advanced by Mush and Garnet that Bell's opinions were novel and unprecedented in England. We can see why they argued that he alone among the English clergy regarded church attendance as in some sense, under the right circumstances, licit; that his opinions were advanced in defiance of the judgement, if not of the entire English Catholic community, then certainly of the English Catholic clergy, and also of those 'virtuous and learned', pious and truly Catholic members of the laity who accepted their authority. Such claims can be construed as responses to, indeed in many ways as simple inversions of, precisely the same claims made by their opponents against them.

What some at least dismissed as the 'seminary opinions' of the 'young clergy', Mush and Garnet therefore defended as the collective judgement of the entire English clergy. This judgement was based, or so they said, on the dictates of Scripture and the authority of the Church, both ancient and modern. It culminated, Garnet alleged in an appendix to his *Treatise*, in the determinations of the council of Trent, and, of course, in the sufferings and witness of so many English martyrs. On this view of the matter, Bell's great fault had been not to defer to the collective judgement of his colleagues and peers in the ministry. Mush's tract of 1588 opened with the example of St Simeon Stylites whose 'new and strange way of life' was suspected to proceed 'from the deceitful spirit of singularity and to be a pernicious illusion of Satan'. It was determined, therefore, to send a deputation to call upon him to 'descend' from his pillar and to 'forsake' his 'strange way'. If he acceded to this request it was to be presumed that his 'vocation was from God' and he was to be let alone; if not, he was to be forcibly pulled down. Simeon, of course, had submitted himself to the judgement of his peers, which Mush proclaimed was something that Bell had signally failed to do. Bell, said Mush, preferred to go public with his opinions without any prior consultation with his clerical peers at all.[19]

Moreover, Bell's subsequent responses to the rebukes and admonitions of his colleagues in the ministry had, Mush feared, revealed him in his true colours. He had lashed out against his critics. He had first reviled them and had then discovered 'to the whole world, the imperfections and faults, either not committed at all, but by yourself surmised, or else by human frailty and now with God forgotten and forgiven and by tears of a contrite heart purged'. Much worse, he had also betrayed them to the authorities with the express intention of bringing 'persecution and manifest danger' upon those who had 'either by writing or words' argued with him about the question of church attendance. In other words, Bell had responded to his critics much as some of the York Catholic community had responded to Mrs Clitherow, by outing her and her alleged moral and sexual faults before the whole world. 'No provocation in the world should have brought a charitable priest to that excess of revenge', Mush concluded.[20]

Mush and Garnet insisted, as we saw, that they had tried in fraternal charity to deal with Bell. But, in fact, what this exercise in Christian charity had entailed was the conduct of a vicious propaganda campaign, as each side took their case to the court of Catholic opinion, doing to one another – naming names and throwing mud – just what Mrs Clitherow's enemies had done to her, and what Mush had done to them in return. Indeed, on Mush's account, the internal dynamics of Bell's altercation with his enemies had been much the same as those of Mrs Clitherow's confrontation with hers. Bell's revelation to the wider world of the moral faults, both real and imagined, of his enemies was matched by his enemies' excoriation of him, to the same audience, as a schismatic and a sell-out, an enemy to the cause of true Catholic religion and a betrayer of the martyrs. In the absence of any effective supervening structure of ecclesiastical authority or jurisdiction, it was likely that serious, even unappeasable, disputes would break out between priests and their followings on issues of central importance to the Catholic cause in England. In these circumstances, such a descent into the muckraking politics of the Catholic public sphere, such a no-holds-barred recourse to all the propaganda tricks, all the manipulations of the available media of the day, could not be avoided. There was simply no other way either for Bell to make his case to the Catholics of England or for his enemies and critics to separate him from his very considerable following.

Thomas Bell and the Politics of Failure

Given the admission of his opponents that he enjoyed widespread support (though, on their account, only among the weakest and most corrupt of Catholics), and also the verdict of some modern historians that the church-papist position was what secured the future of English Catholicism, it is surely remarkable that it was Bell, the proponent of the 'moderate', and arguably the majority, conformist position, who lost. That he did so was a function of a number of political and polemical logics, operating within, without and upon the English Catholic public sphere. As Mush had pointed out, Bell's protestation was not a soft option. Bell himself, despite the accusations of his critics, was anything but an apologist for simple statute conformity and compliance. Conforming by means of a 'protestation', as Bell said you should, would be hard. Indeed as Mush had pointed out, in some places, such as York or London, it would be, if not impossible, then liable to get you into as much, if not worse, trouble than simple recusancy.[21]

In its origins, Bell's position, just like that of Persons and Campion, had been designed both to take seriously and fundamentally to challenge the regime's construction of the line that divided politics from religion and its concomitant claim that it punished Catholics only for their political disobedience and disloyalty rather than for their conscience-based religious beliefs. In order fully to work, that is, in order to do anything other than inflict a certain ideological embarrassment or discomfiture on the authorities, both Bell's and Persons's positions required something like a sympathetic, or at least not an overtly hostile, response from the regime. Bell's position was designed to draw a line between, on the one hand, himself and his followers and, on the other, the proponents of out-and-out recusancy. By demonstrating the superior political loyalty and allegiance of the former and, by implication, the disobedience and disloyalty of the latter, he was surely seeking to win from the regime improved terms, if not for all English Catholics, then at least for his own followers.

While we do not know precisely when Bell took the plunge into protes-tation- based conformity, it seems likely that the public adumbration of his position as the embodiment of majority Catholic opinion and preference, and as the best way forward for English Catholicism, was a product of the heightened levels of persecution consequent on the mission in 1580–1581 of Campion and Persons. But as the resulting persecution continued, and even worsened, this, of course, left him open to precisely the sort of charges levelled by Clitherow, and later by Mush, against Clitherow's conformist neighbours. As the regime's actions revealed it to be precisely the sort of persecutory tyranny which Catholic ideologues such as Persons and Mush claimed that it was, anyone pushing gestures of accommodation towards the regime could be made to look like a spineless weakling. Such a person was, it could be argued, well on the way not merely to schism but even to heresy. Not only that, but the levels of public defiance propagated and performed by the likes of Campion, Persons and Clitherow were unlikely to induce in the regime the sort of compromises and concessions that could alone make Bell's position viable over the long term.

These tensions and contradictions were of course heightened by the wider political contexts of the 1580s. By 1586, as his manuscript tract on the wick-edness of Huntingdon's regime in the North shows only too clearly, Mush had come to view the Elizabethan regime as a tyranny pure and simple, although his account of it as such was still (just) centred on the figure of an evil counsellor – namely Huntingdon. Abroad, similar Catholic estimations of the political and moral temperature of the regime – focused like Mush's on the fate of a series of martyrs at the hands of the regime – were being produced which had taken the final step and unmasked the queen herself as the usurper and tyrant at the centre of the web of persecution, corrup-tion and tyranny that was the Elizabethan court. The beheading of Mary Stuart and the war with Spain served only to heighten these tensions and, indeed, to intensify the persecution. All of this once more turned the screw on Bell. It rendered the State extremely unlikely to concede anything at all to Catholics, even to ones as avowedly 'loyalist' as Bell and his followers. From the Catholic perspective, it made it even easier to portray him as an enabler of, and a would-be collaborator with, a persecuting tyranny.

It was presumably these animosities and passions, mediated through the pressure-cooker atmosphere generated at York by Huntingdon and his min-ions and registered in such vivid language and imagery in Mush's account both of them and their victims that, at some indeterminate point during the 1580s, drove Bell out of Yorkshire and into Lancashire. As Mush had observed in 1588, if Bell's position was going to work anywhere it was going to be in places where Catholicism remained something like the communal norm: where local power lay in the hands of Catholic or crypto-Catholic gentlemen and where even the church-going public remained, in some sense, 'Catholic' in their sympathies and beliefs. What was needed, Bell opined, was 'some obscure parish or chapel, where the gentleman protester is chief and lord of all, or where there is neither hot-spirited minister nor Protestant that will discuss or look into his master's or his neighbour's doings with any malicious complaint to molest them'. In such places, Bell-ite protestations might be made almost as a matter of course. A real constituency for the demonstration of a Bell-ite conformity, or rather for the public expression of a Bell-style combination of political allegiance with Catholic religious profession, might then build up. But, Mush continued, even in such places it was doubtful whether Bell-style protests could go on unmolested for long:

> It is a very hard thing, and morally impossible, that all Catholics which should be redeemed and comforted by this protestation should make it . . . in the presence of well-willers only or such as are Catholicly affected, nay it cannot be that a Catholic can make this protestation in any favourable assembly but in short time the rumour thereof will fly to the ears of some malicious minister, justice of peace or other Protestant that will be glad, for the more vexation of Catholics and protesters, to call it in further question and prefer it to higher powers. And thus the practice of it, in short time, cannot be without extreme danger of the queen's laws anywhere.[22]

As various scholars have shown, during Elizabeth's reign, all over northern England – and indeed even in some parts of southern England – there were places where Catholic belief and practice remained something like the communal norm. By the end of Elizabeth's reign, Christopher Haigh has argued, the place where such pockets of Catholic normality were concentrated most intensely was Lancashire.[23] The fact that, by 1592, Bell's position had proved unworkable even there tells us a great deal about the intensity of the political and polemical forces at work in the county and goes a long way towards confirming Mush's analysis of the realities of late Elizabethan politics, even in Lancashire itself.

Bell's apostasy appeared to corroborate all the dark predictions made by the likes of Mush and Garnet that the only logical end point of his position was not merely schism but heresy. Towards the end of his *Apology* of 1593, which was apparently written before news of Bell's conversion to the Church of England had reached him, Henry Garnet had claimed that Bell and his followers had quite literally gone to the Devil. They had accordingly lost whatever reputation for religious principle or Catholic zeal they had once enjoyed. Moreover, Bell-ite conformists, Garnet claimed, were the victims of God's well-directed providential judgements upon them:

> So many schismatical marriages suddenly turned into mourning; so many conformable men either possessed or distracted or punished with the death of their nearest allies; so dreadful torments of conscience and continual terrors as they worthily are afflicted withal whom God, with Cain, has cast out of his holy sight and left as vagabonds and forelorn of the earth; such sudden deaths of infants baptised by heretics

and so on. As usual, there was something deeply disingenuous about such claims, since, if proponents of the church-papist position were indeed suffering the desperate pangs of a tormented conscience, it was almost certainly at least in part because of the efforts of Garnet and his ilk to scare the living daylights out of them with the certain prospect of mortal sin and damnation if they dared to persist in their current courses.

But, worst of all, Garnet prophesied that 'the favourers of such schism' would, in the end, 'discover themselves' and, through open and shameless apostasy, show what they 'secretly harboured within their rebellious bosoms'. They would then forsake those whom they pretended to feed spiritually.[24] Seldom can such a prophecy of providential judgement have been fulfilled so swiftly or completely as it was in the case of Thomas Bell. On the one hand, we might surmise that we are dealing here with a subtle and sophisticated manipulation of the politics of rumour and the dynamics of Catholic news culture. Garnet, having heard tell of Bell's defection, inserted a prediction of it into a book about to be shipped off to English audiences who were likely to hear news of Bell's conversion more or less at the same time as they either read or heard about Garnet's 'prophesy' of God's judgement on Bell's sin. On the other, if, suspending the hermeneutics of suspicion for a moment, we cut Garnet some slack, we might take the close fit between Garnet's vituperative prognostication and Bell's actions as illustrating just how constraining and predictable the political and polemical lines of force surrounding Bell's church-papist project had become. Squeezed, even in Lancashire, on the one hand between the polemical and pastoral efforts of his clerical rivals and, on the other, the refusal of the State to give ground, Bell found that most Catholic conformists did not see the making of a Bell-ite protestation in open church as a means to reconcile Catholic principle with political allegiance but rather as a way to make an already uncomfortable existence even worse.

The resulting contradictions and tensions were, of course, heightened by the 1591 proclamation. After all, if Bell *had* been selling his position as a way for Catholics to repudiate the siren song of Jesuited extremism, and to eschew the direct confrontation with the regime represented by recusancy and thus to reposition themselves politically, while they waited for better days, under either this Tudor monarch or her next successor, then the proclamation surely seemed to put an end to any such hopes. Garnet's *Apology* of 1593 claimed, as Persons and Mush had done before him, that the visible malice of the authorities in extorting obedience to the law meant that conformity could not in fact be understood as mere temporal loyalty to the queen. The barbarities and spite of the commissioners appointed to enforce the recent proclamation were proof of this. The 'action of going to the church' was always 'exacted in contempt of Catholic religion'. This was quite clear from the 'usages of those poor souls' who had come before the commissioners and had reluctantly agreed to conform. They found that the reward for their compliance was that they were contemptuously 'driven to the church'. At the assizes they were treated with disdain when they tried to register their conformities there. Garnet declared that he knew of one man who, 'purposely coming to the assizes to submit himself', was astounded by the sight of the man in the queue before him, as it were, making 'so shameful a protestation'. The judges were so imperious that, 'very contemptuously', some Catholics were 'like grammar scholars commanded to repeat' their capitulation again, on the grounds that they had not 'pronounced it well, or not spoken' it 'loud enough'. Anyway, 'this man', said Garnet, 'perceiving more to be exacted than he had stomach to bear, withdrew himself' and decided to accept whatever legal proceedings were subsequently taken against him. What could anybody conclude from all this other than that 'the intent of going to the heretics' service is so to obey the prince that God's Church and authority may be condemned'?[25]

Now, left with nowhere to go, and as the full implications of the 1591 proclamation hit home, Bell simply changed sides, just as the likes of Mush and Garnet (and, one dares say, Mrs Clitherow) had always 'known' that he would.

The events that followed Bell's defection merely confirmed such verdicts. In the wake of Bell's apostasy, Garnet described (relying on information passed to him by his confrère Richard Holtby in the North) the furious onslaught launched by the northern administration against Catholics there. In a letter of 17 March 1593 to the Jesuit general Claudio Acquaviva, Garnet directly associated the one with the other. He recorded a torrent of conformity procured by the cruelty of the earl of Huntingdon. In particular Garnet noted how 'schismatic husbands must deliver their Catholic wives into custody, and must bind themselves under heavy penalties to harbour no priest, Jesuit or Catholic, nor to keep Catholic servants; they must themselves frequent the heretical church, or must listen at home to a Calvinistic discourse, or must receive the sacrament at stated times under pain of imprisonment'. Garnet stressed how in Durham the dean, Tobias Matthew, was 'imbued with such malice and fury that scarcely any month passed without three or four sessions of the commissioners, whereby such terror took possession of the fickle souls of the people that many of them forsook the noble cause of religion and joined the heretics outwardly, though inwardly with the utmost reluctance'.

Here Garnet admitted the effectiveness of the new crackdown on recusant Catholicism. He anticipated, quite accurately, that there was worse to follow. 'Twice in this year' Lord President Huntingdon had ridden into Durham. The lord president's intentions were not yet known but he was causing 'intense fear among the Catholics'. His dark presence filled them with foreboding. He 'scattered, throughout various parts of the country, pursuivants and many other persons of notorious dishonesty and malice to harass the Catholics' in their houses.

Garnet described, in extraordinary and vivid detail, the searches which were carried out by the authorities in and around the houses of leading northern Catholics.[26] The intelligent Catholic response to this would, on some accounts, have been a shift, even if only temporarily, into a mode of conformist compliance in the face of such intense official hostility. This is undoubtedly what a number of Catholics were doing. But the chief proponent of that course, Thomas Bell, had just gone over to the enemy. Even though Bell had now cut his ties with the Church of Rome, any widespread movement of the Catholic community's leading men and women into Huntingdonian conformity would be taken as a victory for Bell's account of how such people should position themselves towards the queen and State. This meant that Garnet and his friends, Mush among them, had to insist even more stridently, if that were possible, on the necessity for absolute recusancy, which is what Garnet, assisted in fact, as we will suggest, by Mush, had done with his two recusancy tracts of 1593.[27]

It was grist to Garnet's mill therefore to be able to describe what was happening in the parliament of 1593 which was then in session, and where, as it happened, the crown's law officers were manoeuvring to bring in legislation, virtually by stealth, to allow the authorities to proceed more effectively against women recusants. Some of the parliament's members who had puritan inclinations (and were faced, of course, with other legislation that was intended to punish puritan separation from the national Church) were openly sceptical that the draft bill against Catholic separatism was being introduced for the reasons which the crown's law officers declared.[28] Lord Grey had allegedly said that he 'was under the impression that up to now your purpose in regard to the papists was only to keep them humble and in subjection, so that they would not raise disturbances; but now that they are sucked dry and reduced to the extreme of poverty, and you strive to harass them in this fashion, I see plainly that . . . you are persecuting religion'.[29]

Why should the early 1590s have witnessed what some contemporary Catholics regarded as more-than-customary harshness towards them on the part of the authorities? In fact, the dragging of the confrontation between Bell and his critics out into the open coincided with a series of political realignments in Scotland and France which, even after the failure of the Armada, made the style of Catholicism adopted by some English Catholics look particularly threatening. In Scotland it had appeared to some of James Stuart's Catholic subjects that, following the royal concessions made to the Kirk in 1592, James had decided to pursue a more overtly Protestant path than he had formerly done. This seems to be what drove leaders of the Catholic community there into the arms of the Spaniards and ultimately into rebellion. Some Catholics in the North of England anticipated a victory by their Catholic friends in Scotland, both against the Kirk and, if necessary, against the authority of the king. These events coincided also with the high-point of Elizabethan Catholic resistance theory. Robert Persons, for one, decided that no reliance could be placed now on King James as a friend of Catholics. It seemed right to the Jesuit that Catholics should abandon their former legitimist attitudes on the question of the succession. This mindset produced, in 1594, Persons's most notorious tract, the *Conference about the Next Succession to the Crowne of Ingland*.[30] It was a carefully crafted and outwardly moderate discussion of what factors should be taken into account when considering who had the best claim to succeed Elizabeth. It was, however, a product of the kind of thinking which had characterized the French Holy League's opposition to the blood-right succession of the Calvinist Henry of Navarre. The same case was, *sotto voce*, being made here against James VI. This attitude to the succession was based in part upon the principle that the law of God forbade contamination of the true faith with the poison of heresy.

Of course, many Catholics soon concluded, if they had ever doubted it, that opposition to the Stuart claim was distinctly unwise. The *Conference* was, in some sense, out of date almost as soon as it was published. At the same time, some thought that the rather more relaxed attitude to the question of conformity that seemed to prevail in Scotland might prove an appropriate template for the conduct of Catholics in England, and that it would soon be possible to sort out a *modus vivendi* with the first Stuart king of England, a king who might be persuaded to grant them toleration. In fact, such people said, there was already a model established in Scotland for a royal toleration, a template that was constructed on the basis of Catholic moderation over the issue of separatism.

Garnet, however, refuted those who alleged that the Scottish Catholics had worked out an appropriate compromise with the State. He said that he understood that 'in Scotland (which many perversely will have a pattern for England, whereas it were greater equity, that contrariwise, that country should learn of ours, which hath been with so many holy labours, and bloody conflicts of most holy martyrs, instructed and imbrued)', there was supposed to be a kind of toleration. 'But, of what?', asked Garnet. 'Of going to heretical churches? No sir, of no such thing. But whereas there wants that perfect resolution which ought to be in Catholics, who must bear everywhere Christ's cross and ignominy', this so-called toleration extended only to those who 'being otherwise Catholicly affected, will not refrain from the heretics' synagogues and their schismatical practices'.[31]

The fact that some Catholics in Scotland had a different understanding of the issue of conformity did not, however, make English Catholics' attitudes towards the succession any less threatening. Of course, for the most part, we do not know exactly what most Catholic clergymen thought of the ideological stance which found expression in Persons's *Conference*. Scottish Catholics could claim that they were entirely legitimist, and of course had no intention of blocking James's path to the English crown. But their resort to political resistance and their association with some of the leading Catholic clergy in the North of England were unlikely to be ignored by the Elizabethan authorities who had no wish to see the, in any case unstable and unpredictable, Stuart regime in Scotland interfere in and disrupt the workings of the English polity. As a result, there was, at this point in the 1590s, a determination on the part of the Elizabethan authorities to arrest and even to kill those whom they suspected, with good reason, of engaging in the wrong sort of cross-border politics. There was, for example, a furious hue and cry after the priest John Boste and his harbourers.[32] It seems clear enough that Boste had contacts in Scotland, in particular with the Scottish Catholic peers who were at that point in revolt against James VI. The Elizabethan privy council regarded such people as tentacles of the Habsburg attempt at global dominance, particularly since it was believed that Scottish Catholics were canvassing the court in Madrid for aid against their Protestant enemies in Scotland and even against their king. Boste was arrested in September 1593. The proceedings against his harbourer, Lady Margaret Neville, herself a daughter of the rebel earl of Westmorland, were intended to be a show trial not unlike that which would have taken place in York in March 1586 had Clitherow not refused to plead. Tobias Matthew, the dean of Durham, preached an awe-inspiring sermon about the Protestant faith and Catholics' enmity towards it. Margaret Neville and another harbourer of Catholic clergy, Grace Claxton, were condemned for the same offence with which Clitherow had been charged back in 1586, though Neville and Claxton were both reprieved. The earl of Huntingdon used the occasion to lecture Mrs Claxton about the priests who had said Mass at her house and 'do now as much detest the Mass as ever they embraced it before, and will preach as much against it'. Richard Holtby took this to be a reference to 'those castaway and apostate' clergy, William Hardesty and Anthony Major, or perhaps to Thomas Bell himself.[33]

Another of those who was ensnared and executed at this time, the priest John Ingram, worked as an agent for the Scottish Catholic rebel peers. Ingram was picked up in late 1593 as he came over the border with Scotland. William Hutton, who had helped to compile Mush's life of Clitherow, recorded that 'Father John Ingram, priest, being apprehended in the north country' was 'brought to York to the lord president'. Ingram was 'kept in his porter's lodge about two months close prisoner' and had 'secret conference' with, among others, John Favour, who was Huntingdon's chaplain. He was treated 'both with lenity and extremity'. It appears that they may have been trying to turn him as they tried to turn Clitherow. But 'when they had used all the means they could, and could not prevail against him, they sent him to London to the torturers, where he hung by the joints of his fingers and arms in extreme pain'. He was returned to York in the company of John Boste. They were then sent to Durham for trial at the assizes, after which both were strung up and disembowelled on 24 July 1594. Ingram had tried to pass himself off as a Scot, but Thomas Bell's two friends and fellow converts to Protestantism, Major and Hardesty, had been happy to identify him as an English priest.[34]

The highest-profile victim of the Huntingdon regime in this period was the Jesuit Henry Walpole. His case was yet another demonstration of the centrality during the early 1590s of the conformity issue in the political stand-off between the regime and the queen's Catholic subjects in the North. Bell, Hardesty and Major took part in the disputations with Walpole in York.[35] Nearly 18 months after Walpole had been apprehended, Garnet related, in a letter of 20 June 1595 to the Jesuit general, what had happened to his Jesuit confrère. He described Walpole's landing at Flamborough in December 1593 and his almost immediate arrest. The authorities clearly thought that, coming as he did from service as a chaplain to Englishmen in the Spanish Army of Flanders, Walpole was intending to stir up opinion in the North against the queen's authority there. He was taken to York and remained there until 25 February 1594, when he was sent to London. During that time he was 'visited by a number of ministers' who 'came to have converse with him'.[36] It is clear that what Huntingdon wanted to see was a measure of conformity on Walpole's part. This, presumably, is why Bell was brought in to talk to him. The record of Walpole's examinations suggest that he came close to conceding what his interrogators demanded, in other words, a kind of conformity, verging almost on what some contemporary Catholics would have regarded as apostasy, though it has been claimed that Walpole's 'confessions' are, in part or whole, clever forgeries. Bell obviously saw Walpole's incarceration as an opportunity to reveal the inextricable link between treason and certain erroneous opinions about the connection between spiritual and temporal authority. Bell probably also thought that, if he managed to turn Walpole, this would hand him a remarkable triumph over his Catholic enemies, an enacted vindication of his general philosophy about the relationship between Church and State. Walpole's conformist-sounding statements may, however, have been an attempt to undercut Bell and to retain the approbation of Catholics who did not necessarily want to subscribe either to out-and-out separation or to full-blown resistance theory. Garnet himself conceded that, after Walpole's interrogation, Huntingdon treated him 'much more courteously than he usually does others; and it is believed that he was moved by his disputations and his writings still more, as he himself confessed'.[37] Nevertheless, as Augustus Jessopp points out, Walpole had 'the audacity', after the disputations were over, to 'employ his time in jail in composing a tract with the title "Beware of False Prophets", which was directed at those very ministers who had so lately taken part in the disputation'. Walpole's intransigence and belligerence led, inevitably, to his execution in April 1595.[38]

The result of the confrontations between the regime and these Catholics was, of course, that victory was handed to those who, on one reading, were extremists and impossibilists. In other words, the ideological expression of what, in a seminal article, Christopher Haigh decided to call the 'continuity of Catholicism in the English Reformation' was here rendered untenable for anyone wanting to present himself or herself as a real Catholic. Not merely indelibly tainted with schism and what Garnet had termed 'outward heresy', church popery now seemed to lead inevitably to inward as well as to outward heresy and to apostasy – just as Bell's opponents had claimed that it would.[39] Thus, viewed as an ideological position, a morally and spiritually legitimate identity or stance, to be taken vis-à-vis either one's fellow Catholics or the Protestant State, church popery had been completely discredited. And this had happened, moreover, in Lancashire, the one place, as both John Mush and Dr Haigh would agree, where such a position might have been sustainable, even in late Elizabethan England. Might we, then, be witnessing a moment of major discontinuity in the relationship between

English Catholicism and the English Reformation? Certainly this was a remarkable outcome. The position which, Professor Walsham has argued, ensured the survival of English Catholicism had, at least at the level of self-conscious ideological assertion, as an openly owned, avowed and legitimated religio-political identity, become completely unavailable to anyone who wanted to continue calling himself or herself an English Catholic.

This, of course, is not to argue that, at the level of cultural and social practice, later Elizabethan Catholicism, even in its most stringently recusant forms, did not owe a considerable debt to the earlier survivalist modes of behaviour and practice identified by Dr Haigh. Following in the footsteps of the giant of local Reformation history, John Aveling, Haigh has repeatedly insisted that it did.[40] Nor is it to suggest that, as a series of expedients, a mode of negotiating the toils of the law, of reconciling the demands of religious principle with those of economic or social survival or interest, church popery simply died out. It patently did no such thing. Throughout the period, Catholics of various hues continued to manoeuvre across the line that separated recusancy from conformity, as the promptings of convenience, conscience and the coercive pressure exerted by the State's agents and officials dictated.

We can argue, however, that, after the outing and defection of Thomas Bell, church popery became a position that dared not speak its name; or, rather, it became a position whose name only its opponents wanted to speak. In other words, 'church papist' definitively became the term of derision and abuse that its originators on both the Catholic and hot Protestant sides of the confessional divide had always intended it to be. Haigh's account of a gradual and cultural shift towards a separated community is delivered virtually in the absence of the political and polemical contexts that made that shift so controversial. In fact he portrays the resort of seminarist clergy to gentry households as the means by which Catholicism was whittled down to an elitist minority as these priests, temperamentally unsuited to the rigours of a socially diverse ministry, fled to the luxuries of gentry manor houses, mainly in the South.[41] In Haigh's version, the seminarists, 'at least in the short term . . . had a remarkably slight impact upon the structure of English Catholicism'.[42] And yet, here, in the quarrel between Bell and his antagonists we have a situation in which the gentry houses in Lancashire (the very epicentre of Haigh's research) both harboured a variety of recusant impulses and conformist compromises and provided a venue for the gathering of significant numbers of ideologically committed clergy to meet and to hammer out a new approach to the relationship between, on the one hand, the queen's Catholic subjects and, on the other, the State and the national Church. Bell's defection illustrated how intense these clerical quarrels could become. The normal operation of local politics, office-holding and the 'public sphere' of debate, rumour and gossip became subject to the, in many ways, radical ideological programme of the seminarist clergy and their demand for separatism. This programme, in turn, served as a site where arguments about other politico-religious issues could be conducted as various factions and fractions fought for the soul of English Catholicism.

It is not the least of the ironies in play here that in a struggle between 'moderates' and 'radicals', in other words between those who wanted to make church attendance a sign of political allegiance and those who denied that it could ever be any such thing, it was the policies of the Elizabethan regime that handed victory to the most radically disaffected of the queen's Catholic subjects and definitively stuffed the moderate 'loyalist' tendency among them. Of course, for those contemporaries who firmly believed in the existence of a Catholic threat, and thought that many English Catholics, particularly those who were most uncompromising on the subject of conformity, either were, or were likely to become, politically disloyal – and of course many members of the Elizabethan regime did think precisely that – then closing off the church-papist option in order to turn the likes of Thomas Bell no doubt looked like rather a good deal. After all, Bell was probably losing the debate over conformity anyway. The propaganda value, and indeed the intelligence, to be extracted from his defection were very considerable assets in the linked campaigns both to demonstrate the seriousness and to scotch the practical effects of the popish threat. Bell's defection allowed zealous anti-papists to draw a parallel conclusion to the one drawn in fact by his own Catholic enemies. In other words, those Catholics who did not follow Bell into the national Church were the potential traitors that those anti-papists had always known them to be. In the early 1590s, engaged in a European war with the great Catholic power of the age, and dealing with a queen who perhaps did not entirely share their view either of English Catholicism or of the war itself, this was exactly what the authors and sponsors of the 1591 proclamation wanted, indeed perhaps even needed, to do.

Mrs Clitherow Entirely Vindicated as the Epitome of Catholic Order

Nevertheless, it is quite remarkable how completely the extra pressure exerted through the 1591 proclamation handed the initiative to the most radical of the regime's Catholic opponents. Just how radical they were emerges from the second of Garnet's printed anti-Bell tracts, his *Treatise of Christian Renunciation*. This takes us back to many of the central issues raised by the Clitherow affair. In fact, without once mentioning her name, the tract functions as a gloss on the meaning and significance of Mrs Clitherow's life and fate. For the main purport of its argument was that, on the great questions about how to balance the demands of religious principle and conscience against those of social duty and familial obligation, Clitherow had done the right thing and, in so doing, had provided a model of how other Catholics should conduct themselves when the persecutory policies being pursued by the regime asked the same questions of them.

The starting point of the tract was the prevalence among Catholics of what we might term the conformist or church–papist impulse; that is to say, the impulse to conform in order to preserve the material well-being and the social and political status or clout of one's family. This was a decision taken by many heads of households and then imposed by them, if they could, on the other members of their family. As we have seen, there were indeed very many households headed by a conformist husband, but with a recusant wife. In such households, the education of the children and, in particular, the question of whether the wife and children should conform or not, could become a matter of some tension and disagreement. Here at least, we might surmise, Clitherow was far from unusual. Garnet's *Treatise* was addressed directly to that situation and its consequent dilemmas and moral and practical conflicts.

He came at the subject not through a discussion of the particular circumstances in which English Catholics currently found themselves but rather from the general topic of Christian renunciation. Such renunciation, Garnet explained, was an obligation taken on by every Christian at baptism. Then we all became 'sworn soldiers' of Christ, obliged to renounce 'the Devil and all his works, with all his pomps and vanities'. This, he reminded his readers, was a 'strict obligation . . . homage and promise unto the greatest sovereign which possibly may be, that is to God himself'; and it was a shield against all temptation and all spiritual enemies. However, it was also an obligation all too often forgotten by those who had undertaken it, many of whom behaved as though 'this virtue of renunciation' was a duty only for those who had taken vows in religion. As a result, a spiritual Jerusalem, built by the love of God, was overtaken by a 'confused Babylon' created 'by love of the world'.[43]

At this point Garnet moved from such general observations, applicable to Christians in almost any place and any time, to the current condition of Catholic England. England was full of this kind of iniquity. The failure to practise Christian renunciation did all sorts of harm: 'where do we not see that either parents by children, or children by parents; husbands by wives, or wives by husbands; one friend by another; the subjects by the superiors and superiors by subjects, are hindered from the service of God and that as our Saviour said . . . the enemies of a man are those of his own household?'

These corrupt impulses, Garnet claimed, were to be found working at every level of the social and familial order, corrupting the most intimate and intense of affective relationships – the very relationships, in fact, through which social and moral order was supposed to be created and sustained. As a result, 'those which should, in the holy estate of wedlock, represent the unspotted and inseparable conjunction of Christ and his Church', now trapped and misled by 'base affections', do 'draw one another from Christ . . . whose perpetual link they should resemble'. But what made matters worse was that these corrupting influences were animated and legitimated by recourse to conscience. People sinned and cited as their excuse 'that sacred power which God has ordained, whereby either wives unto their husbands, or children to their parents, or other subjects to their superiors, do owe a kind of duty and obedience', or even, at some level, 'upon the most honest link of human friendship'. This was all wrong, said Garnet. It was tantamount to saying that 'wives had sold both body and soul to be by their husbands mortgaged to perpetual slavery of the Devil', or that 'parents had authority to kill the souls of their children', or that those that were, 'as it were, God's lieutenants, in their several offices, might convert their forces and fight for Hell and lawfully constrain their soldiers and subjects to rebel against God'.[44]

These were remarkable claims. On this view, in England now, under a regime that required, of all its subjects, attendance at heretical services, the normal operation of the links of mutual obligation and obedience that underpinned both the family and 'the State', that created and sustained 'order' in the world, were shown to be the origin of the ultimate in spiritual and moral disorder. Under such circumstances, the disobedience of wives to husbands, of children to parents and of subjects to rulers became not merely a necessary moral duty but in itself the origin of the only (spiritual) 'order' that mattered. Here it is almost impossible not to think back to the problems of the, in some sense, dysfunctional Clitherow household which John Mush had described so vividly in his account of his saintly patroness's life and which, we may conjecture, he would have discussed at some length with his friend Henry Garnet.

Garnet was quick to point out that, under normal circumstances, 'the child is not bound to forsake his parents, but yet he may do it with merit for the service of God. The wife may not forsake her husband at her pleasure, although it were for to be religious.' But what was going on in England was not normal. There good Catholics were being confronted with intolerable choices. In fact, 'if either the son must forsake his faith or his father, or the wife her husband or her maker', then there was no longer a choice in the matter: 'most certain it is that the thing which was lawful before, in the son, is now necessary and that which the wife could not do before but sinfully, now she cannot neglect but damnably'.[45]

Garnet's tract was, in fact, an extended exhortation, indeed a paean of praise, to disobedience. If we transpose Garnet's advice back into the internal disputes that had racked the Clitherow household a decade before, he was quite simply siding with the mother and the son against the father and with the godly woman against the magistrate. Because of the extremely controversial nature of its message, the text took the form of a series of quotations from the Church fathers, arranged so as to answer a basic question and address a series of pendant topics directly germane to the current situation of English Catholics. The 'question', if such it was, recast the issue of church popery in terms already familiar from the other Catholic refutations of Bell: Garnet asked 'whether a child, by the commandment of parents, or a wife, for obedience to her husband, or a servant or inferior, for duty to his superior, or a father, for providing for his children, may lawfully do that which, of itself, is against the law of God and prejudicial to the necessary profession of his faith and contemptuous . . . unto Christ his Church and a very separation from the same?' Since Garnet's *Apology* had been dedicated to the proposition that attendance at church was indeed 'against the law of God' and 'prejudicial to the necessary profession of his faith', this left the reader in little doubt that this was a tract about conformity. The answer to the subsidiary question of 'whether . . . by these respects of temporal duty, these various deformities may be taken away and a contrary bond caused of such temporal obedience or duty?' was a very definite no.[46]

Despite, or rather because of, the discordant and controversial nature of both the topic and of Garnet's argument, he described the book not as any sort of polemical assault on the arguments of Bell or his allies but rather as a pastoral work. It was 'a comfortable sermon' for 'every distressed Catholic . . . whensoever he wants other means of fruitful encouragements'. Because the content (apart from the preface, conclusion and 'some of the third chapter') was composed almost entirely out of the 'uncorrupted judgement' of the fathers, its message, Garnet assured his readers, could be taken neither as a direct emanation of his own wit or pen nor of any spirit of *parti pris*, but rather as a direct product of the 'spirit which dwelled within them'.[47]

Here, as ever in these tracts, were intensely and aggressively polemical and political acts being distributed under the signs of the pastoral and the religious, while a socially and politically insurgent ideology was passed off as the propagation of core Christian doctrine and the alleviation of the sorely tried and tempted consciences of English Catholics. On Garnet's view of the matter, Clitherow's rebukes to her neighbours, Mush's attacks on

Bell, and Garnet's own attempts to scare Bell's followers out of their wits with the spectre of excommunication, mortal sin and damnation, could all be described as signal exercises of Christian charity and the zealous discharge of pastoral duty. So too could Garnet's legitimation of disobedience, indeed of the complete overthrow of the social, familial and moral ties that bound society together, be seen not as any sort of political act but rather as the due and proper exercise of his pastoral concern for English Catholics. Not that his book was innocent of polemical elements; it was merely that the overtly polemical sections – a short treatise designed to prove that attending church with a protestation was simply unlawful (see Plate 20) and an appendix designed to prove that the council of Trent had indeed outlawed such a practice – were appended to the main body of his text as separate items. Indeed the short treatise against attending church appears not to have been written by Garnet himself but rather by somebody else – very possibly by none other than John Mush, although we cannot prove it conclusively.[48]

Garnet's tract was organized around a series of chapters with headings that encapsulated central truths of Catholic religion, the orthodoxy of which was intended to be beyond question for any sincere Catholic believer. For instance, the heading of the second chapter was that 'a man is bound, under pain of eternal damnation, unto a perfect renunciation of all friends, kinsfolk, parents and superiors, their entreaties, examples and commandments, yea and himself also and all that he has, when otherwise he should be hindered from the duty of a Christian'.[49]

The argument then proceeded through a concatenation of quotations from the fathers, with St Cyprian and St Augustine prominent among them, the relevance of which to current English concerns was pointed out largely through marginal notes. At one point, next to St Augustine's praise for 'these men's houses' which, 'excelling in hospitality, do receive the just in the name of a just' man, 'that they may receive a reward of a just' man, Garnet added in the margin: 'receiving of priests and recusants'. At another, next to the claim that 'if the world threaten them for Christ to be bereaved and severed from their friends, they hate parents, brethren, children, wives', and 'if they must bargain with the adversary for the very life of this body, they hate even their own life', Garnet added the marginal comment: 'pecuniary mulcts according to the proclamation', in other words, of 1591. Again, quoting St Augustine on Psalm 136, Garnet juxtaposed this passage: 'Babylon therefore did persecute us when we were little ones but God gave us the knowledge of himself, being great ones, that we should not follow the errors of our parents', with the marginal comment: 'a just revenge to parents for evil bringing up' of children. Next to the Augustinian ejaculation 'alas, alas

I bewail the chaff, I see the ashes', Garnet added in the margin: 'to go to the church'. Quoting St Gregory to the effect that 'Peter had a carnal mind before our Saviour's death, Sarvias his son, with a carnal mind, followed his captain David, yet the one sinned by fear, the other by pride', Garnet added, in the margin, the words 'charitable persuaders to schism'.[50]

For our current purposes the chapter or section of most interest is the third, which, as we have seen, together with the preface and the conclusion, Garnet had marked down as more his own work than that of the fathers. Significantly, this was concerned with relations between spouses. While it started off with the assertion that 'a wife is to be left for the kingdom of heaven', it quickly moved, under the heading of 'God is to be obeyed before husband or any other', to the explication of 'diverse lawful manners of separation of man and wife according to the holy Scriptures and the sentence and practice of holy Church'.[51] The discussion started with first principles and moved through a number of questions concerning divorce and the circumstances under which a wife could leave her husband to become a religious or whether it was lawful for a husband and wife mutually to agree to give up carnal relations and live together 'as brother and sister'. (It was.) Having run through the conventional causes of divorce or separation, Garnet concluded his discussion with the claim that 'there are other causes of divorce which are for a time, until the causes be taken away; as for unreasonable cruelty of the husband, or if the wife or the husband were a witch, or killed the children, or sought the other's death, or were dangerously furious, or, finally, if the one party should draw the other, in whatsoever manner, into deadly sin and could not be reformed; and, in those cases, when necessity urges, the wife may forsake her husband without judgement of the Church'.[52]

Here, of course, we enter not merely Clitherow territory in particular but also church-papist territory in general. Perhaps unsurprisingly, Garnet added that it was 'of this last case' that 'it doth especially behove us to speak a little'. Garnet handled the case through deploying a hierarchy of authorities. He started with Christ's saying 'that if any one come unto me and hates not his father and mother and wife he cannot be my disciple. Also in another place: if your eye scandalizes you, pluck it out and cast it from you.' He moved on to St Paul who, 'in the case of heresy, commands to avoid all persons without exception' and thence to St Jerome's admonition, based upon Matthew 18, not to 'prefer . . . wife nor children nor friends nor any affection which may exclude us from the kingdom of heaven before the love of Our Lord' for 'it is better to lead a solitary life than, for the necessities of this life, to lose the everlasting'. Garnet then followed Jerome's judgement with his own verdict: 'therefore I do conclude that in case a woman by her husband be urged to go to the church or to do any unlawful act of religion, much more than in other carnal sins, she may, yea and is bound, to forsake him, lest loving danger, she perish therein'.[53]

Given the very large number of households headed by conformist husbands yet containing recusant wives this was potentially extraordinarily disruptive, indeed, subversive advice. As we have seen, if Mrs Clitherow is anything to go by, those households may not all have been examples of a consensual division of spiritual and legal labour, with the husband's (sinful) compliance designed to beat back the penalties of the law and the wife's (virtuous) rigorism designed to protect the household as an essentially Catholic space. Rather, they could also be sites of considerable conflict either between husband and wife or, within and between both partners to the union, between the promptings of conscience and the material demands and interests of household and lineage. That certainly was the premise that had framed both Garnet's discourse and the lessons taught by Mush in his account of Mrs Clitherow's tragic fate.

Except, of course, that Clitherow had not left her husband but, instead, had stayed in order to wrest control of both household and children from her unfortunate spouse. That, too, was an option which met with Garnet's approval: 'yet if she perceives herself by God's grace to be so strong and constant that she fears no perversion at all, she is bound . . . to remain with him and so to seek to gain him'.[54] Once again, therefore, Mrs Clitherow had been vindicated. Undoubtedly with her, among others, in his mind, Garnet had located a specific kind of zeal, precisely as she had performed it, up to the point of martyrdom, at the very centre of his own vision of truly Catholic order.

9

Aftermath: The English Catholic Community Tears Itself Apart in the Archpriest Controversy

Had Mrs Clitherow been there to watch the public eviscerations of the likes of John Boste or John Ingram and, doubtless, afterwards to make pilgrimages to the sites of their executions, she would have concluded that the rigorist vision of English Catholic belief and practice had at last triumphed. Some of those who had opposed it, in the name of a deeply compromised occasional conformity, had now embraced not only schism but heresy, just as she had always warned that they would, leaving true believers to follow her, if necessary, to a martyr's crown.

But the victory of what we might term the 'Clitherow tendency' proved to be, if not short-lived, then certainly far from complete. That was in large part because that victory had been achieved over the single issue of conformity; on that topic alone a line had indeed been drawn in the sand. But the issues at stake in the confrontation between Clitherow and her Catholic enemies had never been solely concerned with conformity. After all, Garnet's *Treatise of Christian Renunciation* had confronted the reader not only with two positions on the question of conformity and recusancy, but also with two models of Catholic order, two modes of co-existence between the demands of true religion and those of social and political stability. On the one hand, we have Garnet's own inversionary opposition between a series of social, familial and patriarchal norms and pressures which, if left to run their course, would, as things stood, plunge very large numbers of notional Catholics into mortal sin, which sin, if unacknowledged and unrepented, would ultimately send them to Hell. That was something that we might term the hard-line 'recusant' position. On the other, we have a vision of the inherent compatibility of those same social and gender norms and hierarchies with the promptings of conscience and the demands of true religion. That was a position which we might term the conformist or church-papist model. The latter left the social, gender (and indeed the political) orders more or less intact and claimed that, through the exercise of the conventional authority wielded by husbands over wives or by parents over children or servants, Catholic families and individuals could negotiate their relationship with even an aggressively heretical regime in such a way as to preserve traditional notions of hierarchy and degree, that is to say, of order, conventionally defined, within both the family and the State, while still saving the souls of all concerned. Such claims the former view denounced as not only impossible but also as a snare and a delusion. If believed and, still worse, if acted upon, it would send hundreds, if not thousands, of souls to eternal damnation.

If Garnet is to be believed, in certain circles at least, the latter view was identified with the 'old clergy' of Catholic England, and the former with an insurgent 'young clergy', ordained abroad and sent to England to spread their disruptive and subversive 'seminary opinions' among the people. Garnet, however, equated the former position with the wholly orthodox teachings of the Catholic Church, with the doctrine of the fathers and with the example and witness of the martyrs (both ancient and modern). As for the latter position, he equated that with the perennial forces of spiritual darkness, with worldly corruption, self-love and material self-interest. These were impulses which, in any age, were always completely antithetical to the Christian renunciation that his tract asserted was necessary for the salvation of every true Catholic Christian.[1]

The defection and, in Catholic circles at least, the definitive disgrace, of Thomas Bell rendered any sort of church popery, any mode of conformity, however hedged around with protestations of purely secular allegiance or gestures of religious dissent or principle, entirely unavailable for anyone wanting to appear to be a sincere and orthodox Catholic. But it would be absurd to claim that the tensions between the two versions of English Catholicism, the two visions of a truly Catholic order that were central to the disputes between the recusant and church-papist parties of the 1580s and early 1590s, could have been simply dissolved or dissipated by the apostasy of one man or the resolution of one issue (however central). On the contrary, many of those same difficulties and tensions remained unappeased and unresolved. They would be raised again to the level of coherent articulation and contest in the notorious Archpriest Controversy of the later 1590s.

The triumph of the allies and promoters of Mrs Clitherow, that is to say, of the hard-line proponents of recusancy, had been, in large part, the outcome of a variety of political events and contingencies. It was politics that subsequently reopened many of the central issues here and returned them to the public stage of overt dispute and polemic. For all the inversionary force of his uncompromising recusant vision of order, Garnet had been extremely anxious, for obvious reasons, to claim that this vision had no directly political meanings or implications at all. Garnet, at least, wanted nothing whatsoever to do with the so-called family/State analogy (the simple equation of the authority of husbands and fathers over wives and children with that of princes over their subjects). The otherwise very considerable emotive and ideological force generated by such parallels and analogies were dissipated by his application to these matters of a very sharp distinction between politics and religion, matters spiritual and matters temporal. If, on his view, women like Clitherow were within their rights if they decided to sever themselves from their heretical husbands, the same was not true for the Catholic subjects of heretical princes. For Garnet, the issues involved in the cases of women such as Clitherow were purely 'religious' and the order being preserved by people such as her was entirely spiritual. Accordingly, however intense they may have been, the religious commitments of English Catholics left their political loyalties and their status as loyal subjects of the crown unquestioned and unquestionable. Others, of course, including Thomas Bell, certainly after his defection, but also almost certainly during his Catholic phase, were by no means so sure. As the proclamation of 1591 had reaffirmed, the official view remained that recusant Catholicism was tainted by its association with the globalizing ambitions of the Spanish crown and its Jesuited agents. Just as the likes of Robert Persons, John Mush and Henry Garnet had described recusancy as the only appropriate response for Catholics confronted with a heretical regime and Church, so, from the late 1580s, this hard-line recusant notion of Catholic order had become associated with Hispanophilia and an unwillingness to acknowledge the Stuart claim to the English throne in the person of the Calvinist James VI of Scotland. The leading figure here was, of course, Robert Persons. As we saw, Persons gave public expression to this strand of English Catholic political thought, sympathy and action in his *Conference about the next Succession to the Crowne of Ingland.*

However, within a short time, in fact by the mid 1590s, things had changed. Catholic opinion about these issues, opinion which had never been entirely univocal, started to fracture very openly. Furthermore, this happened in much the same way that Mush and his friends had intended to prevent when they attacked and ideologically destroyed Thomas Bell. This fracture eventually found formal expression in the Archpriest Controversy of 1598–1602. On one level, this was a rather technical argument about the exact circumstances of Rome's appointment in 1598 of an archpriest, George Blackwell, to exercise jurisdiction over the English Catholic secular clergy. On another, however, it was but a part of far wider political forces and events, with roots in the recent political histories both of France and of Scotland as well as of England. The collapse in France of the Holy League, in the face of Henry IV's stunning military successes and then his conversion to Catholicism in 1593, undercut the claims of those English Catholics who had sought to exclude James VI from the throne of England on the basis of the same monarchomach and quasi-republican theories used by the League to block Henry of Navarre's accession in France.

The effects of these events in France were compounded by developments in Scotland. While James VI had appeared to be in the thrall of Protestant courtiers and the Kirk, who were themselves reliant upon the friendship and support of Queen Elizabeth, and while the Spaniards had seemed capable of armed intervention in the British Isles, Persons's disdain for a Stuart succession in England may have been shared by many Catholics, including those who hated, or would eventually come to hate, Persons himself. Even future champions of James, such as the Scottish Jesuit William Creighton, were not prepared to render him obedience until the mid 1590s, after which Creighton openly condemned Persons's *Conference*.[2] But when James appeared to be following a genuinely independent course in Scottish politics and started to extend a measure of tolerance to some of his more powerful Catholic subjects, while at the same time disciplining the Kirk, it became possible for English Catholics to revise their assessment of Scotland's Calvinist king. At this point they could also claim that since the late Elizabethan regime had recognized, albeit tacitly, James's right to succeed Elizabeth, it had now become possible (once again) for loyal English Catholics to seek an accommodation with that regime. This, of course, was to revert to something like the course espoused by Thomas Bell and amounted to the position eventually adopted by the clergy known as the appellants, i.e. those who appealed to Rome against the archpriest George Blackwell's authority.

Faced in the later 1590s by the growing certainty of James VI's accession in England, even Robert Persons, the author of the notorious *Conference*, started gradually to tone down his hostility to the Scottish king. But it appears that even some of those who had once been as strident as Persons in their calls for separation now moved rather faster to abandon their quasi-Leaguer stance on the master-issue of the succession to Elizabeth and the pendant question of the relationship of Catholics to the late Elizabethan State. William Gifford, who became one of Persons's most subtle and determined opponents, had at one time been a League preacher and polemicist.[3] Then, in a superb irony, at some point in the mid 1590s, John Mush himself abandoned his friendship with the Society of Jesus; by the later 1590s he had become one of the appellant critics of the Jesuits. In the process, he adopted a style of rhetoric which, in some ways, was very close to the kind of thing that Bell had been saying in the 1580s and early 1590s about what he took to be the evils of Jesuitical Catholicism.[4] By 1598, Mush had also completely withdrawn any objections that he may once have had to James VI's claim to succeed Elizabeth. In that year he seems to have become a chaplain to Katherine Grey, a daughter of the rebel earl of Westmorland who was now an active supporter of King James.[5]

It is probably worth pointing out that some of the Clitherow clan followed Mush's lead here. Margaret's brother-in-law William was at one time a committed supporter of Mary Stuart. An informer in 1590/1591 stated that 'William Clederow', a client of the Paget family, had been the author of a book 'for the queen of Scots' title', and that he and William Rainolds were, together, 'correcting certain small books and pamphlets' for the press, the expense of which was being met by Persons's friend Richard Verstegan. Charles Paget and his associates did not finally turn against the Spaniards until after the defeat of the Spanish Armada. Paget and his brother had anticipated that they would serve in the invasion force that would be launched from Flanders in summer 1588. But William Clitherow, Paget and William Gifford moved, after the death of Cardinal Allen, to support Owen Lewis (Robert Persons's enemy). They wanted him to be the new focus for English Catholic loyalties and to take over as the unofficial controller and head of the Catholic clerical missionary structure. William Clitherow produced a reply (no longer extant) to Persons's *Conference*. According to Persons, in July 1597 William's nephew, Henry, was also involved in the agitation against the English Jesuits in Flanders.[6]

In part, then, we are seeing here a reorientation of Catholic opinion around political considerations attached to the issue of the succession, as the death of Mary Stuart detached legitimist support for the Stuart claim from support for the Catholic League and Spain, and events in Scotland rendered the prospect of the accession of James Stuart to the English throne a good deal more palatable than it had seemed before. But if the origins of the Archpriest Controversy might be thought to lie, at least in part, in succession politics, and in the rejection of the radical, monarchomach position and Hispanophilia still being pushed by Robert Persons, the roots of that controversy can also be discerned in wider cultural and ideological clashes, clashes that recalled other aspects of the Clitherow affair and of the confrontation between recusants and church papists. For at stake (again) were two visions of order, or rather of the relationship between, on the one hand, the causes of social and political order and, on the other, the imperatives of true (Catholic) religion and reformation. The nature of this clash first showed itself with real clarity in the so-called 'Wisbech stirs', a series of intra-clerical spats which broke out in the mid 1590s among the Catholic clergy imprisoned by the regime in Wisbech Castle in Cambridgeshire.

The issues at stake at Wisbech can appear staggeringly trivial. But they encapsulated, in immediate and personal terms, precisely the same questions about the nature of Catholic order and the different claims to epitomize the cause of English Catholicism that had underpinned the confrontation between Bell and his enemies and which were also to animate the Archpriest Controversy. These tensions and rivalries – both between individuals and between different religious orders and interest groups – were, of course, compounded by the intimacies and impotencies of prison life. Those who supported the Jesuit superior, William Weston, refused to observe the normal, conventionally hierarchical, seating plan at dinner; they sought to suppress traditional festivities at Christmas and to introduce their own austere style of devotions. To other clergymen at Wisbech this seemed not merely disruptive but positively subversive. Indeed, to some of them, it represented a kind of power play on the part of the Society of Jesus; an attempt to convert the holier-than-thou pretensions of the Society into control, not merely over prison life at Wisbech, but ultimately over the entire Catholic community in England.

We can see the quarrels at Wisbech, then, as a local outbreak or emanation of the wider ideological conflicts sketched, for example, in Henry Garnet's *Treatise of Christian Renunciation* of 1593 or laid out in detail in Robert Persons's 'Jesuit's Memorial' for the reformation of English society and government, completed in 1596.[7] Events came to a head in 1598 when these diverse, political and religious, factional and ideological, divisions became attached to, and subsequently organized themselves around, the appointment of George Blackwell as archpriest with jurisdiction over the English Catholic secular clergy. The nomination of Blackwell was intended by its promoters to provide a single source of ecclesiastical authority for the secular clergy, the absence of which had been so lamented by Mush and which had arguably allowed the disputes between Bell and his adversaries to drag on for so long. Unfortunately, Blackwell was inextricably associated with the Jesuits. He had, incidentally, been very hostile towards Thomas Bell (and, as we saw, Thomas Bell had positively loathed him).[8] Blackwell's authority, as his enemies pointed out, extended only to the secular clergy, not to the regulars. In other words, the Jesuits were outside the scope of his jurisdiction. Blackwell's brief instructed him to confer with the Jesuit superior in England. Some seculars saw this as a conspiracy by which the Jesuits would control Blackwell and them as well. The wonderfully ironic result was that an arguably long overdue attempt to impose hierarchy and obedience on the chaotic English mission produced not order and consensus but their very opposite.

Indeed this attempt to give what Mush had called in 1588 the pastorless flock of the English Catholic community[9] both a pastor and a head provoked a return to the sort of factional conflict and public dispute that had characterized the confrontation between Thomas Bell and his adversaries. Again, both sides had recourse not merely to Rome but to wider bodies of public opinion, both Catholic and Protestant. This time around, not only the Jesuit side of the dispute had recourse to print. The appellants, when they launched their appeals to Rome against the appointment of Blackwell, managed to secure the covert backing of powerful men within the Elizabethan regime and thus gained officially sponsored access to the printing press. The result was an outbreak of vicious ideological and factional conflict. This was a public slanging match, with pitches again being made to a variety of publics both at home and abroad. These were publics that were mostly Catholic but also Protestant. After all, a good part of the appellants' message was directed not only to the Elizabethan regime but also to the likely next successor, James Stuart. The aim here was to convince James both of their loyalty to him and of their wider political orthodoxy; that is to say, both of their commitment to James's claim to the English crown and of their assent to his absolutist theories and definitions of free (as he called it) hereditary monarchy. This position was, they said, in stark contrast to that held by Jesuits such as Persons, who were presented as both disloyal to James's person and claim and, in their commitment to populist and monarchomach theories of elective monarchy, as entirely subversive. Here was a threat to all order in Church and State, the appellants claimed, that was easily the equal of that represented by presbyterian puritans. Such assertions echoed those of King James himself and of Richard Bancroft, the rabidly anti-puritan bishop of London and the leading patron of the appellants within the English establishment. The resulting pitches were made through the full gamut of available contemporary media – print, circulating manuscript, and word of mouth. And, with shades of the Clitherow affair, the resulting propaganda campaigns featured, as well as developed pieces of polemical case-making and ideologically informed vituperation, the circulation of the most scurrilous of rumours about the personal and sexual mores of many of the major protagonists and their supporters.

This is no place to retell the story of the Archpriest Controversy. For our current purposes two points stand out. The first is the remarkable similarity, in terms both of form and of content, between these disputes and the earlier confrontation between Bell and his adversaries. After all, both disputes featured the same sort of confrontation between Jesuit or Jesuit-style rigorism and an altogether different account of the right relation between the dictates of true religion and the causes of social and political order. Both disputes were centred on the issue of the relationship between Catholic identity and political loyalty, and, in particular, on the best way to secure, for Catholics, a range of renegotiated and ameliorated terms from the English State, in both its current Elizabethan and its incipient Jacobean incarnations. As the controversy went on, it became clear that there was a radical disjuncture between, on the one hand, the versions of Catholic revival advanced by the Jesuits and their allies, heavily pegged to the original Persons–Campion call to arms and (at least theoretically) to unyielding noncompliance in matters of conformity, and, on the other, the very different line taken by the appellants which, even if it did not endorse anything like occasional conformity, did tend to argue that Catholicism in England could grow and flourish without setting itself up in outright opposition to the regime and the established religion.

The second point is that, in spite of these very considerable, both substantive and structural, similarities between the two disputes, this time round, the issue of conformity and, in particular, the claims about the lawfulness of some form of church popery, were simply not on the table. The issue did feature in the resulting polemical exchanges but only as something of which one accused one's opponents rather than as a characteristic or proposal to be positively owned or propagated by one's own side. For example, the appellants claimed that the Jesuits, for all their much-vaunted hard line on recusancy, were, in practice, inconsistent and weak on the subject. John Mush, in his tract entitled *A Dialogue Betwixt a Secular Priest and a Lay Gentleman*, argued that it was in fact the Jesuits who had corrupted the pure line on recusancy established in the early 1580s by the secular clergy against the scandalous laxity of Jesuits such as James Bosgrave and Thomas Langdale, the nephew of the conformist thinker Alban Langdale. This could be proved by the Society's bad example in Scotland where they 'freely permitted Catholics to go to church with Protestants'.[10] John Southcot alleged, much later on, that, among others, there were sent into Scotland

> three old Jesuits of good reckoning, Father Creighton, Father Hay and Father Gordon. These three Jesuits took another course for converting Scotland than the secular clergy of England had done for England, using more profane and corrupt policy. They gave the Catholics leave to go to church with heretics and to communicate with them in their heretical service and sermons, teaching that there was no sin but scandal. The drift was to save the Catholics from the loss of their livings but this brought all Catholics of Scotland to great dissolution.

Two other Jesuits, the Englishman William Holt and the Scot and future martyr John Ogilvy, 'could never be brought to consent to this impiety, but they were either commanded silence or borne down by authority insomuch that few followed them'.[11] These polemical assertions were picked up and circulated by Edmund Bunny's equally polemically prolific brother, Francis. He observed, from his reading of Robert Charnock's *Reply to a Notorious Libell* that 'the Jesuits taught that lesson in Scotland (we doubt not also but in England too) "that a man might lock up his conscience, after he had heard Mass, and then go to the Protestants' churches", which we suppose too many do believe and practise; whereof also comes that name of church papists'.[12]

There was some truth to these allegations about Scotland. When Henry Garnet had tried to respond to them in his *Apology against the Defence of Schisme*, he had done so with a singular lack of conviction, producing a passage of quite extraordinary syntactical complexity and opacity of meaning.[13] For other Jesuits the best form of defence was attack. Thomas Lister, whom Bell had denounced in 1592, accused the appellant priests of having fallen into schism.[14] Schism here, of course, primarily denoted disobedience to the lawfully constituted authority of the recently appointed archpriest. But the accusation of schism could also be taken to imply that those who rejected the authority of the archpriest were on the verge of rejecting all properly constituted ecclesiastical government and, for their own selfish purposes, were likely to make an accommodation with the Elizabethan regime which would jeopardize the wider interests of the English Catholic community. Thus the Jesuits and their friends made use of the rumour that the notorious appellant priest William Watson had tried, it seems, to follow the prescription laid down by Bell and others. After being arrested, Watson had made a 'protestation' in a prison chapel 'solemnly in the midst of service-time . . . and publicly before all the Protestant congregation calling out aloud unto the minister to hold his peace'. He did this in order to abjure a former act of going to the chapel which he had made, allegedly, mainly for the benefit of other Catholics. But even some of his friends admitted that it was now too late to repair the damage.[15]

As ever, it was Robert Persons who grasped the polemical nettle most firmly. In his account of the history of the Catholic separation in the English Church he argued that division between laity and clergy, as well as among the clergy themselves, in the beginning of Elizabeth's reign, 'some holding with the heretics and politiques by heat of faction, was a great occasion of the total overthrow of religion, whereupon also the same devil brought in the division of opinions about going to the heretical churches and service', which most Catholics 'did follow for many years'. Then, subsequently 'the better and truer opinion was taught them by priests and religious men from beyond the seas, as more perfect and necessary'. But there 'wanted not many that opposed themselves', particularly the Marian priests. This fracturing of Catholic unity was stirred up by the privy council and also by other Catholics. In other words, the appellants of the later 1590s were the spiritual heirs of the (as Persons characterized them) weak, lax, worldly and spineless timeservers and compromisers who, by allowing conformity to the Church established by law in 1559, had betrayed Mary Tudor's achievement of re-Catholicizing the English Church.[16] Persons certainly had no difficulty in equating the actions of the appellants with the sins of the clergy of the 1580s and 1590s who had argued in favour of occasional conformity. Commenting on the preparations made by Thomas Bluet, a critic of the archpriest, for the second appeal to Rome, Persons observed that the two prominent Catholic renegades Anthony Tyrrell and Thomas Bell had never engaged 'themselves further with the council than' the appellants 'seem to have done'.[17]

But according to the appellant clergyman Robert Charnock, it was far more complex than this: 'as for the Catholics their going to the Church, it was somewhat more to be lamented perchance than to be blamed, before it came to be a sign distinctive, by which a Catholic was known from one who was no Catholic'. But the Jesuits had 'made the going to church unlawful in England'. So stark, unnatural and unnecessary was the resulting emphasis on total separation that some priests were driven publicly to oppose it. Charnock could not, of course, be seen to endorse the apostate Bell who was still busily turning out anti-popery tracts. But, as we mentioned above, he did let slip that the priest James Younger had taken a manuscript copy of a defence, written by Bell, to Rome in order to canvass Bell's views there.[18]

Charnock said, in effect, that it was this unnatural, Jesuit-imposed equation of recusancy with true religion that had queered the Catholic pitch in England, causing division where there had been, and needed to be, none. According to Charnock, it was the secular priests who, 'whensoever any troublesome [thing] of any sort has either in teaching or writing nourished this, or any other division, bending this way', had shown 'themselves most vigilant and constant in the defence of unity and the safety of our English Church'. Conclusive evidence for this could be found in John Mush's gallant 'labours against Bell in the North' and also in the struggle which Charnock said had been conducted by Mush and William Watson to confirm and reassure the 'Catholics in Scotland against those Jesuits', notably Alexander MacQuhirrie 'and his fellows', just as John Colleton and Charnock himself had opposed themselves to Henry Garnet and Robert Southwell, 'two Jesuits . . . in the South'.[19]

According to Charnock, the English Jesuits were as lax as their Scottish confrères because they

> did teach the Catholics who were called to the bar openly at assises or sessions, in the yeare 1591, that they might lawfully (to keep themselves out of prison, for not going to the church) yield to go to this or that learned

Protestant to confer with him in matters of their faith; which could imply no other (at the least in the face of the world) than a doubt of their faith, or a contentment to be instructed in their faith by such as, in their conscience, they took for heretics; and consequently it was a denial of their faith before men.

Robert Southwell himself, Charnock alleged, had, in an attempt to limit the damage to the Society, sent him a message (via the pro-Jesuit priest James Standish) that 'he was now of [a] mind that' this practice 'was a thing unlawful'. Also, Henry Garnet had insisted to John Colleton that Southwell's 'meaning was only that the Catholics should go to the houses of the learned Protestants, not to confer with them but, rather as a temporal punishment, to quit them from going to prison', though Charnock thought this was a feeble excuse for an inexcusable practice.[20]

What all these exchanges show is how, after the Bell debacle, the issue of conformity had definitively been taken off the table of available Catholic positions. Associated indelibly with apostasy, church popery was now a dead letter. Any hint of division among English Catholics on the issue of conformity was a positive gift to Protestant polemicists such as Francis Bunny who, just as Francis's brother Edmund had been in the 1580s, were now extremely anxious to use 'church popery' to turn Catholics and church papists into serial conformists and then to turn such conformists into proper Protestants. This put the appellants, who were in many ways the ideological heirs of Thomas Bell, somewhat on the defensive; hence, presumably, the aggression of their assault on the Jesuits' track record on conformity in Scotland.

Of course, the appellants' case about their ideological rectitude and firmness on this issue was greatly aided by the presence in their ranks of none other than John Mush himself, who, as we have seen, had been Bell's severest critic. As Robert Charnock reminded Robert Persons, Mush had written a long casuistical treatise, in other words (as we think) the 'Answere to a Comfortable Advertisment', in reply to Bell.[21] Mush's transformation from the great defender of Mrs Clitherow and ally of Jesuits such as Persons and Garnet, to a proponent of the anti-Jesuit, appellant position is striking. But there is, in fact, no reason to suppose that Mush himself thought that he was being inconsistent here. His public stance in the Archpriest Controversy was that of a detached observer and arbitrator. Reprising the rhetoric of unity which he had deployed against Bell, Mush could claim, as indeed did other appellants, that in resisting Jesuit interference in the regulation of the clergy he was merely trying to preserve Catholic unity in the face of the real (Protestant) enemy. In this sense, Mush's attempt to bring order to the Catholic movement in the later 1590s was very similar, if not identical, to what he, and of course his (at that time) Jesuit friends, had been trying to do in the later 1580s and early 1590s in their campaign against Bell.

We have argued here that, on one level of analysis, the issues at stake in these disputes can be seen as, or assimilated to, a clash of emergent ideologies. These ideologies encapsulated very different visions not only of what the Catholic cause in England was, or should be, but also what the Catholic England of the future would, or ought to, look like. (We might think here of Persons's 'Jesuit's Memorial' and of the furious responses thereto produced by some appellant writers.) But Mush's 'change of sides', not to mention the shift in position of William Clitherow, William Gifford and, undoubtedly, many others, also serves to remind us just how close together the two sides remained. What could, at one moment, or on one view, look like an unbridgeable ideological divide, could, at another moment, and viewed from a slightly different perspective, look like a minor divergence over means rather than ends, as precisely the same sorts of arguments and sources of authority were used by the same cast of characters to argue first one and then the other side of the same questions. But that, too, had been true of the confrontation between Bell and his opponents (with Mush prominent among them), just as it was true now of the divisions between, on the one hand, Mush, in his new persona as a spokesman of the opponents of George Blackwell and, on the other, Mush's Jesuit or Jesuited opponents in the Archpriest Controversy. It was, we might conclude, the very closeness of the two positions, the fact that the two sides were almost always struggling over the same ideological terrain, using the same ideological and polemical weapons to appeal, if not to the same, then at least to largely overlapping constituencies or publics, that explains the personal bitterness and the emotional and polemical intensity that were characteristic of all these disputes.

We might think, of course, that, as the queen's passing drew near and the arrival of James Stuart in England came closer, we are starting to lose sight of the martyr Margaret Clitherow. Her life and death were rooted so firmly in the bloody conflicts of the mid-Elizabethan period, all so different, or so many contemporaries hoped, from what things would be like at the dawning of the new day of the Stuart dynasty in England. Yet the debates in which Clitherow and her associates were involved did carry on right up to James's accession, not only in the trauma of the Archpriest Controversy but even in the politics of the succession itself, of which the Archpriest business was a part. As is well known, the increasingly embattled and desperate earl of Essex, Robert Devereux, had both puritan and Catholic supporters. For those Catholics who positively sympathized with the appellants' rhetoric (and particularly their public rejection of English Catholic reliance on Spain, and their support for the claims of James VI to succeed to the English throne),

Essex's Hispanophobia, his military record against Philip II and his reputation as a champion of James's dynastic rights in England, had everything to recommend him, just as for Essex his capacity to call on the support of loyalist Catholics greatly aided his version of the war effort as not so much a godly Protestant crusade against the papal Antichrist as a war against Habsburg universal monarchy, to which both Catholics (of the right political views) and Protestants could and should sign up. Robert Redhead, the keeper of the York Castle gaol, stated in February 1601, after Essex's failed rebellion, that among the more than 30 recusants in the castle, 'whenever any advertisement came that the earl of Essex was like to have liberty, they exceedingly rejoiced, and prayed to God to prosper him. Contrariwise, when any news came that the earl was like to fall into further trouble, they would mourn exceedingly.'[22]

Among the prisoners in the castle at this point there were still members of the Clitherow circle, principally Margaret's stepson Thomas and her friend Anne Tesh. The authorities tried to badger them into listening to godly sermons which were preached there, week after week, during 1599–1600. In one of these sermons, Robert Cooke took the opportunity to instruct the prisoners about the justice of the regime's proceedings against them. Cooke 'began to tell them . . . out of a Catholic book wherein it was written that the earl of Huntingdon was a tyrant and that he had cruelly executed Mrs Clitherow and banished her husband and children, which latter part he said was false'. The Catholics, determined to refute possible allegations that they had in some sense conformed by listening to Protestant preachers, made the sort of voluble vocal protestations which Thomas Bell had once recommended as a way of fending off allegations of spiritual compliance and spinelessness. Then, in a final remarkable quirk of fate, Bell himself joined the procession of godly Protestant divines who came to the castle to lecture the imprisoned Catholics there.[23]

Epilogue: Margaret Clitherow and the English Reformation

And so, even 15 years and more after Clitherow was done to death for her aggressive passivity in the face of the Elizabethan State's demand for obedience, her agenda was still central to the Catholic issue, and to the internal workings of the Catholic community, as the reign of Elizabeth Tudor faded into oblivion and her subjects looked for the arrival of James Stuart.[1]

Clitherow's recalcitrant recusancy, her intense relationship with and absolute obedience to the most rigorously zealous priests, her addiction to an intense style of Counter-Reformation personal piety and household observance, all maintained in the face of the opposition of her husband, the acid tongues of her detractors among the York Catholics and the vicious repression of a heretic regime, still epitomized what it was to be a good Catholic. Her martyr's death even now served to confirm the rightness of her stand and to condemn her opponents as either persecuting heretics or sadly lapsed, imperfect, indeed schismatic, Catholics.

The deep and painful ruptures at the centre of the Catholic community and movement continued into the seventeenth century. Even the papal attempt to resolve the Archpriest Controversy, by a decree issued in October 1602, never really worked. The divisions which had emerged between different cliques and factions of clerical and lay Catholic opinion in Elizabeth's reign carried on all through the seventeenth century.[2] One of the few times when it appeared that such internal quarrelling would be suppressed was during the late Jacobean period. At this time, the prospect of an Anglo-Spanish dynastic treaty meant that the Hispanophobe and Gallican rhetoric, which had so appealed to some Catholics, of necessity, had to be suppressed. With the possibility of a toleration as a condition of the Spanish match, it was crucial for Catholics, publicly at least, to claim that they were united in their support for royal foreign policy.[3] It may well be significant that, in 1619, there appeared in print an expurgated and truncated version of Mush's narrative of Clitherow's martyrdom. There the first (and major) portion of the book, the part that deals with her life before martyrdom, is pared away to mere generalities about her virtues and graces. The narrative detail about her often fraught engagements with her Catholic neighbours and husband has quite disappeared. All the narrative force of the account is concentrated on her death at the hands of the Protestant authorities. Here the mucky and murky local circumstances, the political and personal rivalries and contingencies that led her to her doom have been completely subsumed into a seemingly timeless archetype, a smoothly inevitable and inexorable narrative of exemplary piety and increasing sanctity topped off by martyrdom.[4]

This reprise of the experience of the mid-Elizabethan Catholic community, allegedly united in suffering, was suddenly far more appropriate, in the late Jacobean period, than the almost endless intra-Catholic bickering of the last 30 years and more. In the context of widespread Protestant opposition to the proposed treaty with Spain, it was highly appropriate for Catholics to summon up the image of bloodthirsty puritanism and to stress its tendency to oppose royal authority and its craving for Catholic victims, such as Clitherow, in order to defend its own nasty political agenda. The Spanish match was, of course, quite unacceptable to many godly Protestants. Indeed, recently, in the North, Lord President Sheffield had gone directly against James's wishes when he secured the execution at Newcastle of William Southern, the last of the Catholic clergy who were put to death in James's reign. This was evidently perceived by Sheffield as a good way to disrupt and even to block negotiations for the proposed Spanish marriage since it would inevitably undermine and discredit the king's promises to the Spaniards that he could guarantee toleration for Catholics in the form which the court at Madrid would require if the marriage were to go ahead.[5] We may speculate that the procurers of the 1619 version of Clitherow's story may, therefore, have been referring implicitly to recent events, in other words to Southern's execution by a cruel successor to the famously cruel former lord president, the earl of Huntingdon. Sheffield found himself dismissed from his post by an angry king who was infuriated, said the Spanish diplomat Julian Sanchez de Ulloa, at his 'harshness and severity'.[6] In these circumstances it made absolutely no sense to refer back to and dredge up the intra-Catholic disputes of the 1580s. Jacobean Catholics now had every incentive to be able to offer an undivided voice to the son of Mary Stuart as he searched for support for his preferred dynastic solution to some of his regime's most pressing foreign and domestic problems. Thus, 30 years after the Clitherow business, all the local detail of the intra-Catholic quarrels in which Clitherow had been involved could be dispensed with, as a conventionally martyrological account of Clitherow's death was recruited, through the medium of print, to serve an altogether different set of confessional and polemical purposes from the one which had been in the mind of John Mush when he first committed it to paper in 1586 and embedded it in the narrative of his patroness's life.[7]

Modern commentators have, however, concentrated on the martyrological frame within which Mush, his editor of 1619 and indeed the Jesuit scholar John Morris chose to set the details of Mrs Clitherow's life and death. This is true also of the beautifully researched modern Catholic hagiography produced by Katharine Longley and of other recent accounts of Clitherow and Mush by Anne Dillon and Christine Peters, all of whom pay more attention to the martyrological, pietistic and patriarchal frames created for the story by Mush and his later editors than they do to the evidence provided by that same text for the religious goings-on in York in the 1580s. For Peters, Margaret Clitherow is, like Anne Askew, a 'helpless, dependent, inferior creature'. Since she was a 'convert from a Protestant upbringing', it was 'psychologically plausible' that she would be dependent on the priests who were the 'instruments of her conversion'. Dillon has, as we have seen, tended to portray Clitherow as a literary archetype.[8] To argue thus is to privilege Mush's interpretative frame, to concentrate on discursive and literary structures, and thus to swallow whole the (covert) polemical purposes that mould his narrative, and moreover to do this at the expense of much of what he actually tells us about Mrs Clitherow. In the first chapter we suggested that we should try to read Mush's text against the grain and to place various of his set pieces and stories in contexts other than those provided by his own discourse. In so doing, we have argued that we have been able to see something of the immediate personal and polemical purposes of Clitherow herself and, more particularly, to reconstruct the multiple contexts for her story, the interlocking levels of gender, local, national and confessional politics, the intersection between which helps to explain this unusual, horrifying and disturbing set of events in Elizabethan York and their implications for the rest of the Elizabethan Catholic community.

To what extent, however, does our recovery and exposure of the factional and ideological divisions among Catholics in this period, as they faced down the representatives of royal authority, tell us anything about that endlessly debated conundrum, the course of the English Reformation? Margaret Clitherow was, of course, not exactly typical of English Catholics of the period. She was one of just three Catholic women executed for their religion during the reign of Elizabeth. But precisely because her death was so unusual it provides us with an almost unique window onto what we might term the micro-politics of religious change in post-Reformation England. At a time when the dynamics of religious change under Elizabeth are being redescribed by scholars under the sign of continuity, of slow and almost consensual processes of 'cultural adaptation', the extraordinary nature of Mrs Clitherow's end and the text that it prompted her chaplain John Mush to write reveal to us the sort of traumatic and tension-filled gender and family politics in and through which religious change was often effected during this period. Without Clitherow's dreadful death – itself a product of a remarkable confluence of circumstances and miscalculations by a number of actors – we would know next to nothing of the household tensions, the petty victories and defeats in and through which this remarkable and tenacious woman wrenched control over large chunks of her own life away from her husband and constructed a stage for herself on the back streets of York on which she could play a massively enlarged role as an exemplary Christian, the carrier of truly Catholic values in the midst of the heresy, laxity and worldliness of her neighbours and kin. Nor could we eavesdrop, as Mush's text enables us so effectively to do, on the gossip and rumour, the rebuke and recrimination with which that performance was greeted by many of Clitherow's contemporaries and neighbours. Without the extraordinary accident of her death and the martyrological text it prompted Mush to write we would be left with just another recusant wife of a conforming husband; another tale of religious difference and division, mediated and contained by kinship and marriage, the politics of good neighbourhood and local connection; a story of Catholic continuity maintained under the very eye of Protestant authority, a perfect example of the peculiar moderation and gradualism of the English Reformations (as some choose to call them), yet another tribute to what Norman Jones, recycling Anglican cliché as post-revisionist sophistication, has recently termed 'the peculiar genius of the Elizabethan settlement'.[9] And yet the tensions and conflicts, the personal agonies of conscience, the mutual recriminations that Mush's text reveals show us that such descriptions are scarcely adequate to convey the experience of many contemporaries. In short, what the accident of Clitherow's death and Mush's text allow us to glimpse very vividly (albeit still imperfectly) are the usually hidden tensions and conflicts underpinning the processes of 'cultural adaptation' whereby Elizabethan England became 'Protestant' and Margaret Clitherow's Catholic enemies became 'church papists'.

For Mrs Clitherow's story allows us to recapture not merely the intensities and stand-offs, the compromises and conflicts, that constituted Catholic–Protestant relations but also a crucial moment in the internal politics of the English Catholic community. By setting Mush's text in its immediate context, and by reading it for the traces of the arguments and persons it was written against (and which its smooth martyrological reprocessing of Clitherow's life and death as a natural, indeed even an inevitable, expression of what it was to be an English Catholic was intended to silence and suppress), we can recover the contours of a moment among the Catholics of the North when it was not obvious that to be a church-papist was to be a bad Catholic, and when recusancy was not obviously the only or even the best way to keep the Catholic cause alive in areas still densely Catholic in sentiment but governed by an increasingly aggressive Protestant regime. Rather than a struggle between (in the main) clerical zealots and a more complaisant and realistic laity, the debate between conformists and recusants emerges from Clitherow's story as one between two factions, each composed of clergy and laity. Both sides took themselves to be good Catholics, armed with what they saw as the best strategy for ensuring the survival of Catholicism under a heretical regime and for seizing (back) a good deal of the political initiative from that regime. It emerges, moreover, as a conflict the outcome of which was by no means obvious to the people involved in it. In the long run, it might be argued, John Mush and Margaret Clitherow won their struggle with Thomas Bell and his followers, just as, in terms of body count at least, they lost their no less pressing battle with Huntingdon and his officials. One might well argue, of course, that the former outcome was considerably eased, indeed enabled, by the latter; that is to say, that the 'martyrs' created by Huntingdon provided the ideological and narratological materials out of which the likes of Mush were able to construct their case against Bell and his friends.

The Clitherow affair also allows us a series of albeit fleeting insights into the relationship between 'gender' and 'religion'; between certain forms of religious rigorism and religious activity, certain claims to spiritual competence, indeed potency, and even sanctity advanced by certain women; claims which allowed those same women considerably to widen their control over their own lives and circumstances and indeed their field of both political and religious operations. It is clear that the religiously divided condition not merely of York society but of the Catholic community in York created circumstances in which Mrs Clitherow could greatly expand her control over the workings of her household and the upbringing of her children into something like an autonomous sphere of religious activity. Her zeal in discharging what she took to be her religious obligations conferred on her a confidence and an authority that enabled her not only massively to defy her husband and to shape the workings of her own household but also to play a far wider, more assertive and contentious role in local society than would have been available to her as the obediently conformist butcher's wife that she would otherwise have been.

Her close association with rigorist priests, working in the inherently unhierarchical context provided by a missionary and underground Church, gave her access to sources of (spiritual and, of course, male) authority altogether separate from those under which she would otherwise have lived out her life as a wife and mother. Playing one source of male authority off against the other she was able to create spiritual and social space for herself, just as, through her co-option of her household's material and social resources, the priests were able to claim spiritual and social space for themselves. The intensity of her relationship with the priests and of her public identification with them as actual or potential martyrs helped mark her off from her less zealous (or holy) co-religionists, let alone from the conformist or heretical throng. It also organized her serial defiance of the wishes and authority of her husband under the sign of religion and conscience rather than under that of female wilfulness and disobedience. (As we have seen, one of the authorities' first acts on apprehending her was to try to reverse that identification by typing her not as a godly matron but rather as a scold.[10]) It was, of course, the intensity of these relationships between Mrs Clitherow and her priestly clients and sponsors that prompted the rumours that pursued her to, and indeed beyond, the grave. But it also guaranteed her status as a woman of outstanding piety, and, at least in her own eyes and those of her immediate circle, even of sanctity.

The very closeness of the resulting relationships between Margaret Clitherow and her priestly clients and sponsors, while essential to her career as a godly woman, also makes it difficult for us, just as it was difficult for her contemporaries, to tell exactly whose purposes were being served here. To contemporaries the crucial question was whether she was, on the one hand, a woman of outstanding piety and principle or, on the other, a disloyal and disobedient wife and mother, a disorderly woman whose spiritual pride and addiction to her own self-righteous piety led her into deeply inappropriate, perhaps even carnally as well as spiritually adulterous, liaisons with her priests. For modern historians, particularly those attempting to gauge the level of female 'agency' at work here, the question might be phrased somewhat differently, albeit crudely: who was manipulating who in these exchanges? Was Mrs Clitherow using her relationship with the priests for her own spiritual and emotional purposes? Or were the priests battening off the simple piety of an unhappy and uneducated woman to gain access to resources both material and spiritual that would otherwise have been denied to them? The urgency of such questions was considerably heightened (both for contemporaries and for us) by her tragic fate. On the one hand, her death seemed to confirm her own claims to martyrdom and sanctity and to provide her priestly mentors with a spectacular vindication of their own claims to represent the cause of true religion and to lead the true Church under the cross of persecution. On the other, it left her husband bereft of a wife and her children motherless.

Mush's narrative makes it clear that there was an important sense in which Margaret Clitherow actually chose to die – and this makes comprehensible the claims that her death was in effect a suicide. In doing what she did, was she pursuing her religious calling to its logical conclusion? Or was she giving final proof both of her own spiritual pride and obstinacy and of the sinister emotional influence exercised over her by a group of priests high on the cult of (their own and others') martyrdom and desperate to vindicate their spiritual authority in and over the community of English Catholics? We might well think (with Brad Gregory) that, pushed too far, such questions risk obscuring the extraordinary nature of Clitherow's witness and suffering. In order to render her ineffably religious commitments and experiences intelligible to a secular age are we recasting the essentially religious categories and emotions that framed her life and death into other reductively material terms and quantities? There might well be some truth to such claims. But, at the very least, as the penumbra of rumour, of claims and counter-claims, surrounding Clitherow before and after her death shows, crudely reductive or not, these are certainly not anachronistic questions. At the most, they are translations, into more modern idioms, of questions and issues with which Clitherow's death confronted her own contemporaries. However, anachronistic or not, followed to their logical conclusion such questions certainly do risk a certain reductionism. Taken too literally, they might prompt us to claim either that Clitherow was guilty of the ultimate act of passive aggression, allowing herself to be crushed to death just to win a series of protracted and bitter altercations with her husband, neighbours and kinsfolk, or that conversely she embraced her fate because she was entirely unable to break free from the sinister hold exercised over her by the likes of John Mush.

The whole point of the densely contextual reading of her life and death essayed above has been to show that while such questions are licit they are neither as mutually exclusive as they might at first appear nor can they wholly either contain or explain the meaning of the life and death of Margaret Clitherow. Answers to them can certainly be attempted without reducing her sacrifice either to (another) example of female victimhood in the face of the all-embracing tentacles of patriarchy or to (another) example of heroic female agency in the face of those same tentacles. Nor is it necessary to choose between a 'religious' account of her actions that merely rehearses, evokes or emotionally inhabits the categories that she herself and (still more) her biographer Mush used to describe them and a secular or material account that treats her religious commitments and actions as coded versions of something else entirely.

We can and must accept the religious nature of her views and commitments. (It is, after all, unlikely in the extreme that she allowed herself to be crushed to death just to make her husband feel guilty.) Over the course of her life Mrs Clitherow had put very considerable emotional and psychic energy into a series of commitments and convictions. Those choices had hardened into a settled identity; an identity based on firm beliefs about herself, about the world, about this life and the next which placed her at odds with many of the most important and powerful people in her life. That stance had attracted the opprobrium and disapproval of many and the approval and admiration of others. It seems from Mush's account of her that Clitherow's sense of herself fed off that process of polarization and her consequent experience of praise and blame, admiration and criticism. At the very least, she consistently took steps and made decisions that were calculated to intensify both the positive and negative reactions to her performance of true Catholic belief and practice. Asked in effect to repudiate those beliefs and to undercut, indeed, by her own standards, to abandon her identity as a truly Catholic Christian she refused, even to the point of death. It seems indisputable that her capacity to make that choice was a function of her belief that such a death constituted a fitting end to her religious profession; that in so refusing she would die a martyr and that as a martyr her witness would not merely prove her right and her enemies and critics wrong but also help to sustain the Catholic cause for which she was sacrificing herself in this world and to ensure her own salvation in the next. But even as we accept that both the causes and meaning of her death were, in these senses, inherently and irreducibly religious, we should also accept that the precise nature and consequences of her religious views and spiritual commitments are unintelligible outside a series of contexts – religious and political, social and cultural – which framed and inflected those views and commitments, giving them, in the process, a good part of their immediate contemporary (and subsequent) meaning and resonance. It has been one of the main purposes of this book to reconstruct those overlapping or concentric circles of context in as much detail as possible.

On our account, Clitherow emerges as both an agent and a victim. She was an agent because her own actions and choices – at the end performed and made alone in her prison cell in the face of a chorus of voices, alternately threatening and pleading with her to do the other thing – determined her fate. If Mush wrote her up as a martyr that was in large part because she had prepared for and chosen to die a martyr's death. She was also clearly a victim; a victim of the Elizabethan State certainly, but also of circumstances; of the machinations and miscalculations of members of the local regime and of her own family; of the extraordinarily high both political and polemical stakes that had come to surround her case and her fate; stakes of which, by the way, she must have been well aware and which her own actions had served very considerably to heighten. And she was also, obviously, a victim of a patriarchal system of power from the constraints of which her religious beliefs and profession – precisely because they were concerned with religion and were grounded on the supervening claims of conscience – had allowed her to escape – for a while and in certain respects, but also anything but scot free.

In the end, we might conclude, the religious divisions and political pressures that made her claims to religious purity so striking and so divisive, and therefore so powerful, also rendered her threatening in the extreme. Clitherow's liminal status as a (relatively well connected) holy woman may well have allowed her for a while to take risks and make claims and gestures closed to many other equally convinced Catholics. Did that privileged condition prompt Clitherow to go too far, in the process rendering her a prime target for a local Protestant regime (and a family) anxious to reimpose order and give the watching world a firm reminder of just who was in charge? Very likely. Was she then targeted not only because her behaviour represented a religious and political challenge to the regime, but also because, as a woman who seemed to be escaping from the control of the male authority represented not only by the council of the North but also by her own husband and stepfather, her defiance was deemed to be peculiarly scandalous and threatening? Very possibly. But if her gender played a role here it may also have been because of what turned out to be the mistaken assumption that, as a member of the weaker sex, Clitherow would be relatively easy to isolate and bully, to break and bend to the regime's purposes. If so, things did not go as planned. Mrs Clitherow's status as a woman, wife and mother rapidly became not an opportunity but rather a liability for the authorities. Even as she played the martyr before the alternately threatening and wheedling attempts of the authorities to get both her and themselves off the hook, she must surely have known as much. Judging from the perfervid discussions, so gleefully recounted by Mush, among the judges on the bench and the puritan ministers sent to counsel and convert her, rather than a triumphant example of (male) Protestant authority being applied to female deviance and Catholic recalcitrance, the trial and death of Mrs Clitherow turned very rapidly into something like a public relations disaster. If the likes of Justice Clench and Giles Wigginton could not be kept onside then things were not going well at all. The Elizabethan regime had recently been accused before the court of both domestic and European opinion of running a vicious religious persecution. Crushing the ribcages of pious and dutiful wives and mothers was no way for that regime to vindicate its claims not to be punishing the queen's Catholic subjects for religion but only for the most heinous of treasons. The York authorities appear to have responded to that dilemma by plunging into the cesspit of sexualized innuendo and rumour, which were deployed in order to tarnish Clitherow's reputation when she proved recalcitrant. That campaign of vilification may, in the short term, have done its job in certain local circles, but such tactics hardly accorded with the Elizabethan regime's chosen self-image as a just but merciful authority visiting condign punishment, more in sorrow than in anger, on only the most traitorous and disobedient of its Catholic subjects. Mush's subsequent accounts both of Clitherow's fate and of Huntingdon's tyranny in the North were, of course, direct responses to that fact, designed to exploit such lapses from grace for his own virulently partisan propaganda purposes. Nor was that reaction to Clitherow's fate restricted to Mush's circulating manuscripts, as her prominence in Richard Verstegan's graphically illustrated accounts of the sufferings of the English martyrs shows. There, at least, the agony of Mrs Clitherow achieved the full apotheosis of martyrdom before a Europe-wide audience.

But if Clitherow was a victim, she was also, perhaps primarily, a victim of herself. Even if she had started out playing a finely calculated (but very dangerous) game of chicken, when her bluff was finally called, she proved up to the challenge. Here the cult of martyrdom that had framed so much of her profession of the Catholic cause both came to her aid and doomed her. And so she died a victim, but then again in her own mind and that of her admirers (and now that of the Roman Catholic Church, which canonized her in 1970) she died as that most paradoxical of figures, the personification of triumphant victimhood, that is to say, as a true martyr and a saint.

Nor, extreme though her experience and fate became, was Mrs Clitherow simply a one-off. On the contrary we might see her experience replicated by other women who used rigorist religion, a deep attraction to the cult of martyrdom and the backing of certain equally rigorist (and often Jesuit or Jesuited) priests to claim for themselves prominent roles in the religious and political life of early modern England which were far in excess of anything that even women of high birth and rank – let alone once illiterate butchers' wives from York – could usually hope to play. We are thinking here first of Luisa de Carvajal. She cultivated the cult of the martyrs in Jacobean London. She collected relics and ferried those physical repositories of the spiritual power generated by the act of martyrdom out of the country. She visited imprisoned Catholics and priests and sought to maintain Catholic unity and defiance in the face of the repressions of an allegedly heretical regime.[11] Carvajal might best be thought of as an aristocratic version of Mrs Clitherow: an aspirant martyr both enabled and ultimately frustrated in her quest for a martyr's crown by Spanish money, her aristocratic connections and a sort of unofficial diplomatic immunity.

But, as Dr Redworth has pointed out, beyond the figure of Luisa de Cavajal stands that of Mary Ward. Ward had at one time had John Mush as a chaplain.[12] There is even an oral tradition, though with no supporting evidence, that the relic of Margaret Clitherow (her hand) now retained in the chapel of the Bar Convent in York was conveyed by Mush to Ward.[13] It is tempting to speculate that he might have imparted to her some of the same spiritual advice which, on his own account, he gave to Clitherow. Ward sought to establish a highly untraditional, uncloistered pattern of life for the religious institute that she founded. She was quite exceptionally stubborn in choosing between some clergy and others when she was seeking ecclesiastical authority and vindication for what she did. For all its professions of moderation and its concerns merely with the education of children and the pursuit of needlework, her organization caused a quite incredible amount of strife in the Catholic community and beyond. (Ward's institute was particularly controversial because it could be seen as a female version of the Society of Jesus.[14])

In the careers of all three of these women we can see how confessional conflict between Catholic and Protestant, and religious division within and between English and indeed foreign Catholics, allowed or created spaces within the structures of ecclesiastical and patriarchal authority. These were spaces within which women, armed with a variety of different claims to sanctity and spiritual power, could claim active roles in the propagation of true religion and the defence of a Church that could be argued to be labouring under the cross of persecution. Crucial in each case were the fragmented structures of ecclesiastical authority consequent upon confessional conflict and persecution and the reserves of sanctity and spiritual power created by the experience of persecution and the fact of martyrdom. Through their close association with martyrs and priests, associations forged in the charged and inherently unhierarchical conditions provided by the mission field and the service of the Church under the cross, these women were able to gain access to these reserves of holiness and spiritual power and use them to legitimate and fuel their own careers as godly women and agents of reformation.[15] If Mrs Clitherow was the only one of these three women to achieve a martyr's crown, that was due, in part, to her relatively lowly status – after all, she lacked both the high birth and patrons in high places enjoyed by both Carvajal and Ward. But, perhaps more importantly, it was also due to her immediate circumstances in York and to the wider political climate of the 1580s, a decade in which, politically, a great deal was at stake and everyone, even lowly butchers' wives from York, was playing for keeps.

In the succeeding decades the tensions and animosities that divided Mrs Clitherow from her contemporaries and kin, both Catholic and

Protestant, did not disappear or dissipate. They merely mutated and rearranged themselves in response to changing political circumstances. We might end, therefore, by concluding that in allowing the accounts and interpretations of the 'victors', both Protestant and Catholic, so comprehensively to dominate our view of English Catholicism during this crucial period, a great deal has been lost that should be central to our understanding of the dynamics of religious (and political) change in post-Reformation England. Luckily, if our account of the history of Mrs Clitherow has anything to recommend it, a good deal of that 'world we have lost' can be reclaimed by the simple expedient of re-reading (against the grain) the very materials designed by the 'victors' to erase it forever.

Notes

1. The Controversial Mrs Clitherow

1   John Mush's 'Trewe Reporte of the Li[fe] and Marterdome of Mrs Margarete
    Clitherowe' found its way into print in the early seventeenth century in an abridged
    version as *An Abstracte of the Life and Martirdome of Mistres Margaret Clitherowe*
    (Mechlin, 1619), but the full text (though still in an expurgated format) was not
    printed until the mid nineteenth century: W. Nicholson (ed.), *Life and Death of
    Mrs Margaret Clitherow* (1849); see also *Oxford Dictionary of National Biography*,
    sub Mush, John (article by William Sheils). The most frequently used version is
    'A True Report of the Life and Martyrdom of Mrs Margaret Clitherow' [hereafter
    TR], in J. Morris (ed.), *The Troubles of our Catholic Forefathers* (3rd series,
    1877). For the textual and publishing history of Mush's work, see Longley, *SMC*,
    appendix 1. We have followed Longley's example in citing from the earliest version
    of the manuscript, retained at York Minster Library (MS T. D. I) and printed by John
    Morris in 1877 though we have, if necessary, used more accurate readings from the
    other full version of the text, produced in 1654, which is kept at the Bar Convent
    in York.
    For an analysis of the text, see Anne Dillon's *The Construction of Martyrdom
    in the English Catholic Community, 1535–1603* (Aldershot, 2002), ch. 6, esp.
    pp. 279–80. Dillon and Katharine Longley conclude that the first part of the
    work, i.e. chapters 1–17, is by John Mush, and the account of her martyrdom, in
    chapters 18–20, is by William Hutton; and indeed those chapters are stylistically
    different from chapters 1–17. Chapter 21 is clearly by Mush, ibid.; Longley, *SMC*,
    p. 191. It is worth pointing out, though, that the 'Yorkshire Recusant's Relation',
    written by Mush, attributes the whole of the 'True Report' to one author, so it is
    possible that Hutton may simply have collaborated with Mush on chapters 18–20
    or just have supplied him with some of the material for them, YRR, p. 86. As sole
    author of chapters 1–17, Mush implies, however, that he is the writer of chapters
    18–20, TR, p. 398. The manuscript of the 'True Report', in its earliest form, was
    written before 3 June 1586, Longley, *SMC*, p. 191. For the title page of the version of
    the manuscript retained in the Bar Convent in York, which was clearly put together
    after 1 December 1586, see Plate 13; Morris, *Troubles*, vol. 3, p. 358.

2   *The Statutes of the Realm* (11 vols, 1810–1828), vol. 4, p. 706.

3 Longley, *SMC*, pp. 157–60; B. Gregory, *Salvation at Stake* (Cambridge, MA, 1999), pp. 280, 292, 313, 322, 341; Dillon, *Construction*, ch. 6.

4 Richard Challoner, ed. J. H. Pollen, *Memoirs of Missionary Priests* (1924), pp. 119–20; Richard Verstegan, *Theatrum Crudelitatum Haereticorum Nostri Temporis* (Antwerp, 1587), p. 77; Dillon, *Construction*, pp. 266–7, 278; ARCR, vol. 1, no. 1297. Verstegan's account was incorporated into John Gibbons's and John Fen's *Concertatio Ecclesiae Catholicae in Anglia adversus Calvinopapistas et Puritanos* (Trier, 1588).

5 See e.g. R. B. Manning, *Religion and Society in Elizabethan Sussex* (Leicester, 1969).

6 P. Hughes, *The Reformation in England* (3 vols, 1954), vol. 3, pp. 338–52.

7 Ibid., pp. 347, 352–3, 367–70; William Cecil, *The Execution of Justice in England* (1583); William Allen, *A True, Sincere, and Modest Defence* (Rouen, 1584).

8 L. Hicks, *An Elizabethan Problem* (1964); Hughes, *The Reformation in England*, vol. 3, p. 351.

9 Aveling, *CR*, p. 48.

10 For example, see Anne Dillon's brilliant and comprehensive analysis of Richard Verstegan's *Descriptiones*, a visual depiction of the sufferings of English Catholics under the lash of Elizabeth's persecution which was used to whip up support for the Holy League in Paris, Dillon, *Construction*, p. 164; Richard Verstegan, *Descriptiones quaedam illius Inhumanae et Multiplicis Persecutionis* (Paris, 1583–1584); ARCR, vol. 1, no. 1283.

11 Cross, 'An Elizabethan Martyrologist', pp. 280–1; Megan Matchinske's take on the Clitherow episode is that it can be recovered only by de-masculinizing it, M. Matchinske, *Writing, Gender and State in Early Modern England* (Cambridge, 1998), ch. 2.

12 Dillon, *Construction*, p. 281. For a discussion of female roles and archetypes in contemporary biography of Catholic women in post-Reformation England, see F. Dolan, 'Reading, Work, and Catholic Women's Biographies', *English Literary Renaissance* 33 (2003): 328–57, esp. 338f.

13 Gregory, *Salvation at Stake*.

14 Dillon, *Construction*, p. 281. Dillon's account of Mush's text leaves in doubt whether many of the things which he describes actually happened at all, or whether they are, instead, a collection of literary and textual references and 'strategies' grouped together to form a narrative, or rather, to construct Clitherow into a 'cosmic image', ibid., pp. 298–9, and *passim*. Dillon suggests that Mush's 'True Report' is a response to John Bale's account of the Protestant martyr Anne Askew, ibid., pp. 303–4. This may be true at one level. But one is inclined to wonder, in the circumstances in which Mush was writing in 1586, whether his concern was first and foremost to produce a reply to Bale. For Katharine Longley's speculation about the sources for the material in the 'True Report' about Clitherow after her arrest in March 1586, see e.g. Longley, *SMC*, pp. 128, 142.

15 Dillon, *Construction*, ch. 6.

16 K. M. Longley (under the name Mary Claridge), *Margaret Clitherow 1556?–1586* (1966); Longley, 'The "Trial"', 335.

17 Wadham, 'Trial', 12–14, 16, 17–19, 20.

18 Ibid., pp. 18–19.

19 Longley, 'The "Trial"', 344. As Longley points out, the search of the Clitherows' house took place in the afternoon, when it might be expected that 'no priest would have been found saying Mass' there, Longley, *SMC*, p. 114.

20 See p. 98 this volume.

21 Wadham, 'Trial', 20; for the Archpriest Controversy and its ramifications, see P. Lake with M. Questier, *The Antichrist's Lewd Hat* (New Haven, 2002), ch. 8; see also Chapter 9 this volume.

22 Longley, 'The "Trial"', 342–3.

23 'Saint Margaret Clitherow: Her Trial on Trial: Reply by Katharine Longley', *Ampleforth Journal* 76 (1971): 23–43, at 36; Longley, 'The "Trial"', 360. Mush does not mention the name of Clitherow's neighbour. Longley, however, has identified those living on either side of her from the mid 1570s as William and Millicent Calvert and Michael and Ellen Mudd. Both of these families were related to her by marriage, Longley, *SMC*, p. 68.

24 Wadham, 'Trial', 15.

25 Longley, 'The "Trial"', 344; p. 102 this volume.

26 TR, p. 418; 'Saint Margaret Clitherow: Her Trial on Trial: Reply by Katharine Longley', 34. Longley denies Wadham's claim that Mr Clitherow left the house on the fateful morning of his wife's arrest so that the authorities could deal with her as they pleased, ibid.

27 Longley, 'The "Trial"', 363.

2. *The Radicalization of the Mid-Elizabethan Catholics*

1 It is not quite clear how this line can be reconciled with, for example, the rising of the earls of Northumberland and Westmorland, a rebellion which convulsed parts of the North in late 1569. For the rising, see K. J. Kesselring, *The Northern Rebellion of 1569* (Basingstoke, 2007).

2 The literature on Catholic recusancy is quite large but, for a technical introduction to the subject, see H. Bowler (ed.), *Recusancy Roll No. 2 (1593–1594)* (CRS 57, 1965), pp. vii–cxiii.

3 Aveling, *CR*, p. 19.

4 Ibid., p. 12; D. Palliser, *Tudor York* (Oxford, 1979), p. 254; Cross, *PE*, pp. 232–3.

5 Aveling, *CR*, pp. 15–16, citing A. G. Dickens, 'Tudor York: Religion and the Reformation' in P. M. Tillott (ed.), *Victoria History of the County of York: The City of York* (Oxford, 1961), pp. 148f.

6 Kesselring, *The Northern Rebellion of 1569*, p. 67.

7 Aveling, *CR*, pp. 34, 37, 39; *CSP Spanish 1568–1579*, p. 241.

8 Aveling, *CR*, p. 42; Longley, *SMC*, pp. 50–3. Comberford had been arrested in November 1570 at Sheffield in the house of the countess of Northumberland. Longley notes how Archbishop Sandys in 1577 regarded Comberford as responsible for the recusancy of most of the separatist Catholics in his diocese, ibid., pp. 52, 50; *Miscellanea XII* (CRS 22, 1921), p. 4.

9 Cross, *PE*, pp. 226, 247. Cross's biography of Huntingdon is a classic and sympathetic

account of Elizabethan puritanism. Cross calls Huntingdon the 'puritan' earl, but he is portrayed by her as a good governor, moderate and godly, and a scrupulously loyal servant of the queen, a civilizing and progressive force in the North: 'a godly man, severe in his own righteousness, unconnected with northern factions, and so the more inclined to impartiality' and 'one who scorned to accept bribes or be diverted from a just decision', ibid., p. 183. Undoubtedly this is how Huntingdon saw himself but, inevitably, not everyone did.

10 Ibid., p. 159.

11 Ibid., pp. 166, 228, 236.

12 Ibid., pp. 201–2.

13 Ibid., pp. 203–5; J. Dawson, 'William Cecil and the British Dimension of Early Elizabethan Foreign Policy', *History* 74 (1989): 196–216; S. Alford, *The Early Elizabethan Polity* (Cambridge, 1998).

14 P. Lake, '"The Monarchical Republic of Elizabeth" Revisited (by its Victims) as a Conspiracy', in B. Coward and J. Swann (eds), *Conspiracies and Conspiracy Theory in Early Modern Europe* (Aldershot, 2004), pp. 87–111; [John Leslie], *A Treatise of Treasons against Q. Elizabeth, and the Croune of England* (Louvain, 1572).

15 When Northumberland was executed at York for his part in the rebellion, this event occurred very close to the Clitherows' house in the Shambles, Longley, *SMC*, pp. 44–5; A. Dillon, *The Construction of Martyrdom in the English Catholic Community, 1535–1603* (Aldershot, 2002), p. 284. The periodic conformist William Tesimond took some hairs from the beard of the beheaded earl, Aveling, *CR*, pp. 41, 68, 171; Longley, *SMC*, pp. 47, 52–3.

16 Aveling, *CR*, p. 44; *TR*, p. 421; Cross, *PE*, p. 237; Cross, 'An Elizabethan Martyrologist', p. 272; Longley, *SMC*, pp. 57–8.

17 Aveling, *CR*, p. 44.

18 Ibid., p. 45; J. C. H. Aveling, *Northern Catholics* (1966), pp. 53f.

19 Aveling, *CR*, pp. 45–6.

20 R. Houlbrooke, 'The Protestant Episcopate 1547–1603: The Pastoral Contribution', in F. Heal and R. O'Day (eds), *Church and Society in England: Henry VIII to James I* (1977), pp. 78–98, at pp. 89–90; Collinson, *Elizabethan Puritan Movement*, pp. 168–79, 182–3, 191–6; P. Lake, 'A Tale of Two Episcopal Surveys: The Strange Fates of Edmund Grindal and Cuthbert Mayne Revisited', *Transactions of the Royal Historical Society* 18 (2008): 129–63, at 132–6.

21 Ibid., p. 133.

22 Ibid., pp. 132–5; see also *idem*, 'The Monarchical Republic of Elizabeth I (and the Fall of Archbishop Grindal) Revisited', in J. F. McDiarmid (ed.), *The Monarchical Republic of Early Modern England* (Aldershot, 2007), pp. 129–47.

23 Aveling, *CR*, p. 46; Cross, *PE*, p. 237; Lake, 'Tale', pp. 136f; BL, Harleian MS 6992, fo. 26r; Longley, *SMC*, p. 58.

24 Aveling, *CR*, pp. 52–3. Aveling describes very well how much of the York administration was Catholic in inclination, ibid., pp. 62f. As David Palliser points out, Cripling was extremely outspoken. He made no attempt to enforce the recusancy laws; he censured a sermon by the minster chancellor, and was said to have uttered '"very unseemly and foul words" against the clergy, which had encouraged like-minded people to post street bills with "filthy and lewd speeches"'. He was therefore

imprisoned by the council and was deprived by the corporation both of his gown and of the freedom of the city. Palliser comments that Cripling had probably 'received much support from lesser citizens', and that 'religious conflict was sharpened by class antagonisms', Palliser, *Tudor York*, p. 254.

25   Clitherow was not the only one in York who may have moved into a more overt and visible rejection of the national Church at this time. Janet Geldard, for example, confessed in August 1577 that she had been a recusant for about a year, Aveling, *CR*, p. 178; see also Longley, *SMC*, pp. 57, 58.

26   Lake, 'A Tale', pp. 137–8. The campaign to save Grindal reached a peak with the arrest, trial and execution of the seminary priest Cuthbert Mayne in late 1577, ibid., pp. 139f.

27   PRO, SP 12/117/9, fo. 20r.

28   For a numerical breakdown of the survey, diocese by diocese, see W. R. Trimble, *The Catholic Laity in Elizabethan England 1558–1603* (Cambridge, MA, 1964), pp. 81–8. The privy council summoned before them the leading gentry recusants named on the returns and tried to coerce them into submission, F. X. Walker, 'The Implementation of the Elizabethan Statutes against Recusants 1581–1603' (PhD, London, 1961), p. 49.

29   *Miscellanea XII* (CRS 22, 1921), pp. 12–38; for Comberford and Clitherow, see ibid., pp. 4, 18, 20; Cross, 'An Elizabethan Martyrologist', p. 272; Longley, *SMC*, p. 58. For a physical description of York Castle and its prison accommodation, see Aveling, *CR*, pp. 63–4; Longley, *SMC*, pp. 60–1.

30   BL, Harleian MS 6992, no. 26, fo. 50r.

31   Aveling, *CR*, p. 43. Aveling shows that by 1578 the 'core of the recusant body was largely composed of women, matriarchs of tradesmen's families'. Of the city's 25 parishes, 19 contained recusants, but 25 per cent of them were resident in the parish of Christ Church, also known as Holy Trinity, King's Court, in other words close to the house of Margaret Clitherow; this group included nine butchers' wives, ibid., p. 65.

32   A. Walsham, *Church Papists* (Woodbridge, 1993), p. 81; F. Dolan, *Whores of Babylon* (Ithaca, 1999), p. 66.

33   See Bowler, *Recusant Roll No. 2 (1593–1594)*, pp. xxxiv–v. In some cases, Catholic wives' spiritual freedom was acknowledged and allowed, even if with a bad grace, by the agents of the State who were supposed to be the guarantors of conformity. For example, in January 1597, Ralph, Lord Eure petitioned Lord Burghley for the release from the common gaol at Durham of his kinswoman Mrs Tempest (Isabel Lampton, the wife of Nicholas Tempest, and the relative of a recent Catholic martyr, Joseph Lampton). Eure urged her release because 'her husband is truly religious, frequenting divine service, sermons and communicates, accompanying me therein at Newcastle the last coronation day of our sovereign'; the rest of his household was similarly obedient. Mrs Tempest was, according to Eure, rather different from Mrs Clitherow (on whom Eure, as vice-president of the council in the North, had sat in judgement in 1586) in that she did not 'persuade child or friend to her religion, neither does she entertain seminary [priest] or offensive person to the State, only blinded in this her devotion, a sickly woman in body, having many young children', BL, Lansdowne MS 82, no. 11, fo. 22r.

34 Aveling, *CR*, pp. 176–7, 186, 187, 194.
35 Ibid., p. 176.
36 Ibid.; S. T. Bindoff, *House of Commons* (3 vols, 1982), vol. 1, pp. 424–5.
37 Aveling, *CR*, p. 206. There are many cases, in the personal statements of prospective candidates for entry into the English College in Rome in the period after 1598, of families which were divided in religion. Some of these divisions were evidently quite acrimonious, A. Kenny (ed.), *Responsa Scholarum* (2 vols, 1954–1955), vols 1 and 2, *passim*. In 1616, a pamphlet described the case of Margaret Vincent. She had killed her two children whom her husband was insisting on bringing up in conformity to the Church of England. A Catholic newsletter narrated how she had been 'long since afflicted together with her husband, a schismatic, by pursuivants and other means'. But when her family tried to force her into conformity and when the authorities tried to remove her children from her 'she fled up into a loft' with her children and 'slew them both'; she was executed at Tyburn, P. Lake and M. Questier, 'Prisons, Priests and People' in N. Tyacke (ed.), *England's Long Reformation 1500–1800* (1998), pp. 195–234, at p. 219; AAW, A XV, no. 98, p. 259; M. Lee (ed.), *Dudley Carleton to John Chamberlain 1603–1624* (New Brunswick, NJ, 1972), p. 204; N. McClure (ed.), *The Letters of John Chamberlain* (2 vols, Philadelphia, 1939), vol. 2, pp. 1–2.
38 On 8 April 1578 Mr Clitherow, along with two other York men, 'took bonds' for 'their wives to return to the castle on 26 June'. In the mean time their wives were 'not to leave their houses except to go to church and not to confer or meet any known disobedient persons', Aveling, *CR*, pp. 58, 180–1. In fact, on 30 June 1578, Margaret Clitherow was dispensed from returning to prison as long as John Clitherow continued to pay her forfeitures, ibid., p. 181. For the payment of these forfeitures, see ibid., p. 182.
39 TR, pp. 409–10.
40 Ibid., p. 414.
41 See p. 37–8 this volume.
42 TR, pp. 406–7; BCA, LD, pp. 73–4.
43 TR, pp. 407–8. John Clitherow was much older than Margaret, who was his second wife, Longley, *SMC*, p. 37.
44 See Aveling, *CR*, pp. 183f.
45 P. Lake and M. Questier, 'Puritans, Papists and the "Public Sphere" in Early Modern England: The Edmund Campion Affair in Context', *Journal of Modern History* 72 (2000): 587–627.
46 Aveling, *CR*, p. 194; Cross, 'An Elizabethan Martyrologist', p. 272; Longley, *SMC*, p. 61.
47 Aveling, *CR*, pp. 194, 196, 197, 198, 201; Longley, *SMC*, pp. 69, 117.
48 Aveling, *CR*, pp. 194, 195, 196, 197–8.
49 Cross, *PE*, pp. 206–7. As Cross points out, 'the rapidly deteriorating situation in Scotland and England's worsening relations with Spain' meant that 1580 was a 'turning-point in Huntingdon's government in the North'. He was granted 'the specifically military office of lord lieutenant' in addition to his powers as lord president, Cross, *PE*, p. 207.
50 Ibid., pp. 208–9.
51 Ibid., pp. 210–11; *CSP Spanish 1580–1586*, p. 85.

52   Cross, *PE*, pp. 233–4; P. Hughes, *The Reformation in England* (3 vols, 1954), vol. 3, pp. 427–40.

53   Aveling, *CR*, pp. 65–6.

54   Ibid., p. 69.

55   Ibid.

56   T. McCoog, *The Society of Jesus in Ireland, Scotland, and England 1541–1588: 'Our Way of Proceeding?'* (Leiden, 1996), pp. 143–5.

57   Aveling, *CR*, p. 73.

58   Longley notes that Bell, who had relinquished his curacy at Thirsk in 1570, was at one point put in the stocks with William Tesimond, Longley, *SMC*, p. 59.

59   A. Kenny, 'A Martyr Manqué: The Early Life of Anthony Tyrrell', *Clergy Review* 42 (1957), pp. 651–68, at pp. 663–5; Longley, *SMC*, p. 77. Since Margaret Clitherow had been released from the castle in April 1581 she presumably would not have met Bell, ibid., p. 61.

60   Kenny, 'A Martyr Manqué', pp. 666–7; Anstruther, vol. 1, pp. 29–30, 203; Archivum Romanum Societatis Jesu, Stonyhurst Anglia MS 30/i, fo. 296r; *CSPD Addenda 1580–1625*, p. 72. Tyrrell had himself been part of the Campion agitation. He claimed to have disputed with Gabriel Goodman and John Aylmer during 1581. He was not tried for treason as Campion and others were, but he broke prison in December 1581, shortly after Campion's execution. It was said in January 1582 that he was being harboured by Lady Paget. He then went north in order to join Bell.

61   For the proceedings against her at the quarter sessions on 8 March 1583, see Longley, *SMC*, p. 79.

62   In June 1584 it was reported by one Thomas Layton that Bell (using his alias of Burton) was a 'sayer of Mass and a preacher in Derbyshire', PRO, SP 12/171/45. By September 1584 he was in Lancashire, when he was nearly arrested, Anstruther, vol. 1, p. 30.

63   PRO, SP 12/153/78, fo. 153r–v; Cross, 'An Elizabethan Martyrologist', pp. 272, 278; Longley, *SMC*, pp. 61, 79, 85; *ODNB* (*sub* Vavasour, Thomas; article by Richard Rex); K. M. Longley, 'Three Sites in the City of York', *Recusant History* 12 (1973): 1–7, at 4–6. Aveling, however, argues that Campion's 'mission tour of the North avoided York', Aveling, *CR*, p. 70; cf. Aveling, *Northern Catholics*, p. 60. Vavasour's eldest son, Thomas, had travelled with Mush to the English College in Rome in 1576, Cross, 'An Elizabethan Martyrologist', p. 276. Longley comments that on 4 August 1581 Huntingdon was instructed by the privy council to raid the homes of Campion's harbourers in Yorkshire; 11 days later, Mrs Vavasour was arrested by a search party which included Clitherow's stepfather Henry May. She spent the rest of her life in prison, Longley, *SMC*, pp. 72–3.

64   Cross, 'An Elizabethan Martyrologist', p. 276. Grindal and Huntingdon had thought it a good idea to shut Dr Vavasour up in solitary confinement at Hull where he would be able to 'talk' only to the 'walls', Cross, *PE*, p. 230.

3. Mrs Clitherow, Her Catholic Household and Her (both Protestant and Catholic) Enemies

1   BL, Lansdowne MS 72, no. 48, fo. 134r; Gregory Martin, *A Treatise of Schisme*

(Douai [imprint false; printed in London], 1578), sig. Diir; P. Holmes, *Resistance and Compromise* (Cambridge, 1982), p. 86.

2 F. Dolan, *Whores of Babylon* (Ithaca, 1999), pp. 50, 87–90 and *passim*; John Gee, *The Foot out of the Snare* (1624), sigs Mr, L2r–v, cited in Dolan, *Whores of Babylon*, p. 88.

3 TR, pp. 368–9, 376; BCA, LD, pp. 15–16, 27.

4 TR, pp. 368–9; Longley, *SMC*, p. 37. Mr Clitherow was a widower who already had two children, A. Dillon, *The Construction of Martyrdom in the English Catholic Community, 1535–1603* (Aldershot, 2002), p. 282. For his protestation of his conformity in July 1593, when he was trying to secure his daughter Anne's release from Lancaster gaol, see BCA, 8C, no. 4.

5 TR, pp. 370, 371–2, 375, 399–400; BCA, LD, pp. 17, 62–3; Longley, *SMC*, pp. 41, 104–5 (for the renewal of the shop's lease in December 1585), but cf. ibid., p. 100.

6 For Henry May's marriage to Jane Middleton in 1567, four months after the death of Thomas Middleton (Margaret Clitherow's father), see ibid., p. 19.

7 TR, p. 375.

8 Ibid., pp. 390–2; BCA, LD, pp. 48–50.

9 TR, p. 394.

10 Ibid., pp. 393–4; BCA, LD, pp. 52–3.

11 TR, pp. 391–2, 394, 396–7; BCA, LD, p. 58; Longley, *SMC*, pp. 50, 53. For Katharine Longley's speculation as to the link between Mrs Clitherow's assistance given to women in childbirth and the services provided by Dr Vavasour's wife to women who were approaching labour, see ibid., p. 50.

12 Dillon, *Construction*, pp. 313–14.

13 TR, p. 377; BCA, LD, p. 29.

14 Longley, *SMC*, p. 50; p. 15 this volume.

15 TR, pp. 389–90; BCA, LD, pp. 46, 47.

16 TR, p. 387. The chronological structure of Mush's narrative is not always entirely clear, but it appears that when he writes that, 'after her deliverance out of prison, she forthwith provided a place, and all things convenient, that God might be served in her house', this is a reference to her release in April 1581, ibid., p. 387; BCA, LD, p. 43.

17 TR, pp. 388, 387, 400–1; BCA, LD, pp. 44, 45.

18 TR, pp. 409–10; Longley, *SMC*, p. 63; p. 21 this volume.

19 As Claire Cross notes, 'fresh from Rome, Mush passed on to . . . Clitherow some of the spiritual practices he had experienced at the English College', Cross, 'An Elizabethan Martyrologist', p. 278.

20 TR, pp. 381–2; BCA, LD, pp. 35–6; Longley, *SMC*, pp. 97, 98.

21 TR, pp. 378–9; BCA, LD, pp. 29–30.

22 TR, p. 375.

23 Ibid., pp. 376, 383–5; BCA, LD, pp. 37–8, 39–40; Longley, *SMC*, p. 69.

24 TR, pp. 402, 403; BCA, LD, p. 67.

25 TR, pp. 385, 386, 398–9, 370–1; BCA, LD, pp. 42, 40.

26 TR, pp. 405, 371, 408, 373.

27 Ibid., pp. 392–3; BCA, LD, pp. 51–2.

28 TR, pp. 377, 376; BCA, LD, p. 27.
29 TR, pp. 405, 404.
30 Ibid., pp. 404–6; BCA, LD, pp. 71–2.
31 TR, p. 385; BCA, LD, p. 41.
32 TR, pp. 404–5.
33 Ibid., pp. 385–6, 366.

4. The Quarrels of the English Catholic Community

1 Alexandra Walsham's account of church papistry in this period suggests that history was on the side of those who rejected the separatist path urged by some Catholic polemicists. The opponents of out-and-out recusancy were more realistic when they argued that, if Catholics were wedged between the rock of obstinate recusancy and the hard place of government displeasure, then that rock was probably not one on which a Church could be built, A. Walsham, *Church Papists* (1993), chs 3, 4. It is impossible in the space available here to do justice to the originality of Professor Walsham's book, which virtually created a new topic in the field and, like John Bossy's *English Catholic Community 1570–1850* (New York, 1975), served as an exemplary exercise in the recovery of post-Reformation religious identity.
2 See Walsham, *Church Papists*. On the impact of the Persons and Campion mission, see P. Lake and M. Questier, 'Puritans, Papists and the "Public Sphere" in Early Modern England', *Journal of Modern History* 72 (2000): 587–627; T. M. McCoog, 'The English Jesuit Mission and the French Match 1579–1581', *Catholic Historical Review* 87 (2001): 185–213.
3 Persons, *Brief Discours*, fos 3r–v, 4v–5r.
4 Ibid., fo. 2r.
5 Ibid., fos 4v–5r.
6 Garnet, *An Apology*, p.125.
7 Lake and Questier, 'Puritans, Papists and the "Public Sphere"'.
8 See p. 27 this volume.
9 See T. McCoog, *The Society of Jesus in Ireland, Scotland, and England 1541–1588: 'Our Way of Proceeding?'* (Leiden, 1996), pp. 145, 156, 166, 167, 169; idem, '"Godly Confessor of Christ": The Mystery of James Bosgrave', *Jezuicka Ars Historica* (Krakow, 2001), pp. 355–75, at pp. 363–4. Alban Langdale wrote in defence of the practice of occasional conformity and, in particular, of some of the positions which were later advocated by Thomas Bell, Walsham, *Church Papists*, pp. 51–6.
10 Persons, *Brief Discours*, *passim*, reasons 4 and 5, fo. 29r; Garnet, *An Apology*, p. 78.
11 BL, Additional MS 39380, fos 18v–19r; Persons, *Brief Discours*, fo. 16v.
12 Ibid., fo. 19v.
13 Ibid., fo. 43v.
14 Ibid., fo. 43r.
15 Ibid., fo. 23r–v.
16 Garnet, *An Apology*, p. 95.
17 Persons, *Brief Discours*, fos 41v–2r.

18 Garnet, *An Apology*, pp. 49–50, 76, 74.
19 Persons, *Brief Discours*, fo. 60v; see also Garnet, *An Apology*, p. 58.
20 Persons, *Brief Discours*, fo. 22v.
21 Garnet, *An Apology*, pp. 42–6.
22 Ibid., pp. 91, 121, 181, 180.
23 Ibid., pp. 100–1.
24 Persons, *Brief Discours*, fo. 64v.
25 Ibid., fos 34v–5r.
26 Garnet, *An Apology*, p. 94.
27 Persons, *Brief Discours*, fos 9r, 14r–v.
28 Garnet, *An Apology*, p. 84; see also Persons, *Brief Discours*, fo. 61v.
29 He had been arrested and was imprisoned in York, whence he absconded in 1576, Aveling, *CR*, p. 62.
30 ABSJ, Stonyhurst MS Anglia VI, no. 19; WHN, p. 300; K. J. Kesselring, *The Northern Rebellion of 1569* (Basingstoke, 2007), p. 16; see also Francis Walsingham, *A Search Made into Matters of Religion* (St Omer, 1609), p. 58; Longley, *SMC*, p. 59.
31 As late as August 1592, however, shortly before his defection to the Church of England, Bell was described by James Younger as one of those Catholics who could be described as 'ill affected' to the queen's government, PRO, SP 12/242/127, fo. 230r.
32 Longley, 'The "Trial"', 354; Richard Verstegan, *Theatrum Crudelitatum Haereticorum Nostri Temporis* (Antwerp, 1587), p. 77; Longley, *SMC*, p. 59; plate 12 this volume.
33 BL, Additional MS 39380, fo. 19r; see also Persons, *Brief Discours*, fos 15v–18r, 59v.
34 Ibid., fo. 62r–v.
35 'An Answere', fo. 5r and *passim* (for the attribution of this manuscript tract to John Mush, see pp. 109, 224 this volume); A. Walsham, '"Yielding to the Extremity of the Time": Conformity, Orthodoxy and the Post-Reformation Catholic Community', in P. Lake and M. Questier (eds), *Conformity and Orthodoxy in the English Church, c. 1560–1660* (2000), pp. 211–36, at p. 220.
36 See e.g. Garnet, *An Apology*, pp. 52–4; *idem*, *A Treatise*, pp. 155–6.
37 Garnet, *An Apology*, pp. 19–20.
38 'An Answere', fo. 35v.
39 Ibid., fos 3r, 5r–6r; Lake and Questier, 'Puritans, Papists and the "Public Sphere"', pp. 623–4; *Statutes of the Realm* (11 vols, 1810–1828), vol. 4, p. 354.
40 See pp. 64, 96, 97 and 159 this volume. The porous nature of the line between conformity and separation was demonstrated also by the case of the priest Richard Simpson. In May 1588, Mush said that he regarded Simpson as one of those who properly understood where to draw the line between recusancy and conformity, even though his negotiations with the authorities had procured him a reprieve, following his arrest in January and trial at the Derby assizes. Mush wrote that 'Mr Simpson in Derby church' had been 'moved' to make his protestation there 'by the spirit of God, zeal to the Catholic faith and hatred to heresy'. This, in fact, appears to have been an exact performance of Bell's prescription for the would-be Catholic conformist. But what might, to some, have looked like an attempt at partial conformity was being

interpreted here, by Mush, as a divinely inspired act of defiance, 'An Answere', fo. 42r. Richard Challoner recorded that Simpson had wavered for a time before steeling himself before his final conflict with the executioner on the scaffold in Derby on 24 July 1588, Richard Challoner, ed. J. H. Pollen, *Memoirs of Missionary Priests* (1924), p. 132; Anstruther, vol. 1, pp. 316–17.

41 Garnet, *An Apology*, pp. 4–5.

42 Persons, *Brief Discours*, fos 44v–5r.

43 'An Answere', fos 57v, 36v.

44 Garnet, *An Apology*, p. 41.

45 Among the conformist arguments which Gregory Martin had had to counter was the claim that 'here be many good men' among the Protestants, and they have 'godly prayers, psalms, Scriptures, although somewhat be lacking, yet that which they have is good, and agreeing with the Catholics', Gregory Martin, *A Treatise of Schisme* (Douai, 1578), sig. Iiiiir. Persons condemned the Protestants who dealt 'too childishly' with Catholics when they said that their service differed 'in nothing from the old Catholic service, but only because' it was 'in English', and thereby thought 'to make the simple people to have the less scruple to come to it', Persons, *Brief Discours*, fo. 39v.

46 Robert Persons, ed. V. Houliston, *The Christian Directory (1582): The First Booke of Christian Exercise, Appertayning to Resolution* (Leiden, 1998); B. Gregory, 'The "True and Zealouse Seruice of God": Robert Persons, Edmund Bunny, and *The First Booke of the Christian Exercise*', *Journal of Ecclesiastical History* 45 (1994): 238–68.

47 Persons, *The Christian Directory*, pp. 5–6.

48 Ibid., p. 7.

49 Ibid., p. 6.

50 See A. Walsham, '"Domme Preachers"? Post-Reformation English Catholicism and the Culture of Print', *Past and Present* 168 (2000): 72–123.

51 Gregory, 'The "True and Zealouse Seruice of God"', p. 243.

52 Ibid., p. 253; Edmund Bunny, *A Booke of Christian Exercise, Appertayning to Resolution . . . and Accompanied Now with a Treatise Tending to Pacification* (1584).

53 Edmund Bunny, *A Book of Christian Exercise* (Oxford, 1585), 'The preface to the reader', sig. *viir–v.

54 Bunny, *A Book of Christian Exercise* (1585), 'The epistle dedicatory', and 'The preface to the reader', sig. *ivr, viiv.

55 Bunny, *A Treatise*, pp. 2–3.

56 Ibid., pp. 9, 13–14.

57 Ibid., p. 31.

58 Ibid., pp. 105–6, 38–40.

59 Ibid., pp. 108–9, 111, 113, 119.

60 Ibid., p. 119.

61 Ibid., pp. 4, 14, 68, 87, 90–1.

62 Ibid., pp. 123, 10–11, 58–62, 124.

63 Ibid., pp. 17–18, 44, 66, 20.

64 Ibid., pp. 63–5.

65 Gregory, 'The "True and Zealouse Seruice of God"', 239.
66 See p. 17 this volume.
67 A. Dillon, *The Construction of Martyrdom in the English Catholic Community, 1535–1603* (Aldershot, 2002), p. 286; Cross, 'An Elizabethan Martyrologist'.
68 TR, p. 408. For Mrs Clitherow's association with William Hart, Richard Thirkeld and Richard Kirkman, see Longley, *SMC*, pp. 78–81.
69 TR, pp. 395–6; BCA, LD, p. 56; Longley, *SMC*, p. 82.
70 Persons, *Brief Discours*, fo. 37v.
71 Longley, *SMC*, p. 69. For the location of the Clitherows' house in the Shambles, currently nos 10–11, see K. M. Longley, 'Three Sites in the City of York', *Recusant History* 12 (1973): 1–7, at 3–4.
72 TR, p. 404.
73 J. Bossy, 'The Heart of Robert Persons', in T. M. McCoog (ed.), *The Reckoned Expense* (Woodbridge, 1996), pp. 141–58; P. Hughes, *The Reformation in England* (3 vols, 1954), vol. 3, pp. 331–2.
74 Langdale had been at St John's in Cambridge with Clitherow's mentor Henry Comberford, M. Questier, *Catholicism and Community in Early Modern England* (Cambridge, 2006), pp. 163–4.
75 Longley, *SMC*, pp. 50–2; Questier, *Catholicism and Community*, pp. 163–4; J. H. Pollen (ed.), 'The Memoirs of Robert Persons', in *Miscellanea II* (CRS 2, 1906), p. 28. John Mush insisted that Langdale, horrified at the fallout from his speculations on this issue, rapidly changed his mind and became a zealous proponent of full recusancy, 'An Answere', fo. 21r.
76 William Clitherow was, however, said in August 1585 to be assisting Charles Paget in writing a reply to the government's case against Francis Throckmorton and the earl of Northumberland, *CSPD Addenda 1580–1625*, p. 150.
77 See esp. ch. 5 this volume.

5. *The Reckoning: Arrest, Trial and Execution*

1 Longley, *SMC*, pp. 118, 123–4.
2 J. H. Pollen, *Acts of English Martyrs* (1891), p. 258.
3 *The Copie of a Leter, wryten by a Master of Arte of Cambridge* (n.p. [Paris or Rouen?], 1584); Dwight C. Peck (ed.), *Leicester's Commonwealth* (Athens, OH, 1985).
4 Aveling, *CR*, p. 71. Mary had always regarded Huntingdon with hostility and suspicion because of his rival claim to the English crown, Cross, *PE*, pp. 148, 150; for Huntingdon's hostility to Mary, see p. 15 this volume. Some contemporaries believed that Huntingdon's elevation to the lord presidency had been obtained by Leicester. For the attribution of 'Leicester's Commonwealth' to Persons, see J. Bossy, 'The Heart of Robert Persons', in T. M. McCoog (ed.), *The Reckoned Expense* (1996), pp. 141–58, at pp. 145–6.
5 Longley, *SMC*, p. 118.
6 Ibid., pp. 54–5, 57, 105–6 and *passim*.
7 Ibid., pp. 110–11; Longley, 'The "Trial"', 338. Longley's biography of Clitherow fully reconstructs the relationship between Clitherow and May. For the renewal of Huntingdon's commission in 1586, see also Cross, *PE*, pp. 207–8. As Longley

points out, in January 1581 May's name had been at the top of a list of jurymen who certified recently detected recusants to the high commission; he was one of the corporation members who was determined to aid the council in the North and the high commission against Catholic separatists, Longley, *SMC*, p. 72. For May's rapid rise in the York corporation, see ibid., pp. 20–1.

8   Ibid., p. 107. For the legal and property implications of this event, see ibid.

9   TR, pp. 365–7; YRR, pp. 84–5; Longley, *SMC*, p. 108.

10 As Claire Cross observed, the council in the North had quite a large membership but 'the nucleus of the council lay in its legal members bound to continual attendance'. Meares and Hurlestone were among the salaried members of the council, Cross, *PE*, pp. 163, 175. Katharine Longley points out that Martin Birkhead, attorney to the council in the North, 'must have played a large part in the deaths of Fr Hugh Taylor and Marmaduke Bowes at York in November 1585, as prosecutor before the council, and it was perhaps he who framed Margaret Clitherow's indictment'. Birkhead had sat as MP for Ripon in the 1585 parliament which passed the new treason statute against Catholic seminarist clergy and their harbourers. Henry Cheke was the non-legal secretary of the council in the North, Longley, 'The "Trial"', 346. Hurlestone took the cause of puritan reform to parliament, and sat for Aldborough in 1586 via Huntingdon's patronage. He spoke in support of Anthony Cope's 'bill and book' on 27 February 1587, and was sent to the Tower on 2 March, P. W. Hasler (ed.), *House of Commons* (3 vols, 1981), vol. 2, pp. 355–6.

11 YRR, pp. 84–5.

12 TR, pp. 409–10; see p. 21 this volume. For Longley's very convincing explanation of why there was a delay in dealing with Mrs Clitherow, namely her stepfather Henry May's interest in making sure that he was involved in and had control over the proceedings to be taken against her, see Longley, *SMC*, pp. 107–8.

13 Ibid., pp. 85, 114; see p. 9 this volume.

14 TR, pp. 410–11; BCA, LD, p. 78; Longley, *SMC*, pp. 67–8, 115–18.

15 See A. Dillon, *The Construction of Martyrdom in the English Catholic Community, 1535–1603* (Aldershot, 2002), p. 280; see also pp. 101, 102 and 207 this volume. Dillon notes that, initially, chapters 1–17 were circulated independently of the account of the trial and execution, though a 'composite' text was 'compiled and circulated before Whitsuntide' 1586, Dillon, *The Construction of Martyrdom*, p. 280.

16 TR, pp. 411–12; BCA, LD, p. 80; Longley, *SMC*, p. 117.

17 TR, pp. 411–12. Longley, citing the lawyer William Blackstone, argues that the arraignment would have been illegal if the indictment had included Mush's name because he was still at liberty, and 'by the old common law the accessory could not be arraigned until the principal was attainted'. (In fact, Longley thinks that Ingleby was still at liberty as well.) See Longley, 'The "Trial"', 356. Juliana Wadham comments that the impediment to the arraignment may have been overcome by referring to them as 'priests unknown', or alternatively, 'the rule may have been waived at the time in connection with recusant trials. But, had Clitherow pleaded, their names would have come out later as the trial proceeded', Wadham, 'Trial', 21.

18 Longley, *SMC*, pp. 118, 184.

19 TR, pp. 412–13; Longley, *SMC*, pp. 121–2. As Longley points out, Rhodes had been

made a justice of the common pleas in 1585 and was also a member of the council in the North. Within little more than six months, he would be at Fotheringhay for the trial of Mary, queen of Scots, Longley, 'The "Trial"', 344–5, 346.

20 TR, p. 413; BCA, LD, p. 84.
21 TR, pp. 413–14; BCA, LD, p. 84; see pp. 8, 9 this volume.
22 TR, p. 414.
23 Ibid.; BCA, LD, p. 85.
24 TR, p. 382; BCA, LD, p. 82.
25 TR, p. 412; Longley, *SMC*, p. 119.
26 TR, pp. 414–15. As Longley points out, after her appearance in court on 14 March she was sent to a prison on the north side of Ouse Bridge, Longley, *SMC*, p. 128.
27 TR, pp. 415.
28 Ibid., p. 416.
29 Ibid. For Giles Wigginton, see Cross, *PE*, p. 264; P. Collinson, *The Elizabethan Puritan Movement* (Oxford, 1967), pp. 130, 208, 394, 403, 405, 424. For Wigginton's intervention, which Longley argues was based on a misunderstanding of the course of the proceedings, see Longley, *SMC*, pp. 133–4. The 1585 statute made Clitherow's offence a felony, whereas accessories to treason were indicted as traitors also; but whereas, in treason cases, two witnesses were required, in felony cases it was only one, Longley, 'The "Trial"', 356.
30 Longley, *SMC*, pp. 186–7. For the statute of Edward I which created this penalty, see Dillon, *Construction*, p. 277.
31 TR, pp. 416–17.
32 Ibid, p. 418.
33 Ibid.
34 Ibid., pp. 418–19; BCA, LD, p. 91. Wadham notes the reprieves in 1594 of Grace Claxton (on the legal grounds of 'benefit of venter', i.e. pregnancy as the basis for a reprieve) as well as of the priest John Boste's harbourer, Lady Margaret Neville, who simply confessed her guilt. Wadham claims that Clitherow could have escaped if she had done either of these things, and that 'Clench had clearly advised her that if she pleaded she would be reprieved. What he was not prepared to do was to reprieve her from the refusal to plead (though even here he offered her the privilege of venter)', Wadham, 'Trial', 22; see also Longley, *SMC*, p. 186.
35 TR, pp. 419–20; BCA, LD, p. 92; Longley, *SMC*, pp. 186–7.
36 TR, p. 420.
37 WHN, pp. 308–9.
38 Bunny had explicitly weighed into the arguments between conformists and their opponents in the 1570s. In his abridgement of Calvin's *Institutes of the Christian Religion*, published in 1576 and dedicated to Grindal, he had argued that 'the sceptre of Christ's kingdom is not so far advanced among us as were expedient, but rather in some things caused to stoop, and restrained more than is seemly for the majesty of it', Edmund Bunny, *The Whole Summe of the Christian Religion* (1576), fo. 2r–v, cited in B. Gregory, 'The "True and Zealouse Seruice of God": Robert Persons, Edmund Bunny, and *The First Booke of the Christian Exercise*', *Journal of Ecclesiastical History* 45 (1994): 238–68, at 245. For Wigginton's battles

with Whitgift, see *Oxford Dictionary of National Biography*, *sub* Wigginton, Giles (article by William Sheils).

39 TR, pp. 420–1. For James Cotterell, see Longley, *SMC*, pp. 145, 187. Longley notes that Bunny and Pease had 'hurled insults' at William Hart when he was at the scaffold in March 1583, ibid.; Bunny 'stepped out and read aloud to the people the bull of Pius Quintus', i.e. *Regnans in Excelsis*, Richard Challoner, ed. J. H. Pollen, *Memoirs of Missionary Priests* (1924), pp. 75–6.

40 TR, pp. 421–2; BCA, LD, pp. 95, 96.

41 See Chapter 4.

42 TR, p. 427. Clitherow's Protestant tormentors also claimed that Henry Comberford (who had died at Hull only a few weeks before this) had allowed a measure of occasional conformity, ibid.; Longley, *SMC*, p. 144.

43 Aveling, *CR*, pp. 73–4.

44 West Yorkshire Archive Service, Ingilby MS 3,655, copy or original of a letter written by William Hart; for another version, see PRO, SP 15/28/58. iv, fos 169r–70r: 'A Shorte Consolatory Epistle to the Afflicted Catholikes'; see also Challoner, *Memoirs*, pp. 76–9; Gregory Martin, *A Treatise of Schisme* (Douai, 1578), sig. Iiiiir–v. While Hart was imprisoned in York Castle he was compelled to take part in two disputations, the first with Matthew Hutton, and the second with Edmund Bunny and William Palmer, Longley, *SMC*, p. 79; according to Challoner, Hart disputed with Pease as well, Challoner, *Memoirs*, p. 74. Hart's letter was published in John Gibbons's and John Fen's *Concertatio Ecclesiae Catholicae in Angliae* (Trier, 1583). We are grateful to Margaret Sena for advice on this point.

45 TR, pp. 422–3.

46 Ibid., p. 423; BCA, LD, p. 99; Longley, *SMC*, p. 150.

47 TR, pp. 423–4.

48 *Oxford Dictionary of National Biography*, *sub* Wigginton, Giles (article by William Sheils).

49 TR, p. 425; BCA, LD, p. 102.

50 WHN, pp. 308–9; TR, pp. 427–8, 429.

51 Ibid., p. 436.

52 Ibid.

53 See pp. 10–11 this volume.

54 Tesimond had already been picked at this point as a juryman for the quarter sessions, Longley, *SMC*, pp. 117, 129–30; Aveling, *CR*, p. 68.

55 Longley, *SMC*, pp. 117, 130–1.

56 TR, p. 416; p. 91 this volume.

57 Longley, 'The "Trial"', 348.

58 Longley, *SMC*, p. 141.

59 According to Mush, Clench gave instructions that the sentence on Clitherow was not to be carried out for a specified time, and made a proviso that he might intervene again, but in fact the power to rescind the judgement of the court had effectively passed out of his hands, ibid.

60 BCA, LD, p. 85; see p. 90 this volume.

61 Cited in 'Saint Margaret Clitherow: Her Trial on Trial: Reply by Katharine M. Longley', *Ampleforth Journal* 76 (1971): 23–43, at 29; see also BCA, LD, p. 113.

62 Laura Gowing, *Domestic Dangers: Women, Words and Sex in Early Modern London* (Oxford, 1996).

63 A. W. Ramsay, *Liturgy, Politics and Salvation: The Catholic League in Paris and the Nature of Catholic Reform 1540–1630* (Woodbridge, 1999), pp. 220–31.

64 As Sarah Ferber points out, much of the 'spiritual vigour' of the early seventeenth century came, even in a Catholic country such as France, from 'private parlours where groups of lay men and women, together with religious, read devotional works and refined their spiritual devotions'. However, 'conspicuous male-female relationships' in this context 'inevitably . . . called up anxieties about sexual contamination', S. Ferber, *Demonic Possession and Exorcism in Early Modern France* (2004), pp. 91, 92.

65 'Saint Margaret Clitherow: Her Trial on Trial: Reply by Katharine M. Longley', 31.

66 TR, p. 433; 'Saint Margaret Clitherow: Her Trial on Trial: Reply by Katharine M. Longley', 29; Longley, *SMC*, pp. 22–3, 178, 179.

67 Persons Correspondence, p. 1199.

68 P. Lake with M. Questier, *The Antichrist's Lewd Hat* (2002), p. 289.

69 TR, p. 404.

70 See p. 205 this volume.

71 'Saint Margaret Clitherow: Her Trial on Trial: Reply by Katharine M. Longley', 29.

72 TR, p. 427.

73 Ibid., pp. 428, 396; Longley points out that the day appointed for the execution was designed partly to comply with the direction issued by Clench in order to delay it, Longley, *SMC*, p. 153; TR, p. 420.

74 YRR, p. 96.

75 TR, p. 429.

76 Ibid., pp. 430–1.

77 Ibid., pp. 431–2; BCA, LD, pp. 111, 112.

78 'Saint Margaret Clitherow: Her Trial on Trial: Reply by Katharine M. Longley', 29–31. According to the Vatican Library's manuscript copy of Mush's 'True Report', Clitherow's body was interred 'in an obscure and filthy corner of the city', but Mush and his friends recovered it six weeks later and, finding it in an incorrupt state, spirited it away for burial, Longley, *SMC*, p. 169; see also YRR, p. 99; p. 123 this volume.

PART II

6. *Mrs Clitherow and the English Catholic Community after 1586*

1 See J. Bossy, *Under the Molehill* (New Haven, 2001).

2 Cross, *PE*, pp. 211–12.

3 P. Holmes, *Resistance and Compromise* (Cambridge, 1982).

4 YRR, p. 87. Katharine Longley argues that this manuscript, the so-called 'Yorkshire Recusant's Relation', was penned by Mush, Longley, 'The "Trial"', 340. The latest event that can be accurately dated in this manuscript is the execution of Richard

Langley, his patron, on 1 December 1586. We might note that, in the text, the writer refers to the whole of the 'True Report', i.e. the life of Clitherow, which is known to be in part or whole by Mush, to have been written by 'a friend of ours', YRR, p. 86, though this may well be simply a crude device to conceal Mush's authorship of the 'True Report' after he had received so much flak for his championing of Clitherow.

5   Ibid., pp. 89–90; TR, p. 411.

6   YRR, pp. 90–1.

7   WHN, pp. 310–11; YRR, pp. 91–2; Longley, 'The "Trial"', 345–6. For the case of Robert Bickerdike, see also 'An Answere', fo. 7r; Richard Challoner, ed. J. H. Pollen, *Memoirs of Missionary Priests* (1924), p. 120. As Aveling points out, the York quarter sessions records contain an indictment in July 1586 of the priest John Boste and of Robert Bickerdike for harbouring him. Since Boste was not arrested at York, Aveling says the indictment remains inexplicable, 'and in form (e.g. the date given) is bogus'. But this does appear to link Bickerdike with the seminarist cleric John Boste, a known associate of David Ingleby, brother of the recently executed cleric, and Clitherow's chaplain, Francis Ingleby, Aveling, CR, p. 204.

8   YRR, pp. 92–3.

9   Ibid., p. 94; Anstruther, vol. 1, p. 240; J. H. Pollen (ed.), *Unpublished Documents relating to the English Martyrs* (CRS 5, 1908), p. 314.

10 PRO, SP 12/193/13. Ironically, in this list of names which Burghley himself endorsed 'extract out of Ant. Tyrrell's last book', Bell is described as 'a dangerous person for sedition, and well learned', but it is not clear whether that was now Tyrrell's opinion of him, ibid.

11 For Tyrrell's recantations, see C. Devlin, 'An Unwilling Apostate: The Case of Anthony Tyrrell', *Month*, new series, 6 (1951): 346–58; Morris, *Troubles*, vol. 2, pp. 287–501; PRO, SP 12/199/41.

12 PRO, SP 12/193/13.

13 'An Answere', fo. 7r.

14 *CSP Scotland 1585–6*, pp. 650, 682, 683; Morris, *Troubles*, vol. 2, pp. 360, 376–8, 381, 384, 387, 473, 492; M. Questier, 'Practical Antipapistry during the Reign of Elizabeth I', *Journal of British Studies* 36 (1997): 371–96, at 382.

15 *CSP Scotland 1585–1586*, pp. 694–5.

16 Ibid., pp. 650, 651.

17 Questier, 'Practical Antipapistry', p. 382; *CSP Scottish 1585–6*, p. 683; Cross, PE, p. 240.

18 *CSP Scotland 1585–1586*, p. 695.

19 Anstruther, vol. 1, p. 44.

20 'Saint Margaret Clitherow: Her Trial on Trial: Reply by Katharine Longley', *Ampleforth Journal* 76 (1971): 23–43, at 40.

21 Anstruther, vol. 1, p. 240; P. Renold, *The Wisbech Stirs* (CRS 51, 1951), pp. 190–2, 312, 315. A letter from the Jesuit Robert Southwell, written on 21 December 1586, noted that Mush had, 'with the help of some saint, escaped the enemy', Pollen, *Unpublished Documents*, p. 314.

22 YRR, pp. 65, 81, 82, 83.

23 Ibid., p. 83; see also Longley, SMC, p. 184. As Cross notes, 'no court could be held

in Huntingdon's absence, or the absence of his deputy', and from 1572 to 1595 he attended two-thirds of all the council's meetings, Cross, *PE*, pp. 163–4. It is highly unlikely, therefore, that he was unaware of the proceedings against Margaret Clitherow, even though Cross claims that 'there seems to be no evidence which connects Huntingdon directly with the condemnation and death of . . . Clitherow, and it is unlikely that he was in York at the time', ibid., p. 303.

24 YRR, p. 65; Cross, *PE*, pp. 207–8.
25 YRR, pp. 65, 66.
26 Ibid., pp. 99–100; Cross, *PE*, p. 249. In 1578 Hutton had supported the dean of Durham, William Whittingham, against Archbishop Sandys in a dispute over Whittingham's clerical orders. In 1585 Hutton quarrelled with Sandys over the York moneylenders' commercial interests, ibid., pp. 250–1, 253.
27 YRR, p. 101.
28 Ibid., pp. 101–2, 76–7, 66.
29 Ibid., pp. 65–7, 68–70.
30 Ibid., pp. 65–6.
31 Huntingdon had refused to allow his name to be bandied about in discussions of the succession. In the 1560s, at the time of the furore caused by John Hales's intervention in the succession debate, Huntingdon described to his brother-in-law Robert Dudley how distressed he was that the queen had 'some jealous conceit of me', and protested 'how far I have been always from conceiting any greatness of myself, nay how ready I have been always to shun applauses'. He was, he said, 'inferior to many others both in degree and any princely quality fit for a prince'. He hoped that Elizabeth would 'be persuaded of better things in me, and cast this conceit behind her; and that a foolish book', i.e. Hales's tract, 'foolishly written', 'shall not be able to possess her princely inclination with so bad a conceit of her faithful servant, who desires not to live but to see her happy', Cross, *PE*, pp. 145–7.
32 YRR, pp. 100–1; D. C. Peck (ed.), *Leicester's Commonwealth* (1985), p. 75.
33 YRR, p. 71.
34 Ibid., pp. 96–9.
35 Anstruther, vol. 1, p. 240; see also note 36 below. Bell himself in 1593 referred back to a circulating manuscript tract by Mush, his 'Answere' to Bell's 'Addition' (mentioned in the title of, and replied to throughout, Mush's 'Answere'), to which Bell had written a 'counterblast', Thomas Bell, *Thomas Bels Motives* (Cambridge, 1593), p. 109.
36 Robert Charnock, *A Reply to a Notorious Libell* (1603), p. 315; Robert Persons, *A Briefe Apologie* (n.p., 1601), fo. 171r. There is no entirely satisfactory explanation as to why the 'Answere to a Comfortable Advertisement' should bear the initials 'I.G.' (i.e. 'J.G.'), though one might speculate that these initials are a fusion of the first letter of John Mush's Christian name and the first letter of Garnet's surname, reflecting the fact that the work may have been the product of a collaboration between them (see Plate 16). It is clear that Garnet was already in touch with Mush, in London one assumes, by 26 August 1587, the date at which Garnet mentioned him in a letter to the Jesuit general Claudio Acquaviva, P. Caraman, *Henry Garnet 1555–1606 and the Gunpowder Plot* (1964), p. 48; Garnet Correspondence, p. 10. Soon after Garnet arrived in England, Mush sued to enter the Society, though his request was not accepted, Caraman, *Henry Garnet*, pp. 53–4. See also A. Walsham, *Church*

Papists (1993), p. 25; A. C. Southern, *Elizabethan Recusant Prose 1559–1582* (1950), pp. 139–40. But Garnet said of Mush in 1587 that it was 'difficult to find anyone' who had 'toiled with greater zeal and charity for the salvation of souls', Longley, *SMC*, p. 85; Caraman, *Henry Garnet*, p. 54.

37 See pp. 153–4 this volume; 'An Answere', fo. 10r–v; Morris, *Troubles*, vol. 2, pp. 489–97.

38 YRR, pp. 82–3; Aveling, *CR*, pp. 44, 343.

39 Cross, *PE*, pp. 214–19.

40 See ARCR, vol. 1, nos 972–9.

41 See e.g. Nicholas Sander, *Nicolai Sanderi de Origine ac Progressu Schismatis Anglicani* (Rome, 1586), pp. 291–2.

42 Ibid., pp. 362–3.

43 William Allen, *An Admonition to the Nobility and People of England and Ireland concerninge the Present War made for the Execution of his Holines Sentence by the highe and mightie Kinge Catholike of Spaine* (Antwerp [?], 1588), pp. 5–6, 9, 11, 17–18, 23, 29.

44 S. Carroll, 'The Revolt of Paris, 1588: Aristocratic Insurgency and the Mobilization of Popular Support', *French Historical Studies* 23 (2000): 301–37, at 319; A. Dillon, *The Construction of Martyrdom in the English Catholic Community, 1535–1603* (Aldershot, 2002), p. 273; Richard Verstegan, *Theatrum Crudelitatum Haereticorum Nostri Temporis* (Antwerp, 1587), pp. 77, 85.

45 Allen, *An Admonition*, pp. 19, 16, 22.

7. *Thomas Bell's Revenge and the 1591 Proclamation*

1 Gregory XIV died, in fact, on 16 October 1591, just before the proclamation appeared.

2 P. L. Hughes and J. F. Larkin (eds), *Tudor Royal Proclamations* (3 vols, New Haven, 1969), vol. 3, pp. 86–93; Throughout the 1590s we can find loyalist Catholics lending their pens to support the case set out by the regime in the 1591 proclamation. In particular Anthony Copley and Lewis Lewkenor constructed a Catholic Hispanophobe case which was drawn in part from the politique critics of the League in France and was broadly compatible also with the arguments of those, for example, around Robert Devereux, earl of Essex who wanted military aggression against Spain but not necessarily as a component of a full-scale war of religion. Copley's Hispanophobia fed into the appellant priests' polemic in the later 1590s which Thomas Bell subsequently both celebrated and ridiculed in a printed tract, his *Anatomie of Popish Tyrannie* (1603).

3 Under the terms of the proclamation, commissioners were to be appointed for each county, and in turn they would set up committees in each parish which would do the basic work of detection, F. X. Walker, 'The Implementation of the Elizabethan Statutes against Recusants 1581–1603' (PhD, London, 1961), pp. 306–9; for the commissioners' instructions, see Hughes and Larkin, *Tudor Royal Proclamations*, vol. 3, pp. 93–5. The commissions seem to have taken rather a long time to start operating, and several had to be renewed. The one for York, for example, was reissued on 4 March 1592, *APC 1591–1592*, p. 227.

4   There was at this time a bureaucratic reorganization of the branch of the royal exchequer which supervised sequestration of Catholic property. It resulted in the institution of the recusancy rolls (PRO, E 377) as a separate series from the pipe rolls (PRO, E 372). This seems to have been a result of, or at least connected with, the 1591 proclamation.

5   The proclamation was published in November 1591 while the earl of Essex's Rouen campaign was in progress. For the date at which the proclamation actually appeared, see A. G. Petti (ed.), *The Letters and Despatches of Richard Verstegan (c. 1550–1640)* (CRS 52, 1959), p. 37; Thomas Stapleton, *Apologia pro Rege Catholico Philippo II. Hispaniae, & caet. Rege. Contra Varias & Falsas Accusationes Elisabethae Angliae Reginae. Per Edictum suum 18. Octobris Richemondiae datum, & 20. Novembris Londini proclamatum . . .* (Antwerp [?], 1592). There was a direct connection between the major propaganda statement in the proclamation about the danger from English Catholics acting as agents of Spain and the current course of Elizabethan foreign policy, pitted against the forces of the League and Philip II in northern France.

6   *APC 1592*, pp. 163–4, 166; BL, Lansdowne MS 72, no. 44, fo. 125r–v (the earl of Derby to the privy council, 30 October 1592, concerning how best to use the information delivered by Bell). On 5/15 October, Richard Verstegan wrote to Robert Persons that 'some supposed papists upon this late persecution have published a pamphlet that it is lawful for Catholics to go to the churches of Protestants', and that the pamphlet was being sent to Flanders. This may be a reference to one of Bell's manuscript treatises, Petti, *Letters*, pp. 79, 81.

7   Bell became friends with some of the leading northern godly, notably Tobias Matthew and the earl of Huntingdon. He spent much of his time writing abusive Protestant theological tracts in order to persuade recusants away from the doctrinal positions towards which he had once coaxed them, J. C. H. Aveling, *Northern Catholics* (1966), pp. 151–2; A. Walsham, '"Yielding to the Extremity of the Time": Conformity, Orthodoxy and the Post-Reformation Catholic Community', in P. Lake and M. Questier (eds), *Conformity and Orthodoxy in the English Church, c. 1560–1660* (2000), pp. 211–36, esp. at p. 219; Walker, 'Implementation', pp. 319–21; Thomas Bell, *The Survey of Popery* (1596), sig. A3r; idem, *A Catholique Triumph* (1610), sig. A3r.

8   PRO, SP 12/215/79, fo. 149r; Walsham, '"Yielding"', p. 219. The informer commented also that Bell, who was resident with Miles Gerard, had 'made a book contrary to her Majesty's laws', presumably a reference to one of his circulating manuscripts concerning recusancy and conformity, PRO, SP 12/215/79, fo. 149r.

9   Garnet Correspondence, p. 102. William Allen, at some point in mid 1593, explained to James Tyrie that the rumour concerning Bell's excommunication was spread in England by James Scudamore, P. Renold (ed.), *Letters of William Allen and Richard Barret 1572–1598* (CRS 58, 1967), pp. 231, 232.

10 Robert Persons, *Elizabethae Angliae Reginae Haeresim Calvinianam Propugnantis Saevissimum in Catholicos sui Regni Edictum . . . Per D. Andream Philopater* (Antwerp, 1592); Stapleton, *Apologia pro Rege Catholico Philippo II.*

11 Robert Southwell, *An Humble Supplication to her Maiestie* (n.p. [printed secretly in England], 1595 [false date of imprint, published 1600–1]); ARCR, vol. 2, no. 717.

12 'An Answere', fo. 79r.

13 *APC 1592*, pp. 166–7, 227; BL, Lansdowne MS 72, fo. 125r; Walsham, '"Yielding"', p. 225.

14 PRO, SP 12/243/51; AAW, A IV, no. 38 ('Copie of an Information given to Henry, Earle of Darbie about the yeare 1589, 1590, 1591 [*sic*] by one [Thomas] Bell, a fallen seminarie priest liveing then in Lancashire'). This manuscript appears to have been retained at Lambeth and was one of the pieces purchased by the secular clergy after the library at Lambeth was broken up in the 1640s. The manuscript is labelled thus: 'The original . . . was found amongst certain writings belonging to the late bishops of Canterbury, and, thus deficient in some pages worn out by time, is come to the hands of Mr Robert Charnock-Manley in whose hands it remains at this present, Anno Domini 1662' (see Plate 18). See also PRO, SP 12/243/52; *APC 1592*, pp. 354–5, 365–6.

15 Walker, 'Implementation', pp. 319–20.

16 Ibid., pp. 320–1.

17 Ibid., p. 320; *APC 1592*, pp. 354–5. In fact, the earl of Derby had to write to the privy council in November 1592 to explain 'why the service took not so good effect for the apprehension of priests', principally because Bell's 'first repair' to Derby had made men suspicious, PRO, SP 12/243/71, fo. 195r. Subsequently, a privy council letter of 13 December 1592 to the earl of Huntingdon noted Derby's information concerning the 'escape of certain seminary priests and others slipped out of Lancaster into the north parts upon suspicion or doubt had of the late search' in Lancashire. The council now issued instructions for an imminent round-up of suspects in 'all the counties within your charge', on the basis of information sent to the archbishop of York and to the council in the North by the earl of Derby, in other words, Bell's new patron. The council trusted that Derby's information described adequately 'what persons are fled out of Lancashire, and who likewise by the detection of Bell are principally to be dealt with in this search'. Huntingdon was to advise them how to proceed, and the privy council had 'thought good . . . to send' him 'the list' enclosed with their letter, 'by the which' he would 'perceive what men of the best account within the several counties charged by the information of Bell are chiefly touched, and in what points they are charged', *APC 1592*, pp. 365–6. For the lists (or, rather, copies of them) which were probably the ones dispatched to Huntingdon by Burghley, see Hatfield House, Cecil MS 21, fos 69r–70r; M. S. Giuseppi *et al.* (eds), *Calendar of the Manuscripts of the Most Honourable the Marquess of Salisbury* (24 vols, Historical Manuscripts Commission, 1888–1976), vol. 4, pp. 240–2; PRO, SP 12/240/139; Anstruther, vol. 1, p. 40; *Miscellanea IV*, pp. 207, 209.

18 M. Questier, 'Practical Antipapistry during the Reign of Elizabeth I', *Journal of British Studies* 36 (1997): 371–96.

19 AAW, A IV, no. 38, pp. 435, 436, 441; PRO, E 368/453, communia section, mem. 2a; P. Hasler (ed.), *The House of Commons 1558–1603* (3 vols, 1981), vol. 3, p. 423.

20 A. G. Petti (ed.), *Recusant Documents from the Ellesmere Manuscripts* (CRS 60, 1968), p. 37. Brereton carried out his very thorough search on 21 November. Though it appears that no priest was arrested there, the searchers found Sir John Southworth's library of Catholic books which included Gregory Martin's *Treatise of Schisme*, ibid., pp. 38, 40, 41; Hasler, *House of Commons*, vol. 3, p. 423.

21 AAW, A IV, no. 38, pp. 453, 459.

22   Ibid., p. 448; *Miscellanea IV*, p. 201. Molyneux was known to use his conformity to shield the Catholicism of the rest of his family, ibid.

23   Philip Woodward wrote in 1607 that Bell had led night-time searches of the houses of those whom he had known in the Catholic community, Philip Woodward, *The Dolefull Knell, of Thomas Bell* (Douai, 1607), p. 390.

24   *Garnet Correspondence*, pp. 102–4.

25   Walker, 'Implementation', p. 312; PRO, SP 12/253/37.

26   PRO, SP 12/235/5. As Joseph Gillow pointed out, Burghley's own working copy is bound with other maps which are annotated with the names of JPs who were selected in 1592 to enforce the 1591 proclamation, *Miscellanea IV*, pp. 162–3. See also PRO, SP 12/235/4 ('A View of the State of the County Palatine of Lancaster, both for Religion and Civil Government'); PRO, SP 12/235/68 ('A Summary Information of the State of Lancashire'). There is a document, assigned in the State Papers series to November 1592, the information in which clearly comes from Bell. It names not just Catholics (the Andertons of Lostock) who had harboured him but also those Church-of-England clergy whom Bell believed 'greatly to favour papists' and those 'ecclesiastical persons' whom he thought were 'very sufficient men to be commissioners' to put the proclamation into effect. The document is extensively annotated by Burghley, PRO, SP 122/243/70, fo. 194r.

27   The report writer probably also had in mind the account concerning the popish culture of the county, written by leading godly Lancashire clergy, which is generally dated to 1590, F. R. Raines (ed.), *A Description of the State, Civil and Ecclesiastical of the County of Lancaster, about the Year 1590. By Some of the Clergy of the Diocese of Chester* (Chetham Society, 1875), pp. 1–48.

28   PRO, SP 12/240/138, fos 222r–3v; Walker, 'Implementation', pp. 314–19. Another document named the JPs in Lancashire who were 'suspected to be inclined to favour papacy and not to seek reformation in religion of any [of] their neighbours that refuse to resort to divine service'; some of them were on the ecclesiastical commission and served as 'intelligencers to the papists', PRO, SP 12/240/139, fo. 225r. This list, though not taken directly from the surviving version of the information which Bell gave to the earl of Derby, almost certainly was compiled with Bell's assistance. See also PRO, SP 12/240/140, fo. 226r–v ('The effect of such articles as are objected against Sir Richard Sherborne', whom Bell had denounced to Derby, AAW, A IV, no. 38, p. 452).

29   W. Richardson, 'The Religious Policy of the Cecils 1588–1598' (D. Phil., Oxford, 1993), p. 82.

30   J. E. Neale, *Elizabeth and her Parliaments* (2 vols, 1953, 1957), vol. 2, p. 280.

31   Richardson, 'The Religious Policy of the Cecils 1588–1598', pp. 89–122; Neale, *Elizabeth and her Parliaments*, vol. 2, pp. 280–91; *CSPD 1591–1594*, pp. 341–2; see also ibid., p. 328. For a narrative of the subsequent passage of the anti-separatist legislation in this session, see Neale, *Elizabeth and her Parliaments*, vol. 2, pp. 291–6.

32   See e.g. J. H. Pollen (ed.), *Unpublished Documents relating to the English Martyrs* (CRS 5, 1908), pp. 212–13; PRO, SP 12/244/8.

33   Thomas Bell, *Thomas Bels Motives* (Cambridge, 1593), dedication. Bell's conversion tract was written in Cambridge and was directed to Burghley with the recommendation of Richard Young, JP, Walsham, 'Yielding', p. 225.

34 AAW, A IV, no. 38, p. 444. Standish was a JP but was also a convinced Catholic and had been a friend of Lawrence Vaux, the last Catholic warden of the collegiate church of Manchester, *Miscellanea IV*, p. 191. Bell asserted that Bishop Edmund Bonner's former chaplain John Murren 'defended going to church' and that the priest called Kinley 'expunged the same in open audience', AAW, A IV, no. 38, p. 453.

35 Ibid., p. 432. For Alice Clifton of Westby, listed as a recusant widow in the first of the exchequer's recusancy rolls, see M. M. C. Calthrop (ed.), *Recusant Roll No. 1., 1592–1593* (CRS 18, 1916), p. 194.

36 AAW, A IV, no. 38, p. 433.

37 Ibid., pp. 442–3, 448–9; *Miscellanea IV*, p. 175.

38 AAW, A IV, no. 38, p. 447; Anstruther, vol. 1, pp. 45–6.

39 AAW, A IV, no. 38, p. 446.

40 Ibid., p. 435.

41 Richard Young, writing to Burghley on 5 July 1593, mentioned that in Bell's correspondence with Sir Thomas Egerton 'he does advertise him of one Hardesty, a priest who has lately submitted himself and is now at Emmanuel College in Cambridge' (Bell at this time was at Jesus College) 'whom he commends to be very learned and well affected', BL, Lansdowne MS 75, no. 20, fo. 40r, no. 21, fo. 42r.

42 A. Jessopp (ed.), *Letters of Fa. Henry Walpole* (1890), p. 19. William Hardesty switched allegiances in 1593 and took part in the debates with Walpole at York after the latter was arrested, ibid., p. 21. Huntingdon used Hardesty and Anthony Major to identify Catholic clergy whom the authorities in the North had arrested on suspicion of being seminary priests, Pollen, *Unpublished Documents*, pp. 242, 272, 282. Walpole was heavily involved with the Habsburg administration in Flanders and also with the English regiment in Spanish service there. Walpole alleged that he had 'relieved' Hardesty 'beyond the seas', Jessopp, *Letters*, p. 21.

43 See Walker, 'Implementation', p. 331; PRO, SP 12/242/121, SP 12/243/6, 88. Younger's naming in August 1592 of 'one Bell . . . a priest . . . who goes as Mush's man', must refer to another cleric (probably Henry Bell), PRO, SP 12/242/122, fos 220v–1r; Aveling, *Northern Catholics*, p. 165. Perhaps significantly, though, Younger reported that Mush had told him that, in the North, the 'gentlemen were much fallen off', in other words, tended to retreat into conformity, 'but the gentlewomen stood steadfastly to it', ibid., fo. 221r. Shortly after, in mid-September 1592, Younger claimed that when he had left Rome in autumn 1589 he had been urged by Persons to 'withstand the opinions of some priests in England that it was lawful to resort to church at the command of the prince, upon which question divers pamphlets were sent beyond the seas on both parts to confirm their opinions', *CSPD 1591–1594*, p. 270.

44 Robert Charnock, *A Reply to a Notorious Libell* (1603), pp. 69–70. It is difficult to substantiate this claim that Younger defended Bell as Charnock describes, Anstruther, vol. 1, pp. 391–3. For Henry Garnet's references to the canvassing of Bell's views at Rome, see Garnet, *An Apology*, p. 13, where he notes that 'a certain other priest, who in England having committed unto writing some fantastical conceits of his own concerning this point, not finding sufficient credit at home, returned to Rome whence he first came, with his conceited writing; there freely and voluntarily making a humble submission and revoking his dreams, [he] burned his

papers'. It seems probable that Cardinal Allen's major pronouncement on the subject of occasional conformity, issued on 2/12 December 1592, was a response to lobbying both for and against Bell's position, T. F. Knox (ed.), *The Letters and Memorials of William Cardinal Allen (1532–1594)* (1882), pp. 343–6; *CSPD 1591–1594*, pp. 291–3; A. Walsham, *Church Papists* (1993), pp. 68–9; In mid 1593 Mush himself travelled to Rome. He arrived in late August. His journey was evidently sponsored by Garnet and was undertaken in connection with the issue of the disputes over recusancy and conformity. Garnet recommended him to the Jesuit general in a letter written on 30 September, Garnet Correspondence, p. 164; Petti, *Recusant Documents*, p. 313. See also P. Renold (ed.), *The Wisbech Stirs (1595–1598)* (CRS 51, 1958), p. 174; cf. Knox, *The Letters and Memorials of William Cardinal Allen*, pp. 356–8.

45 AAW, A IV, no. 38, p. 437; *Miscellanea IV*, p. 205; PRO, SP 12/235/4 describes John Culcheth as a noncommunicant.
46 AAW, A IV, no. 38, p. 435.
47 Ibid., pp. 432, 451; Calthrop, *Recusant Roll No. 1*, p. 192.
48 AAW, A IV, no. 38, p. 433. Lawrence Ireland, who was informed on by both Younger and Bell, was cited in the 'View of the State of the County Palatine of Lancaster' as 'in some degree of conformity, yet in general note of evil affection in religion' and a noncommunicant, *Miscellanea IV*, p. 196.
49 AAW, A IV, no. 38, p. 438; cf. *Miscellanea IV*, p. 209.
50 AAW, A IV, no. 38, p. 448. Bell noted that 'Mr Gilbert Gerard, servant to the master of the rolls, had relieved and greatly aided' Alexander Gerard, the seminary priest, who was now in Wisbech Castle. Alexander Gerard had 'sent two letters from Wisbech to his brother, in which he bitterly exclaimed against his brother going to the church', ibid., pp. 450, 463. Sir Gilbert Gerard died, in fact, in early February 1593. He had been denounced in late December 1586 as a 'Protestant at London and a papist in Lancashire'; the informant claimed that 'there is no man that so much shifts papists from the danger of the law as he does', Hasler, *House of Commons*, vol. 2, p. 184.
51 AAW, A IV, no. 38, p. 435.
52 Ibid., p. 438; *APC 1592–3*, pp. 110–11; BL, Harleian MS 7042, fo. 220r. Bell noted that Miles Gerard's servant, Humphrey Leigh, had told the earl of Derby that, since Bell had changed sides, Gerard had immediately gone to Sir Gilbert Gerard, the master of the rolls, 'to ask counsel what and how he should do in his defence', AAW, B 48, fo. 107v.
53 BL, Harleian MS 7042, fo. 220r. On 30 October 1592, Sir Thomas Heneage, chancellor of the duchy of Lancaster, had been informed by the earl of Derby that both Miles Gerard and his wife had come to church, as Parson Edward Fleetwood of Wigan could confirm. Gerard was a man of 'small reach and easily overruled' and was 'drawn to keep Bell', BL, Lansdowne MS 72, no. 45, fo. 127r. For Miles Gerard, see also Anstruther, vol. 1, p. 30. For his conformity according to statute, see PRO, E 368/497, mem. 55a, which was, however, registered at the exchequer only in 1599. He had first been convicted of recusancy back in 1590 and he publicly conformed again on 7 October 1599 in Chester Cathedral in front of the bishop.
54 BL, Harleian MS 6995, no. 116, fo. 167r.

55 AAW, A IV, no. 38, p. 439; Calthrop, *Recusancy Roll No. 1*, p. 175. James Cowper, ordained at Rheims in April 1585, was reported in 1586 to have said Mass at the lodge in Samlesbury Park, the residence of Sir John Southworth, Anstruther, vol. 1, p. 86.

56 AAW, A IV, no. 38, p. 442; Calthrop, *Recusancy Roll No. 1*, p. 176.

57 AAW, A IV, no. 38, p. 441. Bell's denunciation does not seem to have prevented Southworth obtaining, in 1593, further remission in the exchequer of the sequestration of his property, PRO, E 368/471, mem. 4a.

58 AAW, A IV, no. 38, p. 470.

59 Ibid., p. 449.

8. *Mrs Clitherow Vindicated?*

1 For recent work on the notion of the 'public sphere', see P. Lake and S. Pincus (eds), *The Politics of the Public Sphere in Early Modern England* (Manchester, 2007).

2 'An Answere', fos 3v, 22v.

3 The demonstration, made in many of the recusancy tracts, that since church attendance was simply *malum in se* (that is, contrary both to divine and natural law) it was not to be dispensed with even by the pope himself, was presumably designed to counter such rumours, or lies as Garnet preferred to call them.

4 Ibid., fo. 10v; Morris, *Troubles*, vol. 2, pp. 489–97. Tyrrell's declaration was printed in a new edition of John Gibbons's and John Fen's *Concertatio Ecclesiae Catholicae in Anglia* (Trier, 1588); ARCR, vol. 1, no. 525; Morris, *Troubles*, vol. 2, p. 489. In December 1588, six months after Mush had finished penning his reply to Bell, Tyrrell agreed to preach what was, to the regime, a satisfactory recantation sermon, Anstruther, vol. 1, p. 362; *The Recantations as they were severallie pronounced by Wylliam Tedder and Anthony Tyrrell* (1588); A. Kenny, 'A Martyr Manqué: the Early Life of Anthony Tyrrell', *Clergy Review* 42 (1957): 651–8. The priest Richard Leigh, whose name was appended to Lord Burghley's *Copie of a Letter sent out of England to Don B. Mendoza* (1588), entered at the Stationers in October, had been executed at Tyburn on 30 August 1588, Anstruther, vol. 1, p. 208.

5 'An Answere', fo. 19v. It appears that Garnet and Persons proposed to exploit Tyrrell at the point at which they destroyed Bell's reputation in print. On 20/30 April 1593, Richard Verstegan informed Persons that Garnet had sent him 'a discourse in writing containing 50 sheets of paper, being the confession of Mr Anthony Tyrrell written by himself before his later fall'; Persons prepared it for the press though he did not in fact see it into print, A. G. Petti (ed.), *The Letters and Despatches of Richard Verstegan (c. 1550–1640)* (CRS 52, 1959), pp. 134, 138–9.

6 Garnet, *An Apology*, p. 12.

7 'An Answere', fos 22r, 20r.

8 Garnet, *An Apology*, p. 12.

9 'An Answere', fo. 80v.

10 Garnet, *An Apology*, p. 154.

11 'An Answere', fos 1v, 47r, 79r, 81r.

12 Garnet, *An Apology*, p. 12; for the status of his tract as a communication with a friend, see ibid., title page and p. 2.

13 'An Answere', fos 3r, 12v; see p. 63 this volume.
14 Ibid., fo. 63v. On the Devil's use of schism and heresy to increase his flock, see Garnet, *An Apology*, p. 194.
15 Ibid., pp. 113f.
16 'An Answere', fo. 3v.
17 Garnet, *A Treatise*, pp. 13–14.
18 Ibid., pp. 17–18.
19 'An Answere', fos 1r–2r.
20 Ibid., fos 82v–3r.
21 Ibid., fo. 6v.
22 Ibid., fos 7v–8r.
23 C. Haigh, *Reformation and Resistance in Tudor Lancashire* (Cambridge, 1975).
24 Garnet, *An Apology*, pp. 196, 195.
25 Ibid., pp. 9–10.
26 J. H. Pollen, 'Contributions towards a Life of Father Henry Garnet, S.J.', *Month* 91 (1898), pp. 238–41 (printed version of ABSJ, Stonyhurst MS Anglia I, no. 73), at p. 239; Garnet Correspondence, pp. 94–5. Garnet's account, based on information derived from the leading northern Jesuit Richard Holtby, was one of a number of persecution narratives which were being sent to Rome, presumably to be deployed as evidence to reinforce the case that some English Catholics were trying to make to prove that compromise with Elizabeth's regime was impossible. William Hutton's account of the persecution, penned in December 1594, was sent off to Rome by Holtby, who also annotated it, WHN, p. 307.
27 See p. 177 this volume and p. 233 this volume. According to a letter written by Holtby in 1607, Garnet, in addition to his two printed tracts of 1593 which dealt with or touched on the issue of occasional conformity (his *Apology* and his *Treatise of Christian Renunciation*), also wrote another 'treatise about the sword bearer or noble man going to church for attendance unto the prince', though Holtby was unable to locate it, Archivum Romanum Societatis Jesu, Anglia 37/i, fo. 113r; see also D. M. Rogers, 'The Writings of Father Henry Garnet, S.J. (1555–1606)', *Biographical Studies* 1 (1951–1592): 9.
28 See p. 137 this volume.
29 Garnet Correspondence, p. 101; P. Caraman, *Henry Garnet 1555–1606 and the Gunpowder Plot* (1964), p. 171. Among Richard Verstegan's papers there is a note dated 1 June 1593 that a number of peers including Lord Grey, Lord Strange and Lord Windsor 'would have hindered the bill against the Catholics', ABSJ, Collectanea B, fo. 113r. For the 1593 legislation which imposed penalties on married Catholic women separatists, see J. E. Neale, *Elizabeth and her Parliaments* (2 vols, 1953, 1957), vol. 2, pp. 280–97; F. X. Walker, 'The Implementation of the Elizabethan Statutes against Recusants 1581–1603' (PhD, London, 1961), pp. 337f.
30 R. Doleman *(pseud.)*, *A Conference about the Next Succession to the Crowne of Ingland* (Antwerp, 1594); ARCR, vol. 2, no. 167.
31 Garnet, *An Apology*, pp. 150–1.
32 As we saw, Robert Bickerdike, whose martyrdom Mush had recorded in 1586, had been accused of harbouring Boste. See p. 223 this volume.
33 Cross, *PE*, pp. 244–5; Morris, *Troubles*, vol. 3, pp. 183–90.

34   WHN, p. 314; Anstruther, vol. 1, pp. 44, 183; PRO, SP 12/245/131, fo. 213r; J. H. Pollen (ed.), *Unpublished Documents relating to the English Martyrs* (CRS 5, 1908), pp. 240–3.

35   A. Jessopp, *One Generation of a Norfolk House* (1879), pp. 231–2. Garnet records that Walpole had a disputation with 'various ministers, among whom were two apostate priests, whose impertinences it would be too tedious to set down here', Garnet Correspondence, p. 298.

36   Ibid., p. 285.

37   Ibid., p. 291; Pollen, *Unpublished Documents*, pp. 244–68; W. F. Rea, 'The Authorship of "News from Spayne and Holland" and its bearing on the Genuineness of the Confessions of the Blessed Henry Walpole, S.J.', *Biographical Studies* 1 (1951–1592), pp. 220–30.

38   Jessopp, *One Generation*, pp. 233–4.

39   C. Haigh, 'The Continuity of Catholicism in the English Reformation', *Past and Present* 93 (1981): 37–69.

40   Ibid., p. 41.

41   C. Haigh, 'From Monopoly to Minority: Catholicism in Early Modern England', *Transactions of the Royal Historical Society*, 5th series, 31 (1981): 129–47, at 132–3, 136.

42   Haigh 'Continuity', p. 57.

43   Garnet, *Treatise*, pp. 5, 7–8.

44   Ibid., pp. 8–9.

45   Ibid., pp. 10–11.

46   Ibid., p. 13.

47   Ibid., pp. 11–12, 21–2.

48   In a letter to Robert Persons, written eight years later, Garnet remarked merely that he had 'adjoined a short confutation of such as maintained it was lawful to go to the church with a protestation'; but Garnet did not say who had written it, ABSJ, Stonyhurst Anglia MS Collectanea P II, fo. 553r. There are, however, some verbal similarities between this section of the *Treatise of Christian Renunciation* and the manuscript 'Answere to a Comfortable Advertisement' which we think was almost certainly by Mush, though, of course, this might be explained by Garnet himself having made contributions to the 'Answere'. However, if Garnet wrote this separate final section in the *Treatise of Christian Renunciation*, why would he not simply have incorporated it into his other tract, written at virtually the same time, his *Apology against the Defence of Schisme*? Also, in a passage in the *Treatise*'s final section, describing a letter sent recently from Rome which condemned the frequenting of heretical conventicles, the writer says 'neither must it seem strange to any that herein I go about to publish so private a thing; when I do nothing else but only give a necessary preservative against diverse venomous tongues which, out of so sweet and pleasant a flower having gathered poison, are everywhere busy to disperse the same', Garnet, *A Treatise*, p. 161 (section entitled 'Whether it be lawfull . . .'). In other words, the writer here uses the same metaphor as Mush deployed in the 'True Report' to describe the malice of Margaret Clitherow's enemies, see p. 47 this volume. This metaphor is not exactly an uncommon contemporary conceit; see e.g. Godfrey Goodman, ed. J. S Brewer, *The Court of King James the First* (2 vols,

1839), vol. 2, p. 392. But its appearance here may indicate that Mush was the writer of this section of Garnet's *Treatise of Christian Renunciation* and that he was collaborating with Garnet in order to drive Bell finally out of the Catholic community. It also makes it very likely, in fact almost a certainty, that Garnet and Mush would have discussed the witness and example provided by Mrs Clitherow of exactly the kind of godly disobedience which Garnet prescribes and urges in the main body of the *Treatise.*

49   Garnet, *Treatise*, p. 60.
50   Ibid., pp. 64, 69, 73, 81.
51   Ibid., pp. 78, 83.
52   Ibid., pp. 93, 99.
53   Ibid., pp. 100–1.
54   Ibid., p. 101.

9. *Aftermath: The English Catholic Community Tears Itself Apart in the Archpriest Controversy*

1   See pp. 174–7 this volume.
2   T. M. McCoog, 'Harmony Disrupted: Robert Persons, S.J., William Crichton, S.J. and the Question of Queen Elizabeth's Successor, 1581–1603', *Archivum Historicum Societatis Jesu* 73 (2004): 149–220; V. Houliston, 'The Hare and the Drum: Robert Persons's Writings on the English Succession, 1593–6', *Renaissance Studies* 14 (2000): 235–50.
3   He had, for example, worked with the Leaguer theorist William Rainolds on the text of his *Calvino-Turcismus*. Gifford completed it after Rainolds's death, ARCR, vol. 1, no. 929.
4   Mush was never as violent in his attacks on the Society as some other appellants were. He tried to hold the line against the schism in the Catholic movement which the zealotry of, for example, Christopher Bagshaw threatened to cause. Indeed, it seems that he was his (soon-to-be former) friend Henry Garnet's personal choice as an arbitrator to settle the notorious Wisbech Stirs in 1595, P. Renold (ed.), *The Wisbech Stirs (1595–1598)* (CRS 51, 1958), p. 170. Richard Blount, SJ, clearly regarded Mush as different from the other appellants, AAW, A VII, no. 41, p. 232. In fact, on 10 May 1596 Mush reproved Bagshaw, John Norden and Thomas Bluet concerning the escape from Wisbech and recapture of Francis Tilletson, and accused them of betraying Tilletson to the authorities. The betrayal had brought shame on them all: 'the people, taking advantage of this, add it to the former faults of Bell, Major, Hardesty, [Thomas] Clarke and other apostates, saying the very priests in Wisbech betray one another', Renold, *The Wisbech Stirs*, p. 181. Thomas McCoog suggests that Mush's final break from his friend Garnet came over the attempt by some of the secular clergy to set up clerical associations for the secular priests, which some Jesuits, and particularly Garnet, took to be a threat to the Society of Jesus's position in England. We are grateful to Dr McCoog for information on this point. It appears that Robert Persons, during the Archpriest Controversy, had to strain the evidence, particularly of Mush's visit to Rome in 1593, in order to make Mush appear a natural opponent of the Jesuits, ibid., p. 174; cf. T. F. Knox

(ed.), *The Letters and Memorials of William Cardinal Allen (1532–1594)* (1882), pp. 356–8.

5   Westmorland himself was identified at this time as an enemy to the Spaniards in Flanders where he lived in exile, and by his friends he was, despite his rebel status, being reconstructed as a loyalist and champion of James VI, in expectation that he would be restored to his estates and title once the Scottish king succeeded Elizabeth, J. Strype, *Annals of the Reformation* (4 vols, Oxford, 1824), vol. 4, p. 481. Tobias Matthew, who secured Katherine Grey's arrest, noted that one of her chaplains was called 'Musske', which may be a reference to John Mush, though it might also denote his brother William, ibid.

6   BL, Lansdowne MS 68, no. 70, fos 160v–1r; C. Read, *Mr. Secretary Walsingham* (3 vols, 1925), vol. 2, pp. 422–3; Renold, *Wisbech Stirs*, p. 269; *CSPD 1598–1601*, pp. 456, 460; P. J. Holmes, 'The Authorship and Early Reception of *A Conference about the Next Succession to the Crown of England*', *Historical Journal* 23 (1980): 415–29, at 424; Persons Correspondence, p. 681.

7   See Robert Persons, ed. E. Gee, *The Jesuit's Memorial, for the Intended Reformation of England* (1690). The 'Jesuit's Memorial' was, in many ways, a companion piece to the *Conference about the Next Succession*. It was an exercise in blue-skies thinking about what might happen in England if the political order received the kind of jolt which some Catholics had been actively anticipating and trying to procure for years. It was, in part, a utopian schema of further reformation, Catholic-style and, in part, a series of practical suggestions about how, if the Elizabethan settlement of religion should be overturned, the reform of Church and society could be conducted in order both to avoid the mistakes of the past (notably under Mary Tudor) and to stave off the corrupting effects of the worldliness and carnality, the pride, self-love and faction, that would otherwise inevitably undermine that process of reformation almost before it had begun. This text circulated in manuscript and in that form fell into the hands of the appellants who denounced it in print as entirely symptomatic of the sort of ecclesial dystopia that, unopposed, the Jesuits would seek to visit on Catholic England.

8   See pp. 133, 140 this volume.

9   'An Answere', fo. 3v.

10 John Mush, *A Dialogue Betwixt a Secular Priest and a Lay Gentleman* (Rheims [false imprint; printed at London], 1601), pp. 96–7, 98–103.

11 *Miscellanea I* (CRS 1, 1905), pp. 111–12; see also H. Chadwick, 'Crypto-Catholicism, English and Scottish', *Month* 178 (1942): 388–401. As Chadwick points out, Scottish Jesuits at this point reckoned that attending a heretical sermon was not the same as attending a heretical service in its entirety, though this opinion certainly came in for criticism in the 1590s, ibid., pp. 393–5. Chadwick says that the opinions of Scottish Jesuits on this issue, and their certainty that a different rule should apply from the one on which most English clergy at this point tended to insist, were the product of a sense that, in Scotland, 'during the last twenty years of the sixteenth century . . . there was' frequently the prospect or at least hope 'of a political restoration of Catholicism', ibid., p. 397.

12 Francis Bunny, *An Answere to a Popish Libell* (Oxford, 1607), pp. 115–16; Robert Charnock, *A Reply to a Notorious Libell* (1603), chs 17, 18.

Notes

13 Garnet, *An Apology*, pp. 150–1; p. 169 this volume.
14 P. Milward, *Religious Controversies of the Elizabethan Age* (1977), p. 117.
15 Anthony Copley, *Another Letter of Mr. A.C. to his Dis-Iesuited Kinseman* (1602), pp. 32–3.
16 Robert Persons, *A Briefe Apologie* (n.p., 1601), sig. A5v–6r.
17 Ibid., fo. 210r. In 1602, Persons wrote that the appellants 'go so far in rancour and malice against these men, as they do allow by name Thomas Bell the heretical apostate and relapsed priest his shameless slanders and railings' against the Jesuits, Robert Persons, *A Manifestation of the Great Folly and Bad Spirit of Certayne in England calling themselves Secular Priestes* (Antwerp, 1602), sig. Gv, G4v.
18 Charnock, *Reply*, pp. 69–70; p. 141 this volume. Among the appellants' tracts (including those in manuscript) we find listed an 'imperfect historye' written by the appellant clergy's courier Robert Fisher and an unknown editor; it attacks Cardinal Allen for having insisted on recusancy and points to the 'great inconvenience' that 'has hereupon befallen the Catholics here in England', AAW, OB III/ii, no. 124, fo. 340v.
19 Charnock, *Reply*, p. 70.
20 Ibid.
21 Ibid., p. 315.
22 *CSPD 1598–1601*, p. 576.
23 William Richmond, 'A trewe storie of the Catholicke prisoners in Yorke Castle, theire behavioure and defence of the Catholicke Religion when they were hailed by force to the Protestants Sermons, Anno Domini 1600, with a Confutation of Cooke the Ministers Sermon by C.J. Priest', Stonyhurst MS Anglia A II, fo. 34r; Longley, *SMC*, p. 117; M. Questier, 'Alternative Establishments: Catholics, Puritans and Preaching in Late Elizabethan York' (forthcoming).

Epilogue: Margaret Clitherow and the English Reformation

1 On the ideological ramifications of James's accession, see J. Watkins, '"Out of her Ashes May a Second Phoenix Rise"; James I and the Legacy of Elizabethan Anti-Catholicism', in A. F. Marotti (ed.), *Catholicism and Anti-Catholicism in Early Modern English Texts* (1999), pp. 116–36.
2 See e.g. M. Questier (ed.), *Newsletters from the Archpresbyterate of George Birkhead, 1609–1614* (Camden Society, fifth series, 12, 1998); idem (ed.), *Stuart Dynastic Policy and Religious Politics, 1621–1625* (Camden Society, fifth series, 34, 2009); idem (ed.), *Newsletters from the Caroline Court, 1631–1638: Catholicism and the Politics of the Personal Rule* (Camden Society, fifth series, 26, 2005).
3 See Questier, *Stuart Dynastic Policy and Religious Politics, 1621–1625*.
4 John Mush, *An Abstracte of the Life and Martirdome of Mistres Margaret Clitherowe* (Mechlin, 1619). Antony Allison and David Rogers suggest that the editor may have been the former president of the seminary at Douai, Thomas Worthington, who was reckoned to be a friend of the Jesuits, ARCR, vol. 2, no. 554.
5 A. J. Loomie, *Spain and the Jacobean Catholics* (2 vols, CRS 64, 68, 1973, 1978), vol. 2, p. 113; Richard Challoner, ed. J. H. Pollen, *Memoirs of Missionary Priests* (1924), pp. 358–9.

6   Loomie, *Spain and the Jacobean Catholics*, vol. 2, p. 113.

7   Mush, *An Abstracte of the Life and Martirdome of Mistres Margaret Clitherowe*.

8   C. Peters, *Patterns of Piety* (Cambridge, 2003), p. 287; A. Dillon, *The Construction of Martyrdom in the English Catholic Community, 1535–1603* (Aldershot, 2002); see pp. 6–7 this volume.

9   Norman Jones, *The English Reformation: Religion and Cultural Adaptation* (2002), p. 202; C. Haigh, *English Reformations* (1993).

10 See p. 88 this volume.

11 G. Redworth, *The She-Apostle* (Oxford, 2008).

12 C. Kenworthy-Browne, *Mary Ward (1585–1645)* (CRS 81, Woodbridge, 2008), pp. 111–12, 115, 117.

13 'Saint Margaret Clitherow: Her Trial on Trial: Reply by Katharine Longley', *Ampleforth Journal* 76 (1971): 23–43, at 27–8.

14 See U. Dirmeier (ed.), *Mary Ward und ihre Grüdung: Die Quellentexte bis 1645* (4 vols, Aschendorff, Münster, 2007).

15 As Susannah Monta has argued, the forms and terms of martyrology were a cross-confessional phenomenon. In linking Clitherow with other Catholic women, and seeing her as a kind of precursor for Carvajal and Ward, we do not mean to suggest that other comparisons and connections could not or should not be made to other (both Catholic and Protestant) godly women and martyrs; see S. Monta, *Martyrdom and Literature in Early Modern England* (Cambridge, 2005). Indeed, an account of Clitherow centred on the defining (and changing) characteristics of certain sorts of godly women, and on the relations between gender and religious rigorism in the lives of such women before, during and after the Reformation could be written using both Catholic and Protestant examples. This would link, in fact, the likes of Margery Kempe, Elizabeth Barton (the nun of Kent) and Ann Askew with, on the Catholic side, Clitherow, Carvajal and Ward, and, on the Protestant one, with a variety of godly puritan women, such as Mrs Jane Ratcliffe, and beyond them with the myriad female prophets and activists produced by the English revolution and the rise of Quakerism. (For a pioneering attempt of this kind, see G. Gertz-Robinson, 'Trying Testimony: Heresy, Interrogation and the English Woman Writer, 1400–1700' (PhD, Princeton, 2003.) The literature on these figures is now very extensive and we cannot hope to cite it satisfactorily here; but for a few scattered examples, plucked almost at random from what is now a vast and burgeoning literature, see P. Crawford, *Women and Religion in England, 1500–1720* (1993); C. Peters, *Patterns of Piety: Women, Gender and Religion in Late Medieval and Reformation England* (Cambridge, 2003); D. Watt, *Secretaries of God: Women Prophets in Late Medieval and Early Modern England* (Woodbridge, 1997); E. Shagan, 'Print, Orality and the Maid of Kent Affair', *Journal of Ecclesiastical History* 52 (2001): 21–33; S. Monta, 'The inheritance of Ann Askew, English Protestant Martyr', *Archiv für Reformationsgeschichte* 94 (2003): 134–60; *idem*, 'Foxe's Female Martyrs and the Sanctity of Transgression', *Renaissance and Reformation* 25 (2001): 3–22; T. Freeman, '"The Good Ministrye of Godlye and Virtuouse Women": the Elizabethan Martyrologists and the Female Supporters of the Marian Martyrs', *Journal of British Studies* 39 (2000): 8–33; G. Gertz-Robinson, 'Stepping into the Pulpit? Women's Preaching in the Book of Margery Kempe and the Examination

of Ann Askew' in K. Kerby-Fulton (ed.), *Voices in Dialogue: Reading Women in the Middle Ages* (Notre Dame, 2005), pp. 458–82; P. Lake, 'Feminine Piety and Personal Potency: the Emancipation of Mrs Jane Ratcliffe', *Seventeenth Century* 2 (1987): 143–65; K. Peters, *Print Culture and the Early Quakers* (Cambridge, 2005); B. Kunze, *Margaret Fell and the Rise of Quakerism* (Stanford, 1994); A. Stewart, 'Good Quaker Women, Tearful Sentimental Spectators, Readers and Auditors: Four Early Modern Quaker Narratives or Martyrdom and Witness', *Prose Studies* 29 (2007): 73–85; see also K. Thomas, 'Women and the Civil War Sects', *Past and Present* 13 (1958): 42–62; P. Mack, *Visionary Women: Ecstatic Prophecy in Seventeenth-Century England* (Berkeley, 1992). The present study is conceived as a more narrowly contextual exercise, which seeks to place Clitherow in the local cultural, political and polemical circumstances that framed her life and fate, and thus to use Clitherow's life and Mush's account of it as a window onto the predicament of English Catholics in the 1580s and 1590s and in particular onto their debates about the issue of conformity and more generally about the right relation between their Catholicism and their place within the structures of the English State and social order. While our account does not privilege issues of gender, it does (sometimes directly and sometimes tangentially) address them. But this is only one way to approach such material and our efforts are not intended to preclude or challenge the methodological propriety of other more comparative, cross-confessional exercises in the *longue durée*.

Index